YALE UNIVERSITY PRESS

NEW HAVEN AND LONDON

Indian Survival on the California Frontier

Albert L. Hurtado

The following chapters appeared in somewhat different form as journal articles. They are reprinted with permission:

Chap. 3, " 'Saved so Much as Possible for Labour': Indian Population and the New Helvetia Work Force," *American Indian Culture and Research Journal* 6, no. 4 (1982):63–78.

Chap. 5, "Controlling California's Indian Labor Force: Federal Administration of California Indian Affairs during the Mexican War," *Southern California Quarterly* 61 (1979):217–38.

Chap. 10, " 'Hardly a Farm House—a Kitchen without Them': Indian and White Households on the California Borderland Frontier in 1860," *Western Historical Quarterly* 13 (1982):245–70.

Publication of this book was in part supported by a grant from the College of Liberal Arts and Sciences at Arizona State University.

Designed by Jo Aerne and set in Times Roman with Caslon Antique and Old Western for display by Rainsford Type. Printed in the United States of America by Vail-Ballou Press. Binghamton, New York.

Library of Congress Cataloging-in-Publication Data
Hurtado, Albert L., 1946–
Indian survival of the California frontier / Albert L. Hurtado.
p. cm. — (Yale Western Americana series : 35) Bibliography: p. Includes index.
1. Indians of North America—California—History. 2. Frontier
and pioneer life—California. I. Title. II. Series. E78.C15H87 1988
979.4′00497—dc19 88–1710 CIP
ISBN 0–300–04147–0 (cloth)
    0–300–04798–3 (pbk.)

The paper in this book meets the guidelines for permanence and durability of the Committee on Production Guidelines for Book Longevity of the Council on Library Resources.

10 9 8

To my father,
who taught me to be fair,
and my mother,
who taught me to root for the underdog

Contents

Illustrations

Maps

Figures

Tables

Preface

This book has undergone substantial changes since its inception. Like many other scholarly books, it began as a master's thesis that I expanded into a doctoral dissertation and revised several times until it assumed its present form. But the alterations I made were much more than the editorial emendations that are ordinarily needed to make graduate work publishable. I thoroughly rethought the book as I unexpectedly encountered new materials and ideas. Some of the changes had much to do with the times in which I researched and wrote successive drafts. In the early 1970s the Vietnam War conditioned my feelings about nineteenth-century Indian history. Thus, my thesis was a critique of federal policy in California that demonstrated—at least to my satisfaction—government culpability in the destruction of helpless California Indians.

After passing my qualifying exams in 1977, I would have written a dissertation that was similar to my thesis in tone and content, but there were few academic jobs and little money for half-finished Ph.D.'s. So I left the University of California at Santa Barbara seeking professional employment as a historian. In Sacramento I worked in the State Office of Historic Preservation nominating structures to the National Register of Historic Places. Subsequently, as a consulting historian I collaborated on cultural resource management contracts with anthropologists and archaeologists. In brief, I became a public historian just when that field was struggling to emerge.

The evolution of my professional career is relevant to this book for sundry reasons. First, cultural resource studies required me to write brief histories of several California tribes. This experience convinced me that Indian history varied considerably depending on time, place, and circumstances. Second, this work showed me that Indian survival and social relations were important themes that had not been adequately explored. In addition, public historical work acquainted me with a variety of sources that I had not previously considered, notably the federal and state censuses.

I have been fortunate to have many good critics who have helped me to make this a better book. My mentor at Santa Barbara, Wilbur R. Jacobs, directed my dissertation and has been a constant source of encouragement. Kenneth N. Owens, director of my master's program, read several drafts of this work and made many valuable suggestions. The thoughtful criticism of Roger L. Nichols, who read the manuscript for Yale University Press, helped me to give this work its final form. Many others have criticized portions of the manuscript. They include Bernard Friedman, Rachel Fuchs, Ralph D. Gray, Page Putnam Miller, Fred Nicklason, Richard E. Oglesby, Jan Shipps, Robert A. Trennert, William O. Walker, and David J. Weber. I am also indebted to Howard Lamar for his interest and encouragement.

Several institutions gave financial assistance to this project. The University of California at Santa Barbara provided funds for me to travel to the National Archives. Thanks to Emory G. Evans, the University of Maryland offered assistance in typing an early draft of this manuscript. Dean William Plater of the School of Liberal Arts at Indiana University–Purdue University, Indianapolis, provided funds for research and travel. Samuel Kirkpatrick, dean of the College of Liberal Arts and Sciences at Arizona State University, provided a generous subvention to Yale University Press to defray publication costs and reduce the price of this book. The college also gave me financial assistance for the final preparation of the manuscript, illustrations, and Scott Lecce's maps. Mark Pry prepared the index. The staffs of the following libraries and archives have given me indispensable help throughout this project: the California State Library, California State Archives, Bancroft Library, Henry E. Huntington Library and Art Gallery, Library of Congress, and the National Archives. Jeannie Muñoz, consulting anthropologist, kindly shared a document from the National Archives that shed light on James Savage's final days. Beatrice Orr Smithson graciously permitted me to publish photographs of Miwok Indians working on her family's ranch. I am grateful to Yale University Press editors Charles Grench for his guidance and Harry Haskell for carefully editing the manuscript.

Without the support of some good friends it would have been possible, but far less pleasant, to write this book. My sometime roommates Bill Walker and Bill Chiechi were always interested and willing to talk about my project. At the same time we all became better cooks and more generous food critics. In the last few years Ken Owens and I have taken to backpacking in the Sierra Nevada Mountains, where some of the events described in this book took place. Our long talks beside camp fires under starry skies helped me to sort it all out.

Three compadres on the trail did not live to see this project completed. Ed Brower—horseman, poker player, and champion chili cook—introduced me to *la jaquima*, that marvelous material melding of Hispanic equestrian tradition and Indian technology that set me to wondering about some of the things this book is about. Paige Harper, a redoubtable endurance rider who completed ten Tevis Cup one-hundred-mile one-day races across the High Sierras, led me on rugged canyon trails at a high trot and helped me to know what the horse-raiding Miwok Indians were all about. The old Miller and Lux Ranch vaquero Walter Campbell taught me a few things about the risky business of breaking horses. "Kid," he would say, "take my advice and use your own judgment." That wise counsel ultimately led me away from the horse business and into graduate school, a move that pleased those kindly, knowing old men. To them, "tap 'er light."

Finally, I want to extend special thanks to my wife, Jean, who has been my main source of encouragement and support. She always kept her faith in me and this book. For that and so many other things I will be grateful always.

Abbreviations

Complete bibliographical data appear in the list of sources at the end of the book.

1852 MS Census	1852 Special Census, California State Archives
1860 MS Census	1860 Federal Manuscript Census, California State Archives
CA	Archives of California, 1767–1850, Bancroft Library
FP	Fitch Papers, Bancroft Library
FSP	Fort Sutter Papers, Huntington Library
GWP	Letters Relating to James Savage enclosed in G. W. Patten to M. M. Gardner, Sept. 26, 1852, Records of the U.S. Army Continental Commands, 1821–1920, Department of the Pacific, Letters Received, National Archives
IWP	Indian War Papers, California State Archives
LC	Leidesdorff Collection, Huntington Library
M182	Governor's Letter Books, National Archives
M210	Records of the Tenth Military Department, National Archives
M234	Letters Received by the Office of Indian Affairs, 1824–1881, California Superintendency, National Archives
MC	Marsh Collection, California Room, State Library
MKC	George McKinstry Collection, California Room, State Library
MKP	George A. McKinstry Papers, Bancroft Library
RC	Reading Collection, California Room, State Library
RM	Rudd, Smith, Manuscripts, Lilly Library
RP	Reading Papers, Bancroft Library
SuC	Sutter Collection, California Room, State Library

T135   Selected Records of the General Accounting Office
                Relating to the Frémont Expeditions and the
                California Battalion, 1842–1890, National Archives
T494   Documents Relating to the Negotiations of
                Ratified and Unratified Treaties with Various
                Indian Tribes, 1801–1869, National Archives

Indian Survival on
the California Frontier

Introduction

The grisly statistics of population reduction have overwhelmed most students of California Indian history. When Hispanic settlement began in 1769, about 300,000 native people lived within the current boundaries of the state. At the end of Spanish sovereignty in 1821, perhaps 200,000 remained, and that number dropped to about 150,000 by the time gold was discovered in 1848. During the 1850s, after California became a state, the native population fell by 80 percent to about 30,000. That abrupt, tragic decrease was a consequence of the gold rush: disease, starvation, homicide, and a declining birthrate for native people took a heavy toll. At the same time, the non-Indian population, which had gained only a meagre foothold by the end of the Mexican era in 1846, shot up dramatically to several hundred thousand during the gold rush period. To describe this situation as chaotic hardly does it justice; it was a catastrophe for the Indians. These astonishing numbers represent the human cost of dispossessing California Indians and replacing them with a non-native population.[1]

As the title of this volume implies, my interests extend beyond the calculation of Indian depopulation as a gruesome event in Indian-white relations. The same numbers that illustrate the destruction of native populations also show where and how some Indians survived in a land that was starkly different than the one their grandparents had known. Unlike other western Indians, native Californians often lived and worked with whites, so this book primarily considers the fates of native people in association with white society. In particular, it investigates the ways in which new conditions ultimately impinged on Indians' intimate lives at the household level and affected their ability to persist in a hostile world. California provides a fresh perspective for native American history by presenting a case study of Indian integration with white society in the mid-nineteenth century. Amid the violent disorders of

1. Sherburne F. Cook, *The Population of the California Indians, 1769–1970* (Berkeley, 1976), 43, 44, 59, 65; Rodman W. Paul, *California Gold: The Beginning of Mining in the Far West* (Lincoln, 1965), 23–24; J. D. B. DeBow, *Statistical Review of the United States* (Washington, D.C., 1854), 200–01, 394; and *Compendium of the Tenth Census*, rev. ed. (Washington, D.C., 1885), 337–38.

1

that turbulent age, native Californians became the mudsills of Victorian society in this corner of the American West.

The scholarly foundation for this study is a formidable body of published literature, starting with the comments of the nineteenth-century historian Hubert Howe Bancroft, who described gold rush Indian relations as "one of the last human hunts of civilization, and the basest and most brutal of them all." He was critical of whites for their wholesale murder of natives who "had neither the strength nor the intelligence" to effectively resist. Even though Bancroft obviously had a low opinion of Indian capacities, he genuinely abhorred the destruction of a helpless race, and his depiction of this phase of Indian history as a slaughter of the innocents has influenced historians ever since.[2]

California Indians have intrigued academic scholars for nearly a century. The anthropologist Alfred L. Kroeber studied California's natives for most of his professional life and trained scores of Berkeley students who followed in his footsteps. Kroeber was struck by the rapidity of Indian destruction and attempted to make an informed judgment about its causes. He found that population ordinarily declined "directly in proportion to [the] immediacy and fullness of contact with superior civilization." Kroeber believed that "the richest and most civilized tribes" fared better than those who were "rude even in native culture." Although modern scholars are uncomfortable with Kroeber's characterization of some Indian societies as retarded, he attempted to explain the Indians' survival partly as a function of native cultural traits instead of depicting them merely as passive victims.[3]

The late Sherburne F. Cook was by far the most important and influential twentieth-century scholar to investigate California Indian history. A trained biologist, Cook examined cultural contact as if he were looking at colonies of competing microbes under a magnifying lens. In a series of seminal essays, he explained the overwhelming demographic impact that disease, changes in cultural forms, concentration of Indian populations, dietary modification, and other results of European settlement had on native people. Central to his inquiry was the question of Indian population before contact with white society, which he initially estimated as a little more than 133,000. Over the course of his career he revised his estimate upward until he arrived at the 310,000 figure that is generally accepted today. Like others, Cook issued a devastating critique of California's frontier history, especially the mission and gold

2. Bancroft, *History of California*, 7 vols. (San Francisco, 1886–90), 7:476–77.

3. Kroeber, *Handbook of the Indians of California* (1925; reprint, Berkeley, 1967), 888–89.

rush periods so dear to chambers of commerce, tourists, and school-children. His view, however, emphasized cultural dislocation, starvation, and disease rather than warfare as the principal causes of demographic decline, and his work became a model for subsequent demographic studies of Indians throughout the Western Hemisphere.[4]

The Indians' place in the work force was an important factor in Cook's analysis. He found that differing Hispanic and Anglo attitudes toward Indians had a significant effect on death rates. Hispanics made room for the Indian in their society, placing them first into the communal work environment of the mission and later, when the missions were secularized, settling them into peonage on private ranchos. Cook argued that for California natives Mexican peonage was preferable both to mission life and to the Anglo version of peonage and free labor that came into vogue during the 1850s. Despite abuses by Mexican *hacendados*, Indian *peones* were permitted to live in their own communities and retain tribal customs. When Anglo-Americans adapted peonage, however, they usually broke up native communities and families, thus contributing to Indian demographic decline. Free labor tended to produce Indian migrant agricultural workers and further weakened native social structures.[5]

Although the relationship of community and family life to changing patterns of labor relations is an intriguing and highly important subject, Cook did not proceed to develop solid statistical evidence to examine this problem during the Anglo-American period. And despite Cook's major influence on all serious writing about California Indians, no scholar has systematically tested his ideas about Indian death and survival. Instead, subsequent writers have accepted his analysis and con-

4. Cook's earliest essays include "Population Trends Among the California Mission Indians," *Ibero-Americana* 17 (1940):1–48; "The Mechanism and Extent of Dietary Adaptation Among Certain Groups of California and Nevada Indians," *Ibero-Americana* 18 (1941):1–59; "The Indian Versus the Spanish Mission," *Ibero-Americana* 21 (1943):1–194; "The Physical and Demographic Reaction of the Nonmission Indians in Colonial and Provincial California," *Ibero-Americana* 22 (1943):1–55; and "The American Invasion, 1848–1870" *Ibero-Americana* 23 (1943):1–111. These essays are reprinted in *The Conflict Between the California Indians and White Civilization* (Berkeley, 1976). See also "Mission Registers as Sources of Vital Statistics: Eight Missions of Northern California," in Cook and Woodrow Borah, *Essays in Population History*, 3 vols. (Berkeley, 1971–79), 3:177–311. On Cook's career, see Borah, "Sherburne Friend Cook (1896–1974)," *Hispanic American Historical Review* 55 (Nov. 1975):749–59. For an evaluation of Cook's work, see Wilbur R. Jacobs, "Sherburne Friend Cook: Rebel-Revisionist (1896–1974)," *Pacific Historical Review* 54 (May 1985):191–99.

5. Cook, "American Invasion," 3–4, 46–75; and Cook, "Indian Versus the Mission," 91–101.

centrated on the grossest aspects of population decline. Indeed, two recent books use the word *genocide* in their titles.[6]

Historians of Indian policy have extensively examined the federal government's role in California. Most have been critical of federal administration, finding that bungling administrators mismanaged policies that were basically humane. In this view, California Superintendent of Indian Affairs Edward F. Beale provided a brief glimmer of hope with his reservation plan, which was loosely based on the Spanish mission model; but ultimately the reservations were palpable failures—victims of the inept and corrupt administrators who succeeded Beale.[7]

A half century ago Alban W. Hoopes suggested that California's

6. See, for example, Robert F. Heizer and Alan Almquist, *The Other Californians: Prejudice and Discrimination under Spain, Mexico and the United States to 1920* (Berkeley, 1971); Heizer, ed., *The Destruction of the California Indians: A Collection of Documents from the Period 1847 to 1865* (Santa Barbara, Calif., 1974); Heizer, ed., *They Were Only Diggers: A Collection of Articles from California Newspapers, 1851–1866, On Indian and White Relations* (Ramona, Calif., 1974); Jack Norton, *Genocide in Northwestern California: When Our Worlds Cried* (San Francisco, 1979); Lynwood Carranco and Estle Beard, *Genocide and Vendetta: The Round Valley Wars of Northern California* (Norman, Okla., 1981); and Jack Forbes, *Native Americans of California and Nevada* (Healdsburg, Calif., 1969). Forbes's widely read account describes the "westward movement of a vast horde of armed civilians . . . very much resembling the ancient 'hordes' of Central Asia, in their mobility, warlike nature, and indifference to the boundary claims and property rights of already established but alien peoples." He adds that the "brutality and callousness" of California frontier Indian warfare "closely approaches genocide." Forbes indicts all California whites for Indian murders because "the conquest of the Native Californian was above all a popular, mass enterprise" (pp. 52–53).

7. William Henry Ellison, "The Federal Indian Policy in California, 1846–1860," *Mississippi Valley Historical Review* 9 (June 1922):37–67; Alban W. Hoopes, *Indian Affairs and Their Administration with Special Reference to the Far West, 1849–1860* (Philadelphia, 1932), 35–68; John Walton Caughey, ed., *The Indians of Southern California in 1852: The B.D. Wilson Report and a Selection of Contemporary Comment* (San Marino, 1952); Harry Kelsey, "The California Indian Treaty Myth," *Southern California Quarterly* 55 (Fall 1973):225–38; Michael A. Sievers, "Malfeasance or Indirection? Administration of the California Indian Superintendency's Business Affairs," *Southern California Quarterly* 56 (Fall 1974): 273–94; Gerald Thompson, *Edward F. Beale and the American West* (Albuquerque, 1983), 45–79. On U.S. Indian policy, see Francis Paul Prucha, *American Indian Policy in the Formative Years: The Indian Trade and Intercourse Acts, 1790–1834*, (Lincoln, 1962); Prucha, *The Great Father: The United States Government and the American Indians*, 2 vols. (Lincoln, 1984), 1:354–409; Bernard W. Sheehan, *Seeds of Extinction: Jeffersonian Philanthropy and the American Indian*, (New York, 1973); Ronald N. Satz, *American Indian Policy in the Jacksonian Era* (Lincoln, 1975); Reginald Horsman, *Expansion and American Indian Policy, 1783–1812* (East Lansing, Mich., 1967); and Robert A. Trennert, *Alternative to Extinction: Federal Indian Policy and the Beginnings of the Reservation System, 1846–51* (Philadelphia, 1975). On Indian segregation in the early republic, see Ronald T. Takaki, *Iron Cages: Race and Culture in Nineteenth-Century America* (Seattle, 1979), 55–65.

reservation system was significant because it foreshadowed the creation of reservations elsewhere in the American West. Students of Indian policy no longer accept his conclusions, instead viewing California as an exceptional case that did not influence broader federal policy decisions. Modern scholarship suggests that the establishment of California reservations in the 1850s was part of a larger federal response to post–Mexican War conditions in the Far West, where California offered a difficult testing ground for Indian policy.[8]

Employees of the Office of Indian Affairs found the California situation complicated and often intractable. While some Anglos adopted Hispanic labor practices as expedient, others tried to drive Native Americans out of the work force. Still another group sought to exterminate native people. The reservation system was a stopgap measure, ministering to only a fraction of the Indians. Because federal administration was mostly ineffectual, the state government took an exceptionally powerful role in California Indian affairs. While the state constitution outlawed slavery, the first legislature enacted Chapter 133, "an act for the government and protection of the Indians," which provided for the indenture of loitering and orphaned Indians, regulated their employment, and defined a special class of crimes and punishments for them. Some students of California history have referred to this law as a form of legalized slavery. Certainly it resembled the "black codes" adopted by slave states as a means to control free blacks and bondsmen alike. Simultaneously, the state government subsidized scores of military campaigns against Indian communities considered threatening to white settlement. In fact, these expeditions often killed Indians indiscriminately. Everywhere the United States faced local opponents to its Indian policy, but in California opposition was remarkably widespread and influential, with dire results for the Indians.[9]

Recently James Rawls has explained how changes in Anglo attitudes about Indians in California influenced white behavior toward native people. He reasons that the near extermination of native Californians resulted from changing Anglo needs. When Anglos meant to justify the United States' acquisition of Mexican California, they portrayed Indians

8. Hoopes, *Indian Affairs*, 35–68; Prucha, *Great Father*, 1:315–409.

9. James Rawls, *Indians of California: The Changing Image* (Norman, Okla., 1984), 137–70; Owen Coy, "Evidences of Slavery in California," *Grizzly Bear* 19, no. 6 (1916):1–2; and Heizer and Almquist, *The Other Californians*, 39–58. On "black codes," see Peter H. Wood, *Black Majority: Negroes in Colonial South Carolina from 1670 through the Stono Rebellion* (New York, 1975), 271–84; and Eugene Genovese, *Roll Jordan Roll: The World the Slaves Made* (New York, 1974), 25–49. For documentation of the murder of Indians, see Heizer, ed., *Destruction of the California Indian*, 244–65.

as victims of cruel *hispanos*. To encourage Anglo immigration, pioneer publicists extolled Indians as useful workers. Finally, when Anglo settlement increased and other groups entered the work force, native people became merely obstacles to be swept aside. Rawls observes that the bloody work "went forward with the financial support of local, state and federal governments." But the brutal murder of thousands of California Indians is only part of the story. Useful as his analysis is, Rawls has explicated white behavior without explaining the Indian response to it.[10]

Although a great deal has been written about the destruction and dispossession of California Indians, historians have published comparatively little about their survival. George Harwood Phillips asserts that historians have failed to write about Indians because the stereotypical view that they were merely passive "and therefore historically unimportant has discouraged research." The most important exception is Phillips's own work on southern California Indians. He rightly observes that by concentrating on the theme of Indian abuse, historians have told us more about whites than Indians. His study shows how the Luiseño, Cupeño, and Cahuilla Indians adjusted to successive waves of Hispanic and Anglo colonization. Primarily considering the activities of three important chiefs, Phillips argues that their importance "rests not so much on what they actually achieved for themselves and their followers but in what they attempted to achieve." Both by cooperating with and resisting whites, the chiefs influenced California history and enabled their people to persist during very difficult times. Phillips's study of southern California contributes to a fuller understanding of Indian history and underscores the need for a study of the state's much larger northern region.[11]

This book is an attempt to explain Indian survival in the northern California interior. The plethora of native cultures, each with a distinct history, complicated the effort. Because behavior is culturally determined, we should assume that Indians reacted to new situations in culturally specific ways. A complete understanding of California Indian history would require the detailed study of hundreds of small communities. I do not attempt such a full analysis here. Instead, I intend to show the range of native experiences during a time of enormous cultural

10. Rawls, *Indians of California*, 171–201. The quote is from p. 186.
11. Phillips, *The Enduring Struggle: Indians in California History* (San Francisco, 1981), 1; Phillips, *Chiefs and Challengers: Indian Resistance and Cooperation in Southern California* (Berkeley, 1975), 6, 160–76; and Phillips, "Indians in Los Angeles, 1781–1875: Economic Integration, Social Disintegration," *Pacific Historical Review* 69 (Aug. 1980):427–51.

stress. The evidence clearly demonstrates that Indians were not merely passive victims of white rapacity. While Indian populations were rapidly declining, the survivors adapted to novel circumstances.

Generalization is difficult. Dozens of tribes lived in the interior, speaking distinctive languages and relating to the rest of the world in their own ways. The major differences among these groups are discussed in chapter 1. It should be clear that a study of particular tribal histories is beyond the scope of this work. Instead, I present a historical overview, using the experiences of specific tribes and individual Indians to illustrate particular points.

Although California Indian history seems unrelated to that of other native peoples in the United States, each small community shared a historical link with all other Indians. As the historian Richard White has said, a common theme in the histories of North American Indians was the attempt by whites "to bring Indian resources, land, and labor into the market." Elsewhere, after the fur trade ceased to be important, the land and its resources were the main objects of white attention; but in California native labor became essential for whites who strove to develop the pastoral and agricultural potential of the Golden State. The workplace, therefore, brought Indians into prolonged and intimate contact with whites even as the frontier era was fading. The new market economy was accompanied by changes in Indian subsistence patterns, societies, and cultural landscapes that once had provided for natives' needs. These changes inexorably made formerly self-sufficient Indians dependent on the new order.[12]

Because of the unique position that California Indians held within white society, the concepts and methodologies of social history, family history, and historical demography are important to this study. Reginald Horsman recently called for Native American historians to apply the techniques of the new social history, and California is an appropriate place to do it. Unlike Indians in other parts of the Far West, California natives did not form large and powerful nations with warrior societies that fought the U.S. Army. They lived in much smaller groups and often quickly accommodated to white incursions. When California Indians resisted, they fought whites as individuals and small communities rather than forming grand alliances to "go on the warpath." Moreover, they sometimes knew their enemies well; Indians who had once been employed by whites in many cases raided their former masters. Accommodation and resistance thus went hand in glove as Indians met whites

---

12. Richard White, *The Roots of Dependency: Subsistence, Environment, and Social Change among the Choctaws, Pawnees, and Navajos* (Lincoln, 1983), xv.

on the California frontier. Where they associated closely with whites, Indians can be studied much like other poor, inarticulate people.[13]

California Indians invite comparison with other workers in the industrializing world. But because Indians in nineteenth-century America were distinct racially, culturally, and historically, it would be a mistake to view them simply as another ethnic group in a vast working class. Anglo-Americans were strongly influenced by a heritage that excluded Indians from white society. Most native people could not hope to find work with settlers who had narrowly ethnocentric racial views. Nevertheless, as Frederick Hoxie points out, we would do well to recognize that both Indian and white cultures were in transition, "forming new identities, governmental structures, cultural values, and economic systems." To know the Indian as a laborer is to understand something about the transitions that both societies were experiencing.[14]

Because demographic decline is the outstanding feature of California Indian population history, I have directed special attention to the native family's reproductive and social role. Not all changes in family life can be charted here, but this study delineates the general evolution of household structures up to 1860. Related to the story of the Indian family is the history of native women, who faced particular perils that evidently resulted in death rates exceeding those for men. Consequently, I have specifically examined Indian women's history and analyzed sex ratios and fertility rates, although much of the evidence remains fragmentary, suggestive rather than conclusive.

The nature of household structures has more than passing significance to historians of the modern world, particularly as the history of the family relates to the rise of modern capitalism. We may not agree that a particular type of household structure, such as the nuclear family, led to the development of modern economies; but it is clear that the household was the biological source of the work force and sustained workers with food, clothing, and shelter. In frontier areas, where service industries to support a labor force did not exist, the household economy contributed to the emergence of a capitalist system. In such circumstances capitalist entrepreneurs and native society could establish a symbiotic relationship. But traditional household structures, rooted in hunting and gathering and expressed in complex social relationships, were not invariably amenable to these demands. Immanuel Wallerstein,

13. Horsman, "Well-Trodden Paths and Fresh Byways: Recent Writing on Native American History," *Reviews in American History* 10 (Dec. 1982):234. Herbert G. Gutman, *Work, Culture and Society in Industrializing America* (New York, 1976) provides insights into the history of workers.

14. Hoxie, "Positively Paternal," *Reviews in American History* 13 (Sept. 1985):393.

who has so persuasively described the relationship between capitalist agriculture and the rise of the European world-economy in the sixteenth century, observes that mobile households best serve the needs of capitalism. Therefore, he asserts, capitalism exerts "steady pressure to break the link between household organization and territoriality." At the same time, capitalist economies are based on "a partially waged labor force" and households that are increasingly stratified by race and gender. According to this scenario, as native people are dispossessed, some individuals work for wages—whether full-time, part-time, or seasonally—while others, usually women, continue to provide subsistence in traditional ways and thus support the households that provide labor to the new economy. In this manner the native household subsidizes incipient capitalism even as the native economy is being displaced.[15]

These ideas, which grew out of Wallerstein's study of the sixteenth-century colonial world, have been applied by others to the third world in the twentieth century. Wallerstein designates colonial or underdeveloped areas as the "periphery", serving the needs of the developed nations of Western Europe and the United States, which he calls the "core." The dependent periphery provides raw materials to the industrial core, which in turn manufactures finished goods for resale at home and abroad. Located nearer the core are semiperipheral areas that share some attributes of the core and periphery while remaining dependent on the more powerful core states. This arrangement, in Wallerstein's view, began in the earliest days of the colonial era and continues to the present. Moreover, in the early days the periphery and the core had divergent labor institutions just as they had different economic functions. While the core relied increasingly on wage labor, the periphery and semiperiphery used slavery, debt peonage, and sharecropping. Did nineteenth-century California fit into Wallerstein's scheme? The work of the historian Howard Lamar, who has found many instances of coerced labor in the American West, suggests that Wallerstein's thesis may provide a useful analytical framework for understanding the western frontier.[16]

15. Peter Laslett, "The Comparative History of Household and Family," *Journal of Social History* 4 (Fall 1970):75–87; Immanuel Wallerstein, "Household Structures and Labor-Force Formation in the Capitalist World-Economy," in *Households and the World-Economy*, ed. Joan Smith, Immanuel Wallerstein, and Hans-Dieter Evers (Beverly Hills, 1984), 18–19; and Evers, Wolfgang Clauss, and Diana Wong, "Subsistence Reproduction: A Framework for Analysis," ibid., 23–36.

16. L. S. Stavrianos, *Global Rift* (New York, 1981), 38–39; and Wallerstein, *The Modern World System: Capitalist Agriculture and the Origins of the European World-Economy in the Sixteenth Century* (New York, 1976), 103 and passim; Lamar, "From Bondage to Contract: Ethnic Labor in the American West, 1600–1890," in Steven Hahn and Jonathan

These ideas, like all other generalizations, are not absolute laws, but they ring with special clarity in mid-nineteenth century California, where coerced Indian labor was common before the gold rush. Although it cannot be said that California achieved core status in the 1850s or even during the nineteenth century, it clearly underwent a rapid transition to modern capitalism after the discovery of gold. In the meantime California exhibited characteristics of all of the world-system areas that Wallerstein describes. Disturbing changes were most apparent in the realm of Indian work, where hunting, gathering, peonage, and slave and wage labor sometimes coexisted and sometimes displaced each other. Occasionally Indian labor metamorphosed from traditional to modern forms and back again like quicksilver as Indians struggled to cope with the forces of modernization that transformed California. During this period of difficult adjustment the Indian family was subjected to intense pressure that modified familiar household structures to fit new conditions.

This book, therefore, is concerned with several major themes. The foremost consideration is the survival of the Indians as a result of their efforts to adapt to changing circumstances. The vigorous part that Indians took in the history of California in the mid-nineteenth century, aiding and retarding white settlement as native needs and perceptions dictated, is a concomitant theme. Tragically, Indian participation in the developing capitalist economy contributed to overall Indian demographic reduction as new conditions precipitated the reordering of native institutions—especially the structure of the Indian family—even while permitting some Indians to survive. The especially forceful impact of these events on Indian women is another topic that receives attention. Finally, this book examines the interplay of state and federal Indian policies, their impacts on natives, and the Indian influence on the administration of policy.

The turbulence of the decades under consideration has made it a difficult task to organize this work so as to cover all of the subjects indicated above. The book proceeds chronologically, but some chapters cover long periods, while others focus on particular topics that illuminate major themes. Five of the ten chapters deal with the pre–gold rush period and the remainder with subsequent years.

Geographic considerations have also presented organizational problems. In 1819 the California interior—an immense area approximately

Prude, eds., *The Countryside in the Age of Capitalist Transformation: Essays in the Social History of Rural America* (Chapel Hill, 1985), 293–96, 317; and Richard Slotkin, *The Fatal Environment; The Myth of the Frontier in the Age of Industrialization, 1800–1890* (New York, 1985), 33–47.

STUDY AREA

Culture Area Boundaries

Tribe Area Boundaries

Study Area

Culture Areas and Tribes
Outside Study Area

Tolowa

Shasta

Yurok Karok

NORTH-
EAST

Wintu

Yana

Maidu

Nomlaki

Konkow

Yuki

Pomo

Patwin

Nisenan

Coast Miwok

Miwok

CENTRAL

1 Wiyot
2 Chilula
3 Whilkut
4 Hupa
5 Chimariko
6 Mattole
7 Nongatl
8 Sinkyone
9 Lassik
10 Cahto
11 Wailaki
12 Lake Miwok
13 Wappo

Costanoan

Esselen

Salinan

Yokuts

Monache

Tubatulabal

GREAT BASIN

Chumash

SOUTHERN

0   50   100   150   miles

MAP 1. Culture Areas and Indian Tribes of California

the size of New England plus New Jersey—contained more than one hundred thousand Indians and no non-Indian settlements (see map 1). This country extends some five hundred miles from the Tehachapi Mountains in the south to the Oregon border, and from the Coast range on the west to the crest of the Sierra Nevadas. Topographically diverse, the area includes the fertile Sacramento and San Joaquin valleys; the Sierra Nevada range, which first inhibited immigration because it was so difficult to cross and then attracted immigrants because of its gold deposits; and on the northern border, the Klamath and Cascade mountains with their rugged features, poorer gold deposits, and few river valleys suitable for farming. Although focused on the interior, this study also discusses the coastal regions to clarify the narrative, provide continuity, and make pertinent comparisons.

I have divided the interior into several regions in order to make comparative analyses of the gold rush period. Based partly on the native cultural areas that Kroeber first described, and partly on the delineation of gold rush mining regions by Rodman Paul, the regional scheme is meant to take into account cultural, environmental, and historical differences that are evident in California. Of course, such a division must be somewhat arbitrary; it cannot reflect every cultural subtlety, historical incident, and regional nuance. For example, the vagaries of the gold rush included frequent changes of county boundaries that have complicated the task of comparing census data between 1850 and 1860. Whatever inadequacies these regional designations may possess, they provide a way to refine broad generalizations about the gold rush and Indians.[17]

Regional patterns were further complicated because so many Indian and white cultures were represented in the interior. California became a borderland frontier on the edges of Hispanic colonization, where the first Europeans and Anglo-American settlers quickly adopted the Hispanic traditions of Indian labor. These settlers recruited workers from scores of autonomous native communities with distinct languages and customs. White frontiersmen, therefore, settled a frontier that was densely populated with Indians but balkanized by linguistic, cultural, and historical circumstances.

Anglo- and Hispanic Americans ordinarily observed very different traditions of Indian-white relations. Comparing these customs, Spanish borderland historian Herbert E. Bolton, noted that while in Anglo-America "the only good Indians were dead Indians," in Hispanic America the native peoples were assimilated and exploited. Moreover, as Bolton believed, California and other parts of the Spanish Borderlands were "the meeting place and fusing place of two streams of European civilization." The European "civilizations" that Bolton saw on the frontier, however, were not just simplified reproductions of the mother culture. The frontier was a periphery, the historian Bernard Bailyn observes, "a ragged outer margin of a central world, a regressive, backward-looking diminishment of metropolitan accomplishment" that was primitive, violent, bizarre, and outlandish. The California borderland

17. Paul, *California Gold*, 57–81; and Robert F. Heizer and Albert B. Elsasser, *The Natural World of California Indians* (Berkeley, 1980), 57–81.

lived up to Bailyn's description, especially when seen through the lens of Indian-white relations. Thus, the interior was a meeting ground for competing cultural frontiers; amid numerous and diverse Indian communities, Bolton's Spanish borderlands frontier met with the aggressive entrepreneurial frontier of Anglo civilization that Frederick Jackson Turner postulated.[18]

The fusing of Anglo and Hispanic traditions was not a seamless process in California, especially for the Indians, as the statistics of depopulation show. I have used numbers in an attempt to get behind the gross statistics to show how California Indians improvised strategies for dealing with white settlers and government officials. Violent resistance and servile acquiescence marked the poles of the Indian response to whites, but every subtle variation of accommodation and opposition was used in their quest for survival.

The history of California Indians commands attention as more than a unique episode in the history of the Golden State. Indians participated—as millions of others did—in the fundamental reordering of the world-economy. The adjustments that Indians made stemmed from the exigencies of the new order—Hispanic, Anglo, and capitalist—as well as their cultural predispositions and traditions. Cast in this light, the history of California Indians is not simply an example of how racists ran roughshod over the rights of people of color, nor is it a tale of how Indians blindly resisted the forces of the modern world. Whenever they could, Indians tried to mold their lives according to the revolutionary conditions that overtook them. Their story is a part of the annals of capitalism as it was extended to distant places in modern times, and from this perspective the Indian experience becomes instructive to the world at large.

18. Bolton, "The Mission as a Frontier Institution in Spanish American Colonies" and "Defensive Spanish Expansion and the Significance of the Borderlands," John Francis Bannon, ed., *Bolton and the Spanish Borderlands* (Norman, 1964), 59, 190–91, 211; Frederick Jackson Turner, "The Significance of the Frontier in American History," in Turner, ed., *The Frontier in American History* (New York, 1920); and Bailyn, *The Peopling of British North America: An Introduction* (New York, 1986), 113.

1

Culture and Family on the Borderland Frontier

In the 1850s good California farmland was hard to come by. Much of it had been taken up in the 1840s, when the Mexican government had granted huge parcels to settlers; squatters took most of the rest during the gold rush. James Kilgore was fortunate to have an unencumbered claim to agricultural land on the eastern side of the Sacramento Valley, yet he relinquished it to a young married man because he wanted "to see this country settled up with families." Apparently Kilgore had an extraordinary attachment to the domestic institution that Victorians held most dear, but he might have acted out of farsighted self-interest as well: the family had a strong influence on the Anglo-American frontier. Families brought stability, growth, and white civilization to Indian country. The more quickly families settled the country, the faster prosperity, cities, and sundry opportunities would follow. But not just any families would do. Kilgore meant to see a white family occupy his claim. If he had intended otherwise, he could have turned over the land to one of the Indian families who lived nearby. He would not do so, of course, because Indians lacked the racial and cultural qualifications he had in mind.[1]

If settlement by families had been the sole criterion of a civilized territory, California would have been one of the most civilized places in the trans-Mississippi West before the turn of the eighteenth century. With three hundred thousand native people, California was one of the most heavily populated places in North America. But it was not common for men like Kilgore to think of Indians as family members. White frontiersmen saw them as primitive tribal folk, lacking the sentimental domestic affections that marked Victorian society. Yet family ties bound native people to each other, to their communities, and to the land. Family bonds defined social, political, and economic relationships in

1. Kilgore is quoted in Rufus C. Burrows, "Anecdotes Concerning Early Experiences in California 1848–1858," typescript, California Room, State Library, Sacramento. On the influence of the frontier family, see Walter Nugent, *Structures of American Social History* (Bloomington, 1981), 54–86.

native cultures and were of paramount importance to Indian personal and corporate life. Tragically, the arrival of family-oriented people from other cultures threatened the network of kinship that had supported native society and survival for untold generations (see fig. 1).[2]

Indian Family and Community

The Indian family fit into an elaborate set of social relationships that varied by tribe and locality. To help create order out of this complexity, anthropologists have described general culture areas with similar ways of life and value systems. The interior contained the central and northwestern culture areas. Taking up the central valley and adjacent country, the central culture area included the Nisenan, Maidu, Konkow, Miwok, Yokuts, and other tribes. The northwestern culture area included the Tolowa, Yurok, Karok, Hupa, Shasta, Chimariko, Hupa, Whilkut, and other tribes that lived in the rugged Klamath and Cascade mountains and on the adjacent coast. In both areas several *rancherías* (villages) acknowledging a single chief formed a tribelet, and several tribelets constituted the tribe. Tribelets included as few as three rancherías and as many as thirty and held up to 1,000 people, although 250 was about the average. The conjugal couple and their children formed the basic household unit, which was sometimes augmented by aged relatives and unmarried siblings.

Indian families, however, were not merely a series of nuclear units but were knit into a complex set of associations that comprised native society. For most California Indians, kinship defined the individual's place within the community and family associations suffused every aspect of life. Elites, commoners, poor, and sometimes slaves inherited their status, although it was possible to better one's position by a propitious marriage or by gaining wealth. Because northwestern tribes in particular emphasized acquisitiveness, most marriages in this culture area occurred

2. Rawls, *Indians of California*, 186–201, observes that nineteenth-century whites found native Californians to be nearly devoid of human characteristics. For a comprehensive view of the development of Anglo-American racism toward Indians, see Reginald Horsman, *Race and Manifest Destiny: The Origins of American Racial Anglo-Saxonism* (Cambridge, Mass., 1981), 189–207; James Axtell, *The European and the Indian: Essays in the Ethnohistory of Colonial North America* (New York, 1981); James Axtell, ed., *The Indian Peoples of Eastern America: A Documentary History of the Sexes* (New York, 1981); Robert J. Berkhofer, Jr., *The White Man's Indian: Images of the American Indian from Columbus to the Present* (New York, 1978); and Roy Harvey Pearce, *The Savages of America: A Study of the Indian and the Idea of Civilization* (Baltimore, 1965).

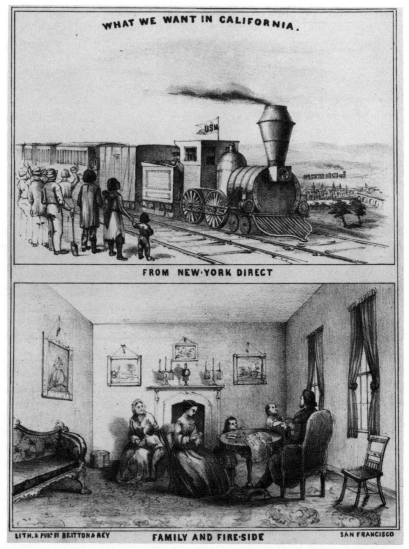

Fig. 1. "What We Want in California". A steam railroad linking California with the East, the cartoonist implied, would help to establish stable Victorian family relations in California. Among the imaginary spectators witnessing the arrival of modern technology was a California Indian family, which evidently would have no place in the idyllic fireside scene below. Modernization and industrialization would help to replace California Indian families with newcomers.

within economic and social ranks, tending to stabilize economic and power relationships.

Chiefs (who were occasionally women) were usually from wealthy families and inherited their positions. Principally they administered economic affairs, governed hunting and gathering on tribelet lands, and assured that food and other goods were fairly distributed. They arranged for public feasting and ceremonial food exchanges with neighboring people. Since secure links with other groups provided insurance against occasional food shortages, a chief would frequently marry several elite women from other rancherías. Diplomatic polygyny provided kinship links, which maintained prosperity and limited the warfare that could result from poaching or blood feuds. In the event of war, kinship considerations helped to determine who would be attacked, as well as the duration and intensity of conflict.[3]

Kinship was important to the daily lives of ordinary people. Families controlled particular hunting and gathering areas; individuals accumulated, shared, or traded resources according to familial associations. In the northwest, where wealth was so important, the owner of a resource could rent, sell, or convey usufructory rights to another family as part of a bride-price to secure an especially desirable marriage alliance. Conversely, the theft of such resources could result in the enslavement of a culpable person who was unable to repay the victim. Northwesterners had a highly developed system of laws that required compensation for any transgression from petty theft to murder. Malefactors and their families, therefore, lost both wealth and status. Throughout California, kinship determined the nature of trading and ordinarily removed the profit motive from the transactions. Marriage and kinship influenced the social structure of each ranchería, depending on tribal customs. Communities were composed of extended residence groups that were linked by family ties. The Yokuts supplemented blood relations with moieties that connected them to a special totem animal such as the eagle or coyote. Children belonged to their father's moiety and were forbidden to kill their totem animal. If someone else killed the totem, the moiety had to purchase and bury the carcass. Since a wide range of commonly hunted animals were moiety totems, this arrangement tended to redistribute wealth and regulate hunting. Moreover, totemic affiliations affected blood ties because an individual had to marry someone from another moiety.[4]

3. Lowell John Bean, "Social Organization in Native California," in *Native Californians: A Theoretical Retrospective*, ed. Lowell John Bean and Thomas C. Blackburn (Socorro, N.M., 1976), 107, 111–12.

4. Ibid, 103–09; Robert F. Heizer, "The California Indians: Archaeology, Varieties of Culture, Arts of Life," *California Historical Society Quarterly* 41 (March 1962):5–6.

Given the significance and complexity of kin and moiety relationships, marriage was an extremely important institution, governed according to strict rules. Unions were prohibited if a couple was related within three to five generations, depending on tribal affiliation. Consequently, men had to look for eligible wives outside their tribelet, and women had to leave their home communities when they married. Because kinship was so important, the departing women formed important new links for their families and communities, strengthening the system of reciprocity that girded native California. The bride-price symbolized women's place in this scheme. The groom gave his parents-in-law a gift to demonstrate his worth, acknowledge the status of the bride's family, and compensate them for the loss of her services. If the family approved, they made a complementary gift, although one of lesser value, to the groom. In the northwest, the value of the bride-price was more important than elsewhere, but it did not signify that the wife was a chattel. No husband could sell his spouse; an unhappy wife could divorce her husband, although social pressure militated against it. Even so, men were considered the family heads, descent was usually through the male line, and residence was at the husband's ranchería (see fig. 2)[5].

California's native household economy was based on hunting and gathering according to a sexual division of labor. Men hunted, fished, and—after the advent of white settlement—raided livestock herds. Abundant deer, antelope, and elk furnished meat, while bountiful salmon runs provided another excellent source of protein. Fish and sea mammals were important foods to the northwesterners who lived near the ocean, and their skillful boatmen constructed graceful redwood dugout canoes. These boats were also useful for transportation in the rugged northern country, where rivers were the main highways. Obviously, the first object of work was to sustain life, but California Indians were able to accumulate surpluses that enabled them to live beyond the mere subsistence level. Through trade, Indians could acquire wealth in the form of such highly prized trade objects as white deerskins and huge obsidian blades, or woodpecker scalps and dentalium beads that served as money.

As important as the male activities were, women did more work and provided the plant foods that comprised the bulk of the Indian diet. The acorn was a staple food, and although men assisted in gathering

5. Bean, "Social Organization," 106–9; and John Bushnell and Donna Bushnell, "Wealth, Work and World View in Native Northwest California: Sacred Significance and Psychoanalytic Symbolism," in *Flowers of the Wind: Papers on Ritual, Myth and Symbolism in California and the Southwest,* ed. Thomas C. Blackburn (Socorro, N.M., 1977), 133.

Fig. 2. Indian Encampment. Charles Nahl's romantic oil painting of an Indian family by moonlight in the San Joaquin Valley is one of the few positive depictions of California Indians in the late nineteenth century. Rendered in 1874, the painting shows Nahl's conception of Indian family life in the 1830s and 1840s. The horse, metal cookware, and cloth—recent innovations in the interior—mingle with traditional articles of bone, shell, and fiber. Nahl's classically posed, smiling parents and cherubic children idealized the Indian family just as other painters romanticized the Victorian family. By using these stock symbols of connubial bliss, Nahl perhaps meant to say that the Indian family was as worthy of admiration as its Anglo-American counterpart.

acorns, women ground them to flour and leached the tannic acid from the meal. In season, women collected grass seeds, roots, pine nuts, berries, and other foods, prepared them, and stored the surplus against lean times. Basket making was also a female task, and elaborate twined pieces, sometimes adorned with precious feathers and shell beads, were esteemed items of trade. All California tribes prized hard-working, productive women.[6]

By bearing children—their most important contribution to Indian

6. Heizer, "The California Indians," 5–6, 10–12; Nona C. Willoughby, "Division of Labor Among the Indians of California," in *California Indians*, Garland American Indian Ethnohistory Series, 6 vols. (New York, 1974), 2:60–68.

society—women created the human resources necessary to sustain their communities. When populations suffered significant reductions, the lack of fertile women meant that the capacity to recover was limited. The complicated rules that regulated marriage and kinship were another consideration. The experience of Ishi, a Yahi man who lived in what is now Tehama County, provides a poignant illustration of this point. After most of the Yahi were killed during the gold rush era, a small remnant hid out on Deer Creek, where a steep canyon afforded them protection. Yahi's band included an old man, a young man, Ishi's mother, and a young woman who was either Ishi's sister or a cousin too closely related for him to marry. When the other young man died, Ishi and his kinswoman were the last potential Yahi parents, but only an incestuous relationship could preserve their tribe. To the end they were true to their cultural values. There were no children; everyone but Ishi died on Deer Creek. He lived to tell his tale to anthropologists who took him to a San Francisco museum, where he, too, died a few years later. The Yahis were not unique. Under ordinary conditions the Indian family was flexible, productive, and viable, but when placed under demographic stress it proved highly vulnerable.[7]

Hispanic Colonization and the Family

When Spanish settlers began to arrive in California in 1769, they brought with them family customs that were well adapted to frontier circumstances. American conditions, especially the lack of Iberian women, modified the ideal Hispanic family in several ways and, as we shall see, impinged on Indian family traditions, with baleful consequences for the latter.

The family was the solid foundation of Spanish-American society. The husband was a patriarch who theoretically controlled all the family's important business. While he went out into the world, his wife took charge of the household, managing child rearing and domestic activities. During most of the colonial era the role of the family was to serve social and economic ends rather than to exemplify romantic love. Especially among the wealthy classes, parents often tried to arrange marriages that would enhance family fortunes, and young couples usually sought their parents' permission to marry. Parental consent, however, was not at first required by Spanish law or the Catholic Church, which upheld the

7. Theodora Kroeber, *Ishi in Two Worlds: A Biography of the Last Wild Indian in North America* (Berkeley, 1961).

right of individuals to marry freely. The Church oversaw the moral aspects of marriage and sexuality and often performed marriages against the wishes of disapproving parents. In New Spain during the sixteenth and seventeenth centuries, the Church frequently assented to unions that crossed class boundaries. Indeed, by 1776 the Spanish crown was so concerned about liberalized marriage practices that it required parental consent for minors and justified parental disapproval if a proposed marriage would offend family honor or threaten the state.[8]

Frontier priests seemed unwilling to undermine prevailing social norms and the economic motives of powerful families. In the archives of the Archdiocese of Santa Fe, for example, there are no cases of clerics overiding parental objections to cross-class marriages. Isolated and exposed on a distant frontier, New Mexican churchmen chose not to subvert the family arrangements and class distinctions that underpinned social order. Nevertheless, as in New Spain, many couples opted for marriages based on mutual romantic love, regardless of parental or Church sanctions, as society became more secular and less concerned with old conceptions of family honor.[9]

Despite long-term changes in connubial habits, distinctive traditions remained evident in the Hispanic family. As among Indians, important families were allied through marriage and such unions were ordinarily considered a matter of duty for the partners. Masculine passion was reserved for prostitutes and mistresses, if they could be afforded. On the other hand, Hispanic culture supposed that wives should be little interested in sexual relations, engaging in sex only for procreation and reserving their love for their children. Brides were supposed to approach the marriage bed with their maidenheads intact, so families strove to protect the virginity of daughters and sisters and the honor of wives— and thus their husbands—by confining them to the home, out of the reach of virile males.

With few exceptions, men were the household's primary economic providers, although women's economic contribution in the form of maintenance, food preparation, and child rearing were by no means incon-

8. Elizabeth Kuznesof and Robert Oppenheimer, "The Family and Society in Nineteenth-Century Latin America: An Historiographical Introduction," *Journal of Family History* 10 (Fall 1985):215–34; and Patricia Seed, "The Church and the Patriarchal Family: Marriage Conflicts in Sixteenth- and Seventeenth-Century New Spain," *Journal of Family History* 10 (Fall 1985):284–93.

9. Ramón A. Gutiérrez, "Honor Ideology, Marriage Negotiation, and Class-Gender Domination in New Mexico, 1690–1846," *Latin American Perspectives* 12 (Winter 1985):81–104; and Gutiérrez, "From Honor to Love: Transformations of the Meaning of Sexuality in Colonial New Mexico," in *Kinship Ideology and Practice in Latin America*, ed. Raymond T. Smith (Chapel Hill, 1984), 237–63.

siderable. It was expensive to maintain the ideal Hispanic family, and poor people simply could not afford to rigorously confine women's activities to the home. Among the lower classes women baked, sewed, and acted as herbal healers (*curanderas*). As a rule, men and women tried to marry as high above their own class as circumstances might permit. The bride's family usually paid a dowry to the husband, but in colonial Peru wealthy *conquistadores* sometimes reversed this procedure so that they could marry women of higher rank than themselves. Regardless of the riches he obtained in the New World, only marriage into the upper classes would confer the highest possible status to the Hispanic frontiersman. In America there were comparatively few Iberian women, so Spaniards took Indian concubines and wives. Moreover, even after a marriage with a suitable Spanish woman had been consummated, rustic husbands were sometimes reluctant to give up their native consorts, so philandering was a part of daily life. These habits were well established by the time the Spanish entered California.[10]

The family that evolved in Hispanic America was not merely a frontier replica of an Iberian model. The Mexican family also reflects the values and traditions of Aztec society, which held the collective family, female chastity, industry, and obedience in high esteem. Thus, the Mexican-American family is an amalgam of European and Indian institutions.[11]

Under frontier conditions Mexican family values could change dramatically. In New Mexico, women seemed far more independent than the usual patriarchal family evidently permitted. New Mexican women ran businesses, divorced their husbands, took lovers, owned property, sued in court, and generally acted as emancipated as their male counterparts. Significantly, New Mexican authorities often upheld female rights. New Mexicans may have been influenced by Indian neighbors who were matrilineal and otherwise regarded women highly.[12]

Californians seem to have followed a more conservative family tradition than New Mexicans. In Los Angeles before the Mexican War, the majority of *californios* lived in extended families. This traditional arrangement engendered strong ties among the head of the family, children, resident in-laws, grandparents, and other relatives. Hispanic Californians augmented familial blood ties with *compadrazgo*, a practice

10. Guillermo Céspedes, *Latin America in the Early Years* (New York, 1974), 56–62; James Lockhart, *Spanish Colonial Peru, 1532–1560: A Colonial Society* (Madison, Wis., 1968), 150–62; and Evers, Clauss, and Wong, "Subsistence Reproduction," 23–36.

11. Alfredo Mirandé and Evangelina Enríquez, *La Chicana: The Mexican-American Woman* (Chicago, 1979), 98–106.

12. Janet Lecompte, "The Independent Women of Hispanic New Mexico," *Western Historical Quarterly* 12 (Jan. 1981):17–36.

that added fictive kin to the family as godparents. Children received one set of godparents at birth and additional *padrinos* at confirmation, first communion, marriage, and other major life events. A californio might have as many as sixteen padrinos, each responsible for giving advice and financial assistance and replacing natural parents who died. Compadrazgo relationships were formalized in church and formed an important part of Hispanic family life.[13]

Early in the conquest of the Americas, the shortage of Spanish women led not only to illegitimate sexual liaisons but to marriages as well. Throughout the Spanish Empire frequent intermarriage along with illicit unions created a substantial mixed blood *mestizo* population. The mestizos were considered to be Spanish *gente de razón* (people of reason), although they were the social inferiors of Europeans. Not surprisingly, mestizos were among the first settlers on New Spain's northern frontier. In California the frontier vanguard included Spaniards, Indians, mestizos, and Negroes. Since few women came along, the familiar process of racial fusion resulted. Not surprisingly, Father Junípero Serra approved of biracial marriages because they helped to establish Hispanic settlements.[14]

Amalgamation in the California borderlands did not mean that Indian and Spanish cultures united on an equal footing. On the contrary, Hispanic Catholic values were meant to supplant native ways. As elsewhere in Spanish America, the Franciscan missions aimed to eliminate marriage and family customs repugnant to Spaniards and the Church. The mission could control only Indians who were under its authority, and Indians were at first slow to volunteer for Christian instruction. As elsewhere in the Western Hemisphere, the Spanish advance was accompanied by epidemic diseases that decimated native populations, and the new pastoral economy disrupted native lifeways. Disease, death, and hunger caused native people to question the efficacy of their old traditions and enhanced the appeal of mission life. By 1785 five thousand Indians had become mission neophytes. Twenty years later there were twenty thousand neophytes in a mission system that eventually expanded

13. Richard Griswold del Castillo, *The Los Angeles Barrio, 1850–1890: A Social History* (Berkeley, 1979), 97–98; and Gloria E. Miranda, "Gente de Razón Marriage Patterns in Spanish and Mexican California: A Case Study of Santa Barbara and Los Angeles," *Southern California Quarterly* 63 (Spring 1981):1–21.

14. Cook and Borah, *Essays in Population History* 3:278–310; and Jack D. Forbes, "Hispano-Mexican Pioneers of the San Francisco Bay Region: An Analysis of Racial Origins," *Aztlan* 14, no. 1 (1983):175–89. Junípero Serra to Antonio María Bucareli y Ursua, Aug. 24, 1775, *Writings of Junípero Serra*, ed. Antonine Tibesar, 4 vols. (Washington, D.C., 1955–66), 2:149.

to twenty-one establishments, all located near the coast between Sonoma and San Diego.[15]

The missions converted Indians to habits of industry as well as Catholic piety. Indian labor had been an important part of the Spanish-American economy from the time of Columbus. Indeed, Spanish colonization could not have advanced without native workers to till the soil and work the mines. Indians were recognized as human beings with souls and certain civil rights, yet the crown and its representatives granted to conquistadors *encomienda* rights to labor and tribute from the conquered Indians. The crown attempted to eliminate the worst abuses of encomienda, eventually resorting to parceling out Indian services by royal authority under the *repartimiento* system. By the seventeenth century debt peonage superseded coerced labor in the new World, but Indian labor remained a necessity on the thinly settled, defensive borderland frontier. The mission functioned as a magnet, drawing Indian workers who established and maintained settlements where labor was otherwise scarce. This was particularly true in California. Since the non-Indian population of Hispanic California never exceeded thirty-five hundred, the missions and Indian labor were the basis for California's economy. Neophytes constructed the buildings, herded the cattle, worked the fields, and did whatever was required to keep the missions running. The Franciscan establishments became the paramount economic institutions of the colony, controlling most of the land and an Indian labor force of many thousands.

To control Indian and Spanish sexual behavior at the missions, single women were locked in sleeping rooms at night. Nocturnal cloistering protected the women's chastity and this made them desirable spouses, but it also made them more susceptible to the infectious diseases that swept through the missions from time to time, killing thousands. Franciscan missionaries were anxious to eliminate polygyny and legitimize native marriages with appropriate Catholic ceremonies. Once these marriages were solemnized, divorce became nearly impossible, although widows and widowers were encouraged to remarry.

Eight northern California missions recorded more than twenty-three hundred marriages between Indians who had previously been joined by native customs, and over five thousand new Indian unions. In addition, more than ten thousand neophyte widows and widowers remarried in the Catholic Church, a statistic that tells as much about mission mortality

15. Cook, "Indian versus the Spanish Mission," 3–56; Robert Archibald, *The Economic Aspects of the California Missions* (Washington, D.C., 1978), 153–54; and Oakah L. Jones, *Los Paisanos: Spanish Settlers on the Northern Frontier of New Spain* (Norman, 1979), 204–17.

rates as about neophyte marriage patterns. Missionaries complained about Indians breaking their marriage vows and secretly keeping up native customs, indicating that the Franciscans were not wholly successful in converting neophytes to Hispanic practices. Nevertheless, the high incidence of Catholic marriages was a hallmark of missionary effectiveness on the frontier. Not only did marriages bind Indian couples to the mission, but Christian Indian parents baptized their children in the Church, increasing the neophyte population with Indians whose links with native culture were weaker than their parents'. By 1834 more than seven thousand Indians had received baptism at six northern California missions. Although infant mortality rates fluctuated between 50 and 60 percent, every birth in the mission tended to weaken native cultures by denying them new members. Thus, mission marriage and childbirth effectively reduced the Indian population as it Hispanicized it.[16]

Indian interracial marriages were uncommon in California, producing fewer than one hundred children, according to northern California mission records. Mexican Californians preferred to marry among themselves, but californio men had illicit sexual liaisons with native women. Franciscan padres often complained that soldiers molested Indian women. Few statistics reflect the extent of casual sex, but contemporary accounts indicate that such liaisons must have been common. The rapid spread of venereal diseases among Indian people was one result of unregulated sexual intercourse. Syphilis was especially devastating; it either killed Indians outright or lowered their resistance to other diseases, often with mortal effects. Women were particularly vulnerable in childbirth, and a mother's death usually resulted in the loss of the infant. Measles, diphtheria, and smallpox likewise caused high mortality rates in the neophyte population, but Spanish frontier family customs and sexual behavior also contributed to native population decline and reduced fertility rates among neophytes. Thus, Hispanic families displaced native families by a long process of attrition.[17]

To maintain mission strength in the midst of Indian demographic decline, missionaries had to look to the interior for new neophytes. The new mission Indians were Yokuts and Miwok, whom the Spanish called

16. Carl O. Sauer, *The Early Spanish Main* (Berkeley, 1966), esp. 31, 35, 76–77; Lesley Byrd Simpson, *The Encomienda in New Spain: The Beginnings of Spanish Mexico* (Berkeley, 1950), esp. 1–28; and Charles Gibson, *The Aztecs under Spanish Rule: A History of the Indians of the Valley of Mexico, 1519–1820* (Stanford, 1964), 58–97, 224–36, 248–52.

17. Cook and Borah, *Essays in Population History* 3:278–310; Daniel J. Garr, "A Rare and Desolate Land: Population and Race in Hispanic California," *Western Historical Quarterly* 6 (Apr. 1975):133–48; Cook, "Population Trends Among the California Mission Indians," 19; and Cook, "The Indian versus the Spanish Mission," 13–34.

tulareños because they lived in the vast tule-choked marshlands of the San Joaquin Valley. The conversion of tulareños was the missions' first important effect on the California interior, setting up conditions for later developments. The arrival of new converts was not an unmixed blessing for the friars, since the tulareños periodically rebelled against mission authority and fled to their homelands. To recover runaways and the livestock that they frequently took with them, military expeditions entered the interior, which remained in Indian hands during the Spanish period. Despite resistance and warfare, the conversion of interior Indians continued, as did the slow, steady transformation of Indian family patterns and labor practices that accompanied demographic decline and frontier settlement. The traditional Indian family was a major casualty on the Spanish borderland frontier.[18]

The Anglo-American Frontier Family

Anglo families also brought well-defined traditions to California. As in Hispanic society, Anglo families were based on the conjugal couple and their children; the husband was the head of the household and the woman's place ideally was in the home. Men were supposed to support and protect their families and theoretically their wives were pure, pious, and domestic. Men confronted the world; women shunned it for household life. Anglo-Americans believed that this sexual dichotomy was fitting because men and women had different natures: males were virile, strong, worldly, coarse, competitive, and forward; women were demure, retiring, passive, spiritual, and maternal. Man's role was to subdue the world; women were supposed to civilize it. In the early years of the nineteenth century a woman could own property, but it became her husband's after she married. Divorce was difficult to obtain and the husband usually retained the children. Some marriages, no doubt, were convenient alliances for combining family fortunes, but the romantic ideal was to marry a loving companion, regardless of social class and economic considerations. Extramarital sex was not condoned, although brothels were common enough to indicate that the ideal was not always attained.[19]

18. Cook, "Population Trends Among the California Mission Indians," 58–67; and Sherburne F. Cook, ed., "Colonial Expeditions to the Interior of California: Central Valley, 1800–1820," *University of California Anthropological Records* 16 (1960):239–292.

19. Carl N. Degler, *At Odds: Women and the Family in America from the Revolution to the Present* (New York, 1980), 3–25; Barbara Welter, "The Cult of True Womanhood 1820–1860," *American Quarterly* 18 (1966):151–74; and Anne M. Butler, *Daughters of Joy, Sisters of Misery: Prostitutes in the American West, 1865–90* (Urbana, Ill., 1985).

The family was basic to the Anglo-American westward movement. In the earliest stages single males went to the frontier. Unlike the Spanish, whose settlements were made according to royal decree, Anglos pushed beyond settled areas on their own initiative and were reluctant to bring women with them until they gained a secure foothold in the new land. Once established, Anglo men looked for spouses and usually returned to settled areas to find them. Since Anglo tradition did not encourage interracial marriages, Indian women were not considered acceptable mates. Fur traders were the only notable exception to this rule, yet they sometimes abandoned their marriages to Indians after the country was settled and white women became available.[20]

Anglo frontier women were extraordinarily fertile and large families were the rule. Unfortunately, the level of health care was so primitive that death in childbirth was an ordinary occurrence. A grieving husband with a cabin full of children remarried as soon as possible, and commonly his new wife produced more offspring. High birthrates and immigration populated frontier areas. As land became scarce and expensive and landless sons moved on to the next frontier where land was readily available, the frontier process was repeated.

Anglo women on the frontier did more than bear children and keep the home fires burning. They pitched in to help with the dozens of chores necessary to operate a family farm in a new country. Whether spinning thread, making clothes, tending a garden, or raising children, frontier women were assets to their husbands and to their communities. Women's domestic work was much more than a mere convenience for their pioneer husbands. Food preparation, household maintenance, child rearing, and clothing fabrication were forms of unwaged labor that subsidized the growing frontier market economy. That is why Anglo men returned to settled areas to find brides. Women provided not only emotional and social stability, but economic contributions as well. Hence, the family was an engine for frontier advancement, casting forth westering sons who came back periodically to take away the excess of unmarried daughters. This dynamic was in force from colonial times until the end of the nineteenth century.[21]

20. Nugent, *Structures of American Social History*, 54–79; Richard A. Bartlett, *The New Country: A Social History of the American Frontier, 1776–1890* (New York, 1974), 343–63; William R. Swagerty, "Marriage and Settlement Patterns of the Rocky Mountain Trappers and Traders," *Western Historical Quarterly* 11 (Apr. 1980):159–80; Sylvia Van Kirk, *Many Tender Ties: Women in Fur Trade Society, 1670–1870* (Norman, 1980), 50–52; and Jennifer S. H. Brown, *Strangers in Blood: Fur Trade Company Families in Indian Country* (Vancouver, B.C., 1980).

21. Evers, Clauss, and Wong, "Subsistence Reproduction," 23–36.

As for Indian families, the United States favored moving them away from settled areas to Indian country, where Indian Office bureaucrats and humanitarians supposedly would teach them Christianity and civilized ways. The transformation of native traditions was the goal of Anglo humanitarians, but it was not a prerequisite for their settlements. Indeed, the elimination of Indians from settled areas was a distinguishing characteristic of the Anglo frontier.[22]

New conditions changed Indian household life even as it was being removed from the scene. As early as colonial times, Anglo society began to alter the native economy and family practices in ways that humanitarians had not intended. The advent of the fur trade and firearms drew Indians into a violent cycle of warfare. High death rates for young men made polygyny a necessity in order to incorporate fertile women into families where they could produce children who would replace the men lost in war. Formerly polygyny had been reserved for chiefs, who required additional female hands to fulfill their ceremonial and entertainment obligations. In New England, colonists sought to restrict polygyny among Christian Indians because it was an affront to God and contrary to colonial statutes. By prohibiting polygyny Englishmen unwittingly legislated continuing demographic decline for Christian Indians, a result that Indians may have foreseen when they protested the Puritans' restrictions.[23]

Farther west and later in time, similar processes occurred among the Sioux and other Plains tribes. There the arrival of horses and the ensuing development of raiding societies once again led to the death of young men, the spread of polygyny, and the adoption of men—including whites—into the tribe. In 1805 the explorer Zebulon Montgomery Pike reported only 3,855 men and 7,030 women among the Sioux. He reckoned, however, that there were 11,800 children, or nearly 1.7 children per woman regardless of age, a statistic that suggests the efficacy of polygyny for buttressing a population under stress. In the 1840s Christian

22. Nugent, *Structures of American Social History*, pp. 54–79; Jack Eblen, "An Analysis of Nineteenth-Century Frontier Populations," *Demography* 2 (1965):399–413; Richard A. Easterlin, "Population and Farm Settlement in the Northern United States," *Journal of Economic History* 36 (March 1976):45–75; Easterlin, "Factors in the Decline of Farm Family Fertility in the United States: Some Preliminary Research Results," *Journal of American History* 63 (December 1976):600–614; Julie Roy Jeffrey, *Frontier Women: The Trans-Mississippi West, 1840–1880* (New York, 1979); John Mack Faragher, *Women and Men on the Overland Trail* (New Haven, 1979); and Sandra L. Myres, *Westering Women and the Frontier Experience, 1800–1915* (Albuquerque, 1982).

23. Axtell, *European and the Indian*, 261–63; and Axtell, *The Invasion Within: The Contest of Cultures in Colonial North America* (New York, 1985), 123–24, 152–53, 155, 169–70, 253.

missionaries who attempted to convince the Sioux to give up polygyny met with staunch resistance. Even while accepting a religion that promised life everlasting, the Sioux understood the brutal arithmetic of biological survival. Polygyny would be discarded grudgingly.[24]

Anglo-Americans had little regard for Indian kinship patterns. Believing that the native family could be changed at will in order to conform to the norms of white society, they preferred that Indians be transformed at a distance, separated by a frontier line, and isolated on reservations until the metamorphosis was complete. In California, however, complete racial segregation was impossible and Anglos had to adjust to a closer association with Indians.

A Social Vision Realized

There were both similarities and important differences among Indian, Hispanic, and Anglo families. Each group revered the family and made it a central part of their lives. For each the family served social, biological, economic, and occasionally political purposes. Hispanics and Indians commonly married out of their communities, but only the Spanish intended to destroy an alien culture while integrating new spouses. Both Anglo and Hispanic families were part of a structure of empire building, yet they had quite different effects on native families: one sought to draw them to its bosom; the other strove to drive them away. However, Anglos excluded Indians and Spaniards included them for the same purposes: to regulate the cultural context of newly settled areas so that frontier resources could be conveniently exploited. Native people were accustomed to marrying outlanders to secure diplomatic and trade advantages, but they had no idea that exogamy could be detrimental to their interests. Nor could they foresee how inclusion in non-Indian society would affect their own family structures and their prospects for survival.

Between 1820 and 1860 these contradictory and complementary traditions blended on the California borderland frontier. With hardly a thought, Anglos accommodated to Mexican California, Indian labor, and even miscegenation. But in asserting control over California, they quickly reestablished their old family customs as they adapted new technology and labor arrangements. By 1860 Anglo families far exceeded

24. Donald Jackson, ed., *The Journals of Zebulon Montgomery Pike, with Letters and Related Documents*, 2 vols. (Norman, Okla., 1966) 1:220–22; and Gary Clayton Anderson, *Kinsmen of Another Kind: Dakota-White Relations in the Upper Mississippi Valley, 1650– 1862* (Lincoln, 1984), xi, 17–18, 169–70.

native and Hispanic families in numbers and power, and the newcomers viewed their position with a sense of self-satisfaction that was common in the age of Manifest Destiny. In 1864 Fannie Reading, the wife of the Anglo pioneer Pierson B. Reading, described the wheat harvest for her mother back east. In one week twenty-two men, a steam engine, thresh-ing machine, two heading machines, two wagons, and twenty-two horses would finish a job that used to take up to three months and require the services of scores of Indians. The new heading machines, which Reading was the first to use in his part of the state, made all the difference. "About ten or fifteen minutes after the grain is standing in the field," Mrs. Reading wrote, "it is cut, threshed and sacked, ready for market." She had been watching wheat harvests on her husband's farm since they were married in 1856. Then the process had been carried out mostly by Indians using sickles and cradles. Later they assisted when Reading switched to combine harvesters, a technological advance that still re-quired two or three months to finish a harvest. The arrival of steam-powered threshers, horse-driven headers, and other innovations reduced the need for Indian agricultural labor and inexorably diminished an important source of subsistence for Indian families. But Indian survival was not Fannie Reading's concern. She happily reported that even dur-ing the bad drought year of 1864 the farm had produced a bountiful crop.[25]

The Readings' marriage followed a common Anglo pattern. He was a widowed overland pioneer of 1843 who established his Mexican land grant, Buenaventura Rancho, the next year. Fighting on the American side in the Mexican War and gaining financial success in the gold rush, Reading became one of the most prominent men in California. Fannie was from Virginia's prominent Washington and Lee families. Her uncle Richard Lee introduced them when Reading was in Washington, D.C., to quiet the title to his land grant rancho. During their courtship she took the trouble to inquire about his reputation in California. After receiving the necessary assurances, her grandmother, Elizabeth Lee, gave Pierson a lock of George Washington's hair, a "sacred relic" that was presented as a token of Mrs. Lee's affection. Suitably overwhelmed by the grave symbolism of the occasion, Reading hoped that his life would be "not unworthy of the signal favor" and married Fannie three weeks later. In California she lived a leisured but rustic life in the north end of the Sacramento Valley, attended parties, feted guests, doted on

25. Fannie Reading to her mother, July 8, 1864, RP; Reading Ranch Journal, 1854, RC; and Gertrude A. Steger, "A Chronology of the Life of Pierson B. Reading," *California Historical Society Quarterly* 22 (Dec. 1943):365–71.

her children, and vacationed near Mount Lassen. Her domestic duties were eased by Indian servants and two native nurses.[26]

Fannie's family attachments and household life were in many ways typical of middle-class Victorian women. Her sentimental love for her husband, children, and kin were much in keeping for a woman of her status and background. That she never inquired—in writing, at least— into the family lives of her domestic help also speaks of the cultural blindness and class presumptions that were common to women of southern birth. People of color were born to serve whites in the world of Fannie's youth. If Fannie thoughtlessly accepted the exploitation of people who were not white, she was hardly alone.

For Fannie, Indian servants' labor was not so much a frontier economic necessity as it was a badge of the Readings' social rank. Had Fannie arrived a decade earlier, she would have found a much different situation. She would have seen Indian trappers going with her husband into the Trinity River country for beaver and otter. She would have seen Indian women living with white men and raising their children. She would have seen an Indian majority that could still speak up for its interests and isolated white settlements protected by Indian soldiers. This world was fast fading when she arrived in California. Indeed, she may not have realized that it had ever existed. To discover it—and a time when Indians could shape the terms of their accommodation and survival—we must turn our attention to the end of the Spanish Empire in America, when California was one of the most remote places on the continent.[27]

26. Pierson B. Reading to Mrs. Elizabeth Lee, Feb. 23, 1856, RC; Fannie Reading to her grandmother, Jan. 1, 1857, RP; and Fannie Reading to her mother, July 8, 1864, RP.

27. New Helvetia Account Book, 1845, RC.

2

California's International Frontier, 1819–1846

The large willow trees that stood in the valley of the San Joaquin provided lookouts for Yokuts Indians who watched for intruders. In the autumn of 1819 they saw a party of Spanish soldiers and their mission Indian allies enter the valley near the now dry Tulare Lake. They were expecting the Spanish, since two Wowol Yokuts had returned from a September fiesta at the Mission San Miguel with a rumor that a force would come to the valley to capture all the runaway neophytes and all the gentiles, as well. Moreover, the Wowols believed that the Spanish intended to kill anyone who resisted. When the Indians spotted the expedition from the coast, they fled to hiding places deep in the great tule swamps. To the north, another Spanish expedition went after runaway neophytes in Miwok country near the modern city of Stockton.[1]

These expeditions represented the waning power of the Spanish Empire in America. Spain's colonies were in revolt and in two years Mexico would become independent. In 1819 California was on the periphery of these changes, ruled by loyal government officials and Franciscan missionaries who were more concerned about the immediate problem of controlling the numerous Indian population than about the outcome of events in distant Mexico. East and north of the missions, presidios, and pueblos lay thousands of square miles of country that remained in the hands of native people (see map 2). Occasionally Spanish forces entered the interior to explore, capture runaway neophytes, and to reclaim the livestock that mission fugitives had taken.[2]

In theory, Spaniards sought to incorporate Indians peacefully into frontier society by training them in Franciscan missions. In practice, the

1. Anna H. Gayton, ed., "Estudillo Among the Yokuts," in *Essays in Anthropology Presented to A. L. Kroeber in Celebration of His Sixtieth Birthday*, ed. Robert H. Lowie (1936; reprint, Freeport, N.Y., 1968), 68, 83.

2. Francis F. Guest, O.F.M., "An Examination of the Thesis of S. F. Cook on the Forced Conversion of Indians in the California Missions," *Southern California Quarterly* 61 (1979):1–77; David J. Weber, *The Mexican Frontier, 1821–1846: The American Southwest under Mexico* (Albuquerque, 1982), 15–42, 60–67.

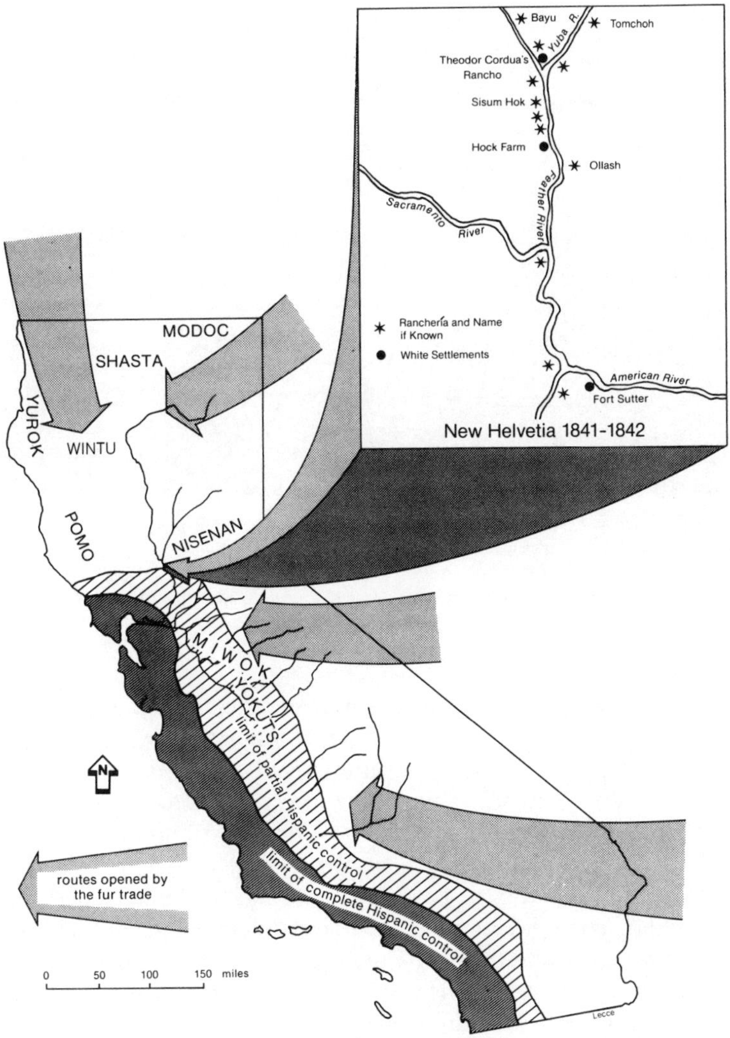
Bayu
Tomchoh
Yuba R.
Theodor Cordua's Rancho
Sisum Hok
Hock Farm
Ollash
Feather River
Sacramento River
Ranchería and Name if Known
White Settlements
American River
Fort Sutter
New Helvetia 1841-1842
MODOC
SHASTA
YUROK
WINTU
POMO
NISENAN
MIWOK
YOKUTS
limit of partial Hispanic control
limit of complete Hispanic control
N
routes opened by the fur trade
0 50 100 150 miles
Lecce

Map 2. Hispanic and Anglo Influences on California's Interior Indians, 1820–1840

results were not ideal. Sadly, violence was common, for Indians often resisted alien invaders and the Spanish fought to protect their small, isolated settlements. Demographic decline and the friars' coaxing convinced many Indians that the missions provided a safe haven, but others—especially Yokuts and Miwoks in the interior—believed that resistance was the key to survival.

FIG. 3. Plain between the San Joaquin and Kings Rivers. This scene shows a Yokuts man in the San Joaquin Valley around 1853, looking like a Plains Indian ready to hunt buffalo. Note the leggings with a knife tucked in the knot just below the knee. During the Mexican era, horse raiding Indians probably dressed and rode much like this. From R. S. Williamson, *Report of Exploration in California for Railroad Routes to Connect with Routes Near the 35th and 32nd Parallels of North Latitude* (Washington, D.C., 1856).

Whatever strategy Indians chose, survival depended on adapting to the Spanish presence on the coast. The development of Indian livestock raiding illustrates this point. Soon after Spanish colonization began, native people started stealing and eating mission livestock, but the seriousness of livestock raiding increased after missionaries began to search out interior Indians to replace the coastal neophytes who had died from infectious diseases. To prevent raiding, the Spanish had considered building some inland missions that would have given the Franciscans a new field while opening church lands on the coast to private settlement, but Indian resistance and lack of adequate government support prevented the construction of any institutions in the interior. Without permanent Spanish defenses in the interior, the Indians became a troublesome and then a formidable foe. Interior neophytes who learned the skills of Spanish horsemanship could avoid capture by taking horses and driving them swiftly to their interior homeland. In the central valley, horses proved useful to Miwok and Yokuts Indians, who used them to hunt antelope and elk much as Plains Indians hunted buffalo (see fig. 3). In addition, the interior Indians commonly ate horsemeat, thus making complete use of their newfound beast of burden. In 1819 Father Mariano Payeras claimed that all the valley Indians rode horses and even held horse fairs where they traded stolen stock. Payeras may have exaggerated, but his concern reflected the importance of Indian horse raiding to Spanish Californians.[3]

The 1819 expeditions were, as usual, looking for livestock thieves and new mission sites. Lieutenant José María Estudillo commanded the force that the Yokuts had spotted, while Sergeant José Sanchez directed the northern contingent. Estudillo proceeded to the Wowol Yokuts ranchería, where he was surprised to find the community deserted. From two captured Indians he learned that the others had fled because they were afraid to go to the missions, although they were willing to give up the runaway Christians. Estudillo assured them that he wanted only to reclaim stolen horses and return Christians to the missions.[4]

The lieutenant and his troops spent nearly a month reconnoitering the rancherías in the valley and in the Sierra Nevada foothills near modern Fresno. Many Indians hid to avoid capture until Estudillo reassured them of his intentions. Some foothill people—probably Western Mono—who had not met Hispanic people before, said that they were anxious to trade, so Estudillo gave their headman a pass to go to the missions. Despite the proclaimed peaceful intentions of both sides, however, the foothill Indians kept their young women and children hidden from the soldiers.[5]

While Estudillo saw the bones of many slaughtered horses and recovered one alive, he did not report seeing any mounted Indians or feral horse herds in the San Joaquin Valley. The southern Yokuts referred to the "horse-killers of the north," possibly to encourage Estudillo to take his expedition elsewhere. In the meantime Sanchez's operations in the north and an unrelated expedition farther south, headed by Lieutenant Gabriel Moraga, gave native people reasons to doubt Estudillo's bland promises of peace. Moraga, searching for escaped Santa Barbara neophytes, surprised them in a canyon and captured nine. One neophyte who escaped walked for four days and nights to report the news to the ranchería where Estudillo was camped.[6]

On the same day that Estudillo heard about Moraga's foray, he learned that Sanchez had fought the Muquelemne Miwoks on the Ca-

3. Hubert Howe Bancroft, *History of California*, 2:335, n. 30; Sylvia M. Broadbent, "Conflict at Monterey: Indian Horse Raiding, 1820–1850," *Journal of California Anthropology* 1 (1974):86–101; Anna H. Gayton, "Yokuts and Western Mono Ethnography," *University of California Anthropological Records* 10, nos. 1–2 (1948):183–84; and George William Beattie, "Spanish Plans for an Inland Chain of Missions in California," *Historical Society of Southern California Annual Publication* 14 (1929):243–64.

4. Gayton, "Estudillo," 70.

5. Ibid., 74.

6. Ibid., 76, 79.

laveras River, killed twenty-seven gentiles, wounded twenty more, and captured sixteen. Sanchez also recovered forty-nine stolen horses, but the Miwok killed a neophyte ally and wounded five soldiers. Alarmed at the news of Spanish casualties, Estudillo sent an Indian messenger to tell native people that no soldiers had been injured, fearing that knowledge of the army's losses might inspire Indian resistance. The lieutenant spent another week examining the foothill country, but gave up the idea of going farther north, believing that intelligence of Sanchez's battle would cause the Indians to hide at his approach. In the middle of November the small force returned to Monterey presidio.[7]

These expeditions, and the Miwok and Yokuts response, illustrate the variety of Indian-white relations in the interior at the end of the Spanish era in California. Valley Indians feared the Spanish would take all native people to the missions and kill any who resisted. In the south, whole rancherías fled; women and children hid while chiefs and headmen promised to cooperate in returning stock and Christian Indians to Spanish authority. There was evidence of horse raiding throughout the valley, but horse carcasses and bones were found in greatest abundance towards the north along the San Joaquin River. The Muquelemne Miwoks in the San Joaquin delta region had dozens of live horses in their possession that showed the extent of their rustling. They vigorously resisted the Spanish invaders. Miwok country, the geographic center of the interior, was the focus of Indian horse raiding.

In 1821 the Mexican Revolution changed the institutions that governed the relations between Hispanic and Indian people. The 1824 constitution made Indians citizens. Two years later California's governor, José María Echeandía, acting on instructions from the central government to convert the missions to secular parishes and grant lands to the Indians, cautiously began to emancipate neophytes from mission authority. Under Spanish law the missions did not own the vast estates that they controlled. Instead the crown granted the missions a usufructory right to administer lands for the benefit of the Indians. After neophytes had been trained, mission lands were supposed to be turned over to the Indians and the surplus would become part of the public domain. The Franciscans had resisted secularization for decades, but the new Mexican government meant to carry it forward. Franciscan resistance and political turmoil forestalled secularization until 1833, when governor José Figueroa proposed a plan for congregating former neophytes in native-owned towns on former mission lands. While the governor's ap-

7. Ibid., 79, 83; and Bancroft, *History of California*, 2:335.

pointees administered surplus real estate, non-Indians acquired the new Indian lands and other ex-mission property by fair means and foul. Some emancipated neophytes farmed for themselves or worked for californios, making a poor living as farm laborers and servants. Others ventured into the interior to live in Indian communities.[8]

In 1824 a dramatic neophyte revolt illustrated some changes that were underway. On February 21 the Santa Ynez neophytes, angry because a presidio soldier had flogged one of them, attacked the garrison and burned most of the mission buildings. The La Purísima neophytes joined the rebellion on the same afternoon, taking possession of their mission. The next day the Santa Ynez rebels marched to La Purísima, which they fortified. The missionary Juan Cabot said that the barricaded Indians sent "two sacks of beads to persuade all the villages to join them in annihilating the soldiers." By Cabot's account, the Tachi Yokuts on the western side of the valley and the Kaweah River Telamni Yokuts refused to accept the beads; the Kings River Nutunutnu Yokuts took the beads, but did not go to the neophytes' aid. The hitherto peaceful Wowol and Suntache Yokuts accepted the beads, and Cabot believed that "some of them from each village started out for La Purísima."[9]

On February 22 news of the revolt reached the Mission Santa Barbara, where the Indians armed themselves. After a missionary intervened, the neophytes agreed not to join the revolt if the local presidio troops would disarm and leave the mission, but two soldiers refused to give up their weapons and fighting broke out. The neophytes looted the mission except for the church, then fled to the mission dam. Soldiers ransacked the neophyte quarters and killed several innocent Christian Indians. Rebel neophytes stayed at the dam for about two weeks, simultaneously asking for pardons from the Mexican authorities and trying to make alliances with the gentile Indians in the interior. Finally convinced that

8. Weber, *Mexican Frontier*, 15–42, 62–68; Manuel P. Servin, "The Secularization of the California Missions: A Reappraisal," *Southern California Quarterly* 47 (1965):133–49; C. Alan Hutchinson, "The Mexican Government and the Mission Indians of Upper California," *Americas* 21 (1964–65):335–62; and Daniel Garr, "Planning Politics and Plunder: The Missions and Indian Pueblos of Hispanic California," *Southern California Quarterly* 54 (1972):291–312. For the text of the approved secularization order, see Bancroft, *History of California*, 3:342–44, n. 4.

9. Bancroft, *History of California*, 2:527–30; Cabot to Gov. Luis Argüello, Feb. 28, 1824, in Sherburne F. Cook, ed., "Expeditions to the Interior of California: Central Valley, 1820–1840," *University of California Anthropological Records* 20, no. 5 (1962):152. Suntache does not appear in the Southern Yokuts synonymy given in Robert F. Heizer, ed., *Handbook of North American Indians*, vol. 8, *California* (Washington, D.C., 1978), 448, 461.

they would not receive amnesty, the Santa Barbara Indians withdrew to the San Joaquin Valley.[10]

In March reinforcements from the Monterey presidio attacked La Purísima, where about four hundred neophytes held out. The rebels took heavy casualties, then surrendered. The Wowol and Suntache Indians, enroute to the scene, learned of the defeat and returned to their rancherías. The authorities condemned and shot seven Indian rebels, and sentenced twelve others to presidio labor for eight to ten years.[11]

Approximately 450 Santa Barbara neophytes remained in the San Joaquin Valley near Buenavista Lake. They had rebelled against the excesses of presidio soldiers rather than against the missions; but once they were free from the restraints of mission life neophytes ceased to observe Catholic customs. They exchanged women with Yokuts gentiles—regardless of their Christian marital status—took frequent sweat baths, gambled much, and were never seen to pray "or even tell their beads," as one neophyte put it.[12]

Besides flouting Catholic conventions, the "Indians worked in the daytime digging ditches across the trails" to foil Mexican cavalry. Andrés, who had been a mission alcalde, assumed a leader's part, visiting gentile rancherías and sending them presents to cultivate alliances. With these new allies, Andrés hoped to return to Santa Barbara, kill the neophytes who had stayed behind, and attack the presidio. Mexicans even received an unconfirmed report that someone from the Russian settlement at Ross, north of San Francisco Bay, was instructing Andrés and his followers in the use of firearms, although subsequent Mexican operations did not turn up the mysterious foreigner.[13]

Despite Andrés' efforts, only a part of one ranchería decided to join the Santa Barbara Indians; but they never had an opportunity to attack

10. Bancroft, *History of California*, 2:530–31; Fernando Huilaset (neophyte), reply to *interogatorio*, June 1, 1824; Fray Antonio Ripoll to Vicente Francisco de Sarría, May 5, 1824, in Cook, "Expeditions, 1820–1840," 152–53.

11. Cabot to Argüello, Feb. 28, 1824, in Cook, "Expeditions, 1820–1840," 152; and Bancroft, *History of California*, 2:531–32.

12. The responses of Indians Leopoldo, Senen, and Fernando Huiliaset to the *interogatorio* of June 1, 1824, in Cook, "Expeditions, 1820–1840," 153–54; and Heizer, *Handbook*, 453, 455.

13. The responses of Indians Leopoldo, Senen, Pelagio, Alberto, and Fernando Huiliaset to *interrogatorio*, June 1, 1824, in Cook, "Expeditions, 1820–1840," 153–54. Pelagio and Alberto saw the Russian alive, and Senen heard from Christian Indians that "members of the expedition killed the Russian," meaning apparently the April expedition. There is no known formal report from the April foray; a subsequent letter by Gov. Luis Argüello states only that four rebels were killed in the interior, without mentioning anything about a Russian (Argüello to José de la Guerra y Noriega, May 5, 1824, in Cook, "Expeditions, 1820–1840," 152).

the coastal settlement. In April a Mexican force went to the interior and took part in two skirmishes before retreating because of inclement weather. Two months later Pablo de la Portilla took another detachment to the valley, promised the rebels pardons, and arranged for their peaceful return to the mission. Portilla even reappointed Andrés as an alcalde, with authority to round up recalcitrant Christians in the tulares. The Portilla expedition ended the mission revolt, but at least 163 neophytes wise to the ways of Mexican California remained in the interior.[14]

The mission revolt demonstrated changes in the attitude of interior Indians. In 1819 the Yokuts bowed and scraped before Estudillo. Five years later some of them were willing to risk Mexican wrath by harboring neophyte fugitives. Resistance and flight to the interior was becoming an increasingly viable strategy for survival.

Amidst growing Indian militance Jedediah Strong Smith entered California in 1826, initiating the Anglo-American fur trade. His expedition added a new dimension to Indian-white relations in the California interior. Smith and his band of trappers represented United States' fur interests, and his venture made the interior an international frontier. He stopped first at Mission San Gabriel near the little pueblo of Los Angeles, rested for a few weeks, then moved into Southern Yokuts territory near Kern Lake and headed farther north looking for beaver. Everywhere the Yokuts gave him friendly receptions, provisions, and Spanish-speaking fugitive neophyte guides. Yawelmani Yokuts on horseback came to Smith's camp carrying "small sack[s] of down and sprinkled [Smith] from head to foot." They told Smith that there were beaver farther north and the trappers moved on. At the Sukuwutnu Yokuts ranchería, they invited Smith to sit on a grass mat, where, he reported, they poured "grass seed . . . on my head until I was nearly covered." The American gave presents to his hosts and arranged to have the seed ground into meal. The Sukuwutnu then feted him with a meal of "roasted fish . . . a mush made of grass seed," and a dance.[15]

As the mountain men pushed north along the San Joaquin River, Smith noticed fewer Indians, "the greater part of them . . . having . . . gone into the missions" in earlier years. On the Stanislaus River Smith hired another mission runaway to guide him; but after crossing into Miwok territory, he had more trouble convincing the Indians of his

14. Portilla to Argüello, June 28, 1824, in Cook, "Expeditions, 1820–1840," 156–57.
15. Smith's journal of the first part of his expedition is found in George R. Brooks, ed., *The Southwest Expedition of Jedediah S. Smith: His Personal Account of the Journey to California, 1826–1827* (Glendale, Calif., 1977). The account of his stay at San Gabriel is on pp. 100–10 and 126–30. Unless otherwise noted, all of Smith's quotations are from this source, pp. 136–57.

friendly intentions. At several Mokelumne River rancherías the Miwoks
ran "screaming into the woods." In desperation Smith captured two
Indian women, "my object being to convince them of our friendship,"
but their meeting ended abruptly when a "party of Indians rushed . . .
from concealment . . . with intentions apparently not the most friendly,"
forcing him to retreat "without delay."

On the Cosumnes River Miwoks apparently stole some traps, and
when an Indian ventured "within long shot, [he] was fired upon by a
Rifleman and killed." Smith and his men continued north into Nisenan
territory on the American River, where there were "Indians by the
hundreds but wilder than antelopes running and screaming in every
direction" when they saw the whites. Looking for a pass over the Sierra
Nevadas, the trapper turned east up the American, but heavy snow
forced him back. In the mountains the Nisenan twice surrounded Smith's
party. He believed that they thought the rifles were "solid sticks which
we could use only in close contest," so they pressed in on the trappers
in such numbers that Smith ordered two of his men to fire into the
crowd. "At the report of the guns . . . two Indians fell. For a moment
the Indians stood still and silent as if a thunder bolt had fallen among
them then a few words passed from party to party and in a moment
they ran like deer." The next day there was a similar "affray," except
that "more guns were fired and more Indians were killed." In May
Smith took his men back to the Stanislaus River and left most of them
camped near present-day Oakdale. He promised to return by late September, then went up the Stanislaus with two men and crossed the Sierra
at Ebbetts Pass.[16]

While Smith's men waited through the summer, the Muquelemne
Miwok chief Te-mi came to their camp bringing grass seed, "meal,
currents and raspberries & c." to make friends. In return American
hunters "loaded him with meat." Te-mi also returned two horses that
had been stolen earlier in the spring, convincing the Americans that the
Muquelemne were "very honest . . . and entirely friendly." Ordinarily
that part of the Stanislaus was the home of the Lakisamne Yokuts, but
they had been Christianized and then lived at the Mission San José.
The Lakisamne neophytes learned about the fur trappers and the Muquelemne when an Indian messenger went to the mission with a letter
from Smith explaining his activities to Father Narciso Duran. On the
evening of May 15, four hundred neophytes bolted from the mission
and returned to the interior. Father Duran insisted that they left because
the Americans had offered them "protection to abandon the mission

16. Ibid., 166.

and Christian obligations and to return to their villages to live and die gentiles." Ignacio Martínez, the Mexican officer who investigated the incident, found that it had been planned by the neophyte Narciso "using the pretext of the Americans." In any event the neophytes remained at large, leaving Father Duran to predict that it was only "the beginning of such troubles and happenings at other missions." His statement proved prophetic.[17]

The previous year there had been fighting in the interior between vacationing San José neophytes and Cosumnes River Miwok. Intertribal animosity may have been a cause of Narciso's exodus, especially since the Muquelemne were ranging into Lakisamne country. Even so, the Muquelemne harbored some of the fugitives and suffered a Mexican attack as a result, although the runaways there may have been ethnic Miwoks. Apparently most of the neophytes remained in the interior during the summer, but there is no evidence that they contacted the Smith brigade.[18]

Soon after the flight from mission San José, Martínez took an expedition to the Stanislaus to detain the Americans, but the trappers convinced him that they meant no harm and intended to leave the country as soon as Smith returned. Martínez acquiesced, perhaps thinking the task of evicting the well-armed mountain men and their Miwok friends too difficult a job.[19]

Smith returned to his men late in the year. After some trouble with Mexican authorities, he purchased 250 horses and mules for ten dollars each, planning to sell them at the Rocky Mountain rendezvous for fifty dollars a head. In January 1828 his men trapped the lower reaches of the Calaveras, Mokelumne, and Cosumnes rivers, where Smith found the Indians "almost universally friendly." He then proceeded north through the Sacramento Valley, where the Indians were less cooperative. On the American River two of Smith's men fired on Nisenan Indians they had discovered near their beaver traps, killing one and wounding another. Near modern Red Bluff Smith turned northwest,

17. Smith quoted in Maurice S. Sullivan, ed., *The Travels of Jedediah Smith: A Documentary Outline Including the Journal of the Great Pathfinder* (Santa Ana, Calif., 1934), 35. This volume includes Smith's journal of his journey from Bear Lake, Utah, back to California. Heizer, *Handbook*, 462; and James A. Bennyhoff, *Ethnogeography of the Plains Miwok*, Center of Archaeological Research at Davis, Pub. no. 5 (Davis, Calif., 1977), 114–17; Brooks, *Southwest Expedition*, 146; Jack Holterman, "The Revolt of Estanislao," *The Indian Historian* 3 (Winter 1970):43–44; and Duran to Ignacio Martinez, May 16, 1827, quoted in Dale Morgan, *Jedediah Smith and the Opening of the West* (Indianapolis, 1953), 208–09, and Martinez quoted, ibid., 209.

18. Bennyhoff, *Ethnogeography of the Plains Miwok*, 114.

19. Sullivan, *Travels of Jedediah Smith*, 36; and Morgan, *Jedediah Smith*, 209.

taking the Hay Fork of the Trinity River through the mountains. The Indians (either Wintu or Nomlaki) shot arrows at his horse herd and shouted at him from the high ground. The Indians harassed Smith all the way down the Trinity. More than once he shot Indians "to intimidate them and to prevent them from doing further injury." Near the junction of the Trinity and Klamath rivers Smith's expedition encountered Yurok Indians who were inclined to trade, although one of them stole a knife, an ax, and a pet kitten. Indians north of the American River who had little or no experience with whites were not willing to immediately accept the newcomers into their midst, and Smith was all too willing to resort to violence to force his way to Oregon.[20]

Smith's troubles with northern California Indians were merely a prologue to the disaster that befell him in the Oregon country, where Umpqua Indians killed most of the mountain men and stole their horses and pelts. Smith escaped and managed to make his way to the Hudson's Bay Company post at Fort Vancouver. The "honorable company" factor, Dr. John McLoughlin, alarmed at the encroaching Americans as well as Umpqua audacity, sent an expedition under Alexander McLeod to recover Smith's property, punish the Indians, and proceed to the Sacramento Valley to preempt the beaver hunting grounds. McLeod recovered some of Smith's things but refrained from inflicting reprisals because the Umpquas claimed that they had attacked Smith after one of his men tried to rape an Indian woman. McLeod postponed the California trip until the next year. From 1829 to 1842 Dr. McLoughlin usually sent a company brigade to California, but it was too late to stave off American competitors who followed the southwestern route that Smith had pioneered.[21]

Smith's entry into California was important to Indian affairs because he initiated the American fur trade from the southwest. Moreover, Smith recognized that California's horse trade was potentially valuable, inaugurating a commerce that would involve mountain men and California Indians for decades. He demonstrated that a trans-Sierra crossing was feasible. Henceforth, California Indians would contend not only with Mexicans to the west but with Americans and British from the south, the north, and eventually from the east. The aftermath of Smith's in-

20. Morgan, *Jedediah Smith*, 257–61; and Harrison C. Dale, ed., *The Ashley-Smith Explorations and the Discovery of a Central Route to the Pacific, 1822–1829*, rev. ed. (Glendale, Calif., 1941), 247–55.

21. Maurice S. Sullivan, ed., *Jedediah Smith: Trader and Trail Breaker* (New York, 1936), 107–9, 148; John S. Galbraith, "A Note on the British Fur Trade in California," *Pacific Historical Review* 24 (Aug. 1955):253–60; and Joseph J. Hill, "Ewing Young in the Fur Trade of the Southwest," *Oregon Historical Society Quarterly* 24 (1923):1–35.

trusion included new opportunities and problems for interior Indians. Some, like the Miwok Te-mi, would attempt to take advantage of the fur trade by establishing commercial relations with the mountain men. Other Indians would react like those north of the Sacramento Valley, violently resisting trespassers who entered Indian country. After Smith's arrival, the circumstances of Indian accommodation, resistance, and survival became more complex, chancy, and dangerous.

Whether the fur trade caused it or not, Father Duran's prediction of increasing Indian trouble was accurate. A few months after Smith's party left the Stanislaus camp, the San José mission neophyte Estanislao led some Indians from the mission, sent word that he was in revolt, and established a fortified settlement near the abandoned American camp. There were several apparent reasons for Estanislao's rebellion. Narciso's 1827 revolt had set an example for discontented neophytes. The failure of the Mexican military to arrest Smith's men may have contributed to Estanislao's conviction that the soldiers were "few in number . . . very young," and that they could "not shoot very well." Moreover, Estanislao and his followers were Lakisamne Yokuts who may have been concerned with the Muquelemne Miwok's activities in what had been Yokuts territory.[22]

His contemporaries described Estanislao as about six feet tall, with "skin more pale than bronze, of slender figure, with a head of heavy hair and a beard on his face." He had been born before 1800 at the Mission of San José, where he worked as a vaquero and mule trainer. From his Stanislaus stronghold he raided Mexican livestock herds, encouraged other Indians to leave the missions, and became a formidable enemy of the californios. Some of his recruits became well-known native leaders in their own right: Cipriano from the Mission Santa Clara; Yozcolo, a Lakisamne Yokuts alcalde from Santa Clara. A rebellious Miwok alcalde from Mission San José, José Jesus, would also take up horse raiding in the valley of the San Joaquin. He proved to be a remarkably resourceful leader who would help shape events in the interior until the 1850s, as we shall see in later chapters.[23]

In the meantime, Mexican authorities regarded Estanislao as the ringleader of the horse-raiding Indians in the San Joaquin Valley, and rightly so. He defeated the first three military expeditions sent against

22. Cook, "Expeditions, 1820–1840," 174; Duran to Martinez, Nov. 9, 1828, ibid., 169; and Holterman, "Estanislao," 43–44.

23. Juan Bojorques, quoted in Cook, "Expeditions, 1820–1840," 166; Holterman, "Estanislao," 44; Jack Holterman, "The Revolt of Yozcolo: Indian Warrior in the Fight for Freedom," *The Indian Historian* 3 (Spring 1970):19–23; and Bancroft, *History of California*, 6:75–76.

him in 1828 and 1829. Finally the Mexicans put together a force under twenty-one-year-old Ensign Mariano Guadalupe Vallejo. This army consisted of more than one hundred soldiers from the San Francisco presidio, accompanied by fifty or more neophyte auxiliaries captained by the neophyte Marcelo, all reputed to be long-standing enemies of the Lakisamnes. The army attacked Estanislao's stronghold in late May. After several hours of hard fighting, they breached the stockade walls with cannon fire and then retreated for the night. In the morning Vallejo found the camp deserted, so he ordered his troops to attack another stockaded Indian community about ten miles away, thinking these people had assisted the rebels. The coastal force set fire to the brush around the stockade and shot the Indians who tried to escape; but Estanislao was not found among the dead.[24]

While Vallejo marched back to the coast, Estanislao secretly returned to Mission San José and asked Father Duran for a pardon. Duran permitted him to return to the mission after he promised not to raid again, a turn of events that irritated the Mexican soldiers who had spent so much time, energy, and blood seeking the Yokuts leader. Vallejo and his men were accused of atrocities in their campaign and one soldier was found guilty of killing an old woman. Nevertheless, the campaign gave young Vallejo a military reputation and the grudging respect of California's politicos, like his nephew, future governor Juan B. Alvarado. Vallejo became commander of the northern frontier at Sonoma, gaining popularity because of his forays against the Indians. Evidently Estanislao died at the mission, but skeptical Mexicans still considered him to be the scourge of their horse herds and reported seeing him driving one hundred horses before him in the interior.[25]

Estanislao's exploits marked the beginning of an era when fur traders in the valley provided access to an international market for stolen horses. Independent American trappers and New Mexicans, collectively known as *chaquanosos* (adventurers of all nations), participated in a trade that eventually involved Colorado Ute Indians as well as Miwok and Yokuts. In 1829 the infamous mountain man, Thomas L. "Peg-leg" Smith, stole three or four hundred horses and drove them out of the province. Californios knew him as "El Cojo Smit" (lame Smith) and accused him of riding with Miwok and Yokuts raiders. Much of Smith's stolen loot wound up in Missouri, but not all horse trading was illicit. In 1831 David E. Jackson purchased seven hundred horses and mules from the missions and drove them back to Santa Fe. The illegal trade, however, continued

24. Cook, "Expeditions, 1820–1840," 169–75; Holterman, "Estanislao," 44–47.
25. Cook, "Expeditions, 1820–1840," 180; Holterman, "Estanislao," 52–53; and Bancroft, *History of California*, 3:360–62, 471–74.

to worry Mexican authorities. The same year that Jackson came to California, Governor Manuel Victoria complained that New Mexicans were "establishing trade relations with the wild Indians, Christian fugitives and actually some of the mission neophytes." The traders induced the Indians to steal horses that the whites took to "their own country by various routes," including a route through the San Joaquin Valley.[26]

The relationship among interior Indians, trappers, and traders was uneasy. Mountain men wanted a peaceful atmosphere for trading and trapping, and to keep their own stock safe from depredations. Moreover, they did not want to unduly arouse Mexican authorities. Like Jedediah Smith before them, traders used force against Indians when it suited their purposes. An 1830 incident illustrates how conflicts could arise. Ewing Young's trapping party, including young Christopher "Kit" Carson, was camped on one of the tributaries of the San Joaquin when they were approached by Francisco Jímenez, Indian alcalde of the mission San José. Jímenez, with neophyte auxiliaries and some interior Indians, was after mission runaways harbored by the Ochejamne Miwoks, but the Ochejamnes had defeated the neophyte and gentile force. Jíminez wanted a letter from the Americans verifying that he had tried to recover the fugitives. Instead, Young sent some of his men, including Carson, to help him get the job done. Carson recalled that they "fought for one entire day," killed many Indians, "entered the village in triumph, set fire to it, and burned it to the ground." Then the Americans took some captives to the mission, where they "were well received by the missionaries." Young used the occasion to trade some furs for horses before riding back to his foothill camp. The Americans' role in reclaiming neophytes did not intimidate the Sierra Miwoks, who subsequently stole about sixty of Young's horses. Carson and others chased the Indians

26. David J. Weber, "American Westward Expansion and the Breakdown of Relations between Pobladores and 'Indios Barbaros' on Mexico's Far Northern Frontier, 1821–1846," *New Mexico Historical Review* 56 (July 1981):221–38; Elinore Lawrence, "Mexican Trade between Santa Fe and Los Angeles, 1830–1848," *California Historical Society Quarterly* 10 (March 1931):27–39; Elinore Lawrence, "Horse Thieves on the Spanish Trail," *Touring Topics* 23 (Jan. 1931):22–25, 55; Broadbent, "Conflict at Monterey," 86–101; Thomas N. Layton, "Traders and Raiders: Aspects of the Trans-Basin and California-Plateau Commerce, 1800–1830," *Journal of California and Great Basin Anthropology* 3 (Summer 1981): 127–36; Holterman, op. cit.; Bancroft, *History of California*, 3:172–79, 4:208–09; Sardis Templeton, *The Lame Captain: The Life and Adventures of Pegleg Smith* (Los Angeles, 1965); Alfred Glenn Humphreys, "Thomas L. (Peg-leg) Smith," in *The Mountain Men and the Fur Trade of the Far West*, 10 vols., LeRoy R. Hafen, ed., (Glendale, Calif., 1965–72), 4:311–30; Hill, "Ewing Young," 18–31; Gov. Victoria to commanders at San Diego and Santa Barbara, March 10, 1831, quoted in Cook, "Expeditions, 1820–1840," 162. Layton argues that the inter-regional Indian horse trade may have begun as early as 1800, but this remains to be proven.

nearly one hundred miles into the Sierra, then charged the native camp, "killed eight Indians, took three children prisoners," and recovered their animals—except for six that had already been eaten.[27]

Despite occasional cooperation with California authorities from traders like Young and Carson, the commerce between mountain men and Indians alarmed Mexicans and restrained settlement on Mexico's borderland frontier from Texas to California. California Indians seemed to have more horses than ever. At the time of the Ochejamne fight, José Berreyesa asserted that there was "not a village which does not have horses" in the San Joaquin Valley. The Muquelemne Miwok alone had fifty horses, not counting their chief, Te-mi, who had one hundred animals. Jímenez had seen "about 30 wild Indians chasing deer on horseback." In 1833 californios sought to control the interior horse trade with a law that set prices for horses and required traders to carry both proof of livestock ownership and an official permit to visit ranchos. The law was ineffective. In the spring Governor José Figueroa still was concerned about trappers who identified themselves "with the wild natives, following the same kind of life." Because of their influence "the natives have dedicated themselves with the greatest determination to the stealing of horses from all the missions and towns in this territory," trading them for "intoxicating liquors and other frivolities."[28]

While Mexican governors were most concerned about the social and economic discord that accompanied the fur trade, Hudson's Bay Company trappers inadvertently brought a virulent form of malaria from Oregon to their campgrounds in the swampy lowlands of the interior. In the spring of 1833, infected anopheles mosquitos spread malaria that killed an estimated twenty thousand Indians, virtually depopulating parts of the central valleys. A decade later there still remained macabre reminders of the malaria epidemic: collapsed houses filled with skulls and bones, the ground littered with skeletal remains. Malaria remained endemic in the interior, an invisible insurgent that permanently debilitated many Indian survivors and newcomers as well.[29]

27. José Berreyesa, July 15, 1830, in Cook, "Expeditions, 1820–1840," 187; and Carson quoted in Harvey Lewis Carter, ed., "Dear Old Kit:" The Historical Christopher Carson, with a New Edition of the Carson Memoirs (Norman, 1968), 47–48.

28. Berreyesa, July 15, 1830, quoted in Cook, "Expeditions, 1820–1840," 187; Figueroa to minister of war and navy, Apr. 12, 1833, quoted ibid., 188; Weber, "American Westward Expansion," 221–38; Lawrence, "Mexican Trade," 27–39; and Anna H. Gayton, "Yokuts and Western Mono Ethnogeography," University of California Anthropological Records 10 (1948):183–84.

29. Sherburne F. Cook, "The Epidemic of 1830–1833 in California and Oregon," University of California Publications in American Archaeology and Ethnology 43, no. 3 (1955):303–25; Alice Bay Maloney, ed., Fur Brigade to the Bonaventure: John Work's

The ravages of malaria caused a temporary decline in raiding as survivors abandoned their lowland rancherías and resettled in the foothills. But raiding never stopped entirely, and after 1835 interior Indians were again plaguing the Mexican herds. In 1838 the situation was so alarming that Governor Juan Alvarado asked Michel Laframboise, then leader of the Hudson's Bay Company brigade in the Sacramento Valley, to chastise the Indians who stole from the californios. The trapper agreed, but according to his superior James Douglas, he had been "completely scared" by the idea and quickly left California. Douglas ordered him back with instructions to use his influence to constrain Indians from attacking settlements, but not to "identify [company] interests with [Mexican interests] by resorting to violent measures." The Hudson's Bay Company intended to stay in California on its own terms rather than the Mexican government's.[30]

Shortly after Laframboise packed his traps and fled north, a new arrival, John A. Sutter, asked permission to establish a permanent settlement in the interior. A German-born Swiss, Sutter was a man of good appearance and gentlemanly bearing who embellished his reputation with a bogus French captaincy, a charade that often impressed his frontier associates. In addition to his pretensions, Sutter had gained wide experience on the North American frontier. He had made two trading trips from Missouri to New Mexico, been an Indian trader, gone to the American trappers' rendezvous, seen the Hudson's Bay Company's operation at Fort Vancouver, sailed to the Sandwich Islands, then to the Russian-American post at Sitka, and on to California.[31]

Sutter had asked Governor Alvarado for permission to plant a colony on the Sacramento River at a propitious time. Besides discouraging Indian raiding, the governor hoped Sutter's settlement would reduce the power of Alvarado's ambitious uncle, Mariano Guadalupe Vallejo, who had become commander of the northern frontier. Operating out of Sonoma, Vallejo assaulted interior rancherías and sent captured na-

California Expedition, 1832–1833 (San Francisco, 1945); and Lansford W. Hastings, *The Emigrant's Guide to Oregon and California* (Cincinnati, 1845), 116.

30. Douglas to the governor of the Hudson's Bay Company, Oct. 14, 1839, quoted in E. E. Rich, ed., *The Fort Vancouver Letters of John McLoughlin*, 3 vols., (London, 1941–44), 2:217–20; Bancroft, *History of California*, 3:396; Lawrence, "Mexican Trade," 31; and Galbraith, "Note on the British Fur Trade," 253–60.

31. James Peter Zollinger, *Sutter: The Man and His Empire* (New York, 1939), 1–59; John A. Hawgood, "John Augustus Sutter: A Reappraisal," *Arizona and the West* 4 (Winter 1962):345–56; Richard Dillon, *Fool's Gold: The Decline and Fall of Captain John Sutter of California* (New York, 1967), 15–81; Doyce B. Nunis, "A Mysterious Chapter in the Life of John A. Sutter," *California Historical Society Quarterly* 38 (Dec. 1959):321–27; Johann August Sutter, *The Diary of Johann August Sutter* (San Francisco, 1932), 3.

tive workers to californio ranchos. Thus, Vallejo kept Indian society in turmoil and built a loyal following among rancheros who needed Indian labor. Alvarado authorized Sutter's settlement and subsequently gave him official civil authority and a land grant. As a result, Sutter and Vallejo became bitter rivals for power on California's northern frontier.[32]

With the governor's blessing, Sutter sailed up the Sacramento in three boats bringing a party that included a few trappers, ten Hawaiians, and an Indian boy from the Rockies. The Indians stayed out of sight until Sutter had reached the upper section of the delta region, about twelve miles south of the mouth of the American River. There two hundred painted Gualacomne Miwok men confronted him. Guessing that they were former neophytes, he waded ashore and began to explain in broken Spanish that he did not want to make war or force them into the missions, but to be friends, give them presents, and live among them. The Miwoks seemed agreeable to his proposal, but provided a guide who quickly ushered him out of Miwok territory north into Nisenan country.

One of the Miwok headmen, Anashe, remained a loyal Sutter ally until the gold rush, but other Indians did not regard Sutter's arrival favorably. Sutter found no warm welcome among the Nisenans, who had rather tenuous relations with whites. Unlike the Miwok, Nisenans did not raid the coast, although they sometimes stole livestock from trappers. Since 1837 Nisenans had traded at the Hudson's Bay Company camp on the Feather River that Laframboise had vacated in the spring of 1839. A British trader described them as living in "extreme destitution," coming to their camp "in crowds" to have their "wants relieved." Weakened by malaria and facing competition from trappers who used firearms, the Nisenan needed to trade with whites. Nevertheless, the Nisenans at the mouths of the American and Feather rivers fled from Sutter. The Hudson's Bay men may have warned Nisenans against trading with other whites, or they may have feared that Sutter and his Miwok guides heralded a military campaign. In any case, Sutter soon gained their confidence, promised them presents, and settled near the Pusune Nisenan ranchería at the mouth of the American River. To be on the safe side, he demonstrated his cannons; the Indians, he reported, "did not care to have them tried on them."[33]

32. Sutter, "Reminiscences of General John Augustus Sutter," MS, Bancroft Library, Berkeley, California (hereafter cited as Sutter, "Reminiscences"); Sutter, *Diary*, 3–4; *A Faithful Translation of the Papers Respecting the Grant Made by Governor Alvarado to John A. Sutter* (Sacramento, 1942); Cook, "Nonmission Indians in Colonial and Provincial California," 9–10, 25 n., 33, 35–36; and Rawls, *Indians of California*, 89.

33. Sutter, "Reminiscences"; Sutter, *Diary*, 5; William Heath Davis, *Sixty Years in*

Making good on his promises, Sutter gave the Indians beads, blankets, Hawaiian sugar, and shirts as a first step in securing their friendship and their labor. He also sold them liquor, that staple of the Indian trade, although he attempted to restrict its use. Soon Nisenan and Miwok Indians began to trade work for goods from Sutter's store. To keep track of their credit, Sutter issued his workers metal disks that he punched with a distinctive hole for each day of labor. The Indians wore the disks on necklaces and redeemed them at Sutter's store, where it took approximately two weeks of labor to purchase a plain muslin shirt or material for a pair of cotton trousers. Thus, Sutter controlled wages, prices, and the Indian trade by creating a primitive cash economy and a system of debt and credit.[34]

To gain secure control over native labor, Sutter sought the allegiance of ranchería headmen and required them to send workers to New Helvetia. Those who failed to honor the levy were subject to Sutter's armed force. Cooperative leaders received gifts from Sutter, who reinforced the authority of headmen among the Indians. Among the Miwok captains was Maximo, a powerful headman who sent Miwoks to work at the secularized Mission of San José. Sutter courted Maximo, who soon supplied him with Indian labor. Anashe, Maximo, and other Indian captains became important middlemen who managed the movement of Indians into the market economy that Sutter established in the California interior. But the interests of Sutter and his captains were not identical, and the white colonizer and Indian middlemen would eventually clash as history took its course in the Sacramento Valley.[35]

In the meantime, the lure of trade goods proved to be a potent force that attracted Indian labor to New Helvetia. Except for a few overseers, Indians did all the work on Sutter's rancho, where wheat was the most important crop. During the harvest season he employed as many as six hundred Indians. Indians also worked in nonagricultural enterprises, operating a distillery, hat factory, blanket works, and a tannery. Native

California (San Francisco, 1889), 17–19; James Douglas quoted in Rich, *Fort Vancouver Letters*, 2:252–54; and "The Launch of a Tug Boat," *Sacramento Union*, Sept. 29, 1862, 1 [Sutter's account of meeting Anashe].

34. Sutter, "Reminiscences"; Marguerite Eyer Wilbur, trans. and ed., *A Pioneer at Sutter's Fort, 1846–1850: The Adventures of Heinrich Lienhard* (Los Angeles, 1941), 7, 68; Sutter to John Marsh, Oct. 7, 1840, MC; and Sutter et al., *New Helvetia Diary: A Record Kept by John A. Sutter and His Clerks at New Helvetia, California, from September 9, 1845, to May 25, 1848* (San Francisco, 1939), 27.

35. Zollinger, *Sutter*, 104–05; "An Aged Indian Chief," Sacramento Union, May 25, 1885, 4; "The Dead Chieftain," Sacramento Daily Record Union, May 25, 1886, 2. Raphero's relationship to Maximo is a matter of oral tradition told to me by the Miwok Dwight Dutschke, my former colleague in the California State Office of Historic Preservation.

men trapped beaver and sailed Sutter's launch between New Helvetia and Yerba Buena. They caught salmon for shipment to the coast. They killed deer, rendered their tallow, and packed it in barrels for customers in South America. They built the thick adobe walls and bastions of Sutter's Fort and manned the army that protected New Helvetia. Hawaiians taught Indian women to wash and sew cloth. Sutter sometimes used native handicrafts to curry favor with whites, giving feather blankets and baskets to important visitors. In sum, Indian labor created New Helvetia.[36]

Sutter tried to stop Indian livestock raiding, but he met with indifferent results and Mexican contemporaries did not always appreciate his efforts. Soon after his arrival, he returned some stolen animals to their Mexican owners. Because he claimed to have purchased the horses from native rustlers, Sutter required repayment from resentful rancheros. When Mariano Castro reported that Hudson's Bay Company men had sold Sutter forty stolen horses from San José, it looked like Sutter was the horse thieves' accomplice. Living among the horse thieves, Sutter seemed a suspicious character, but he always claimed that he worked against the Indian raiders.[37]

It was in Sutter's interest to eliminate horse raiding. After all, he had his own vast herds to protect. To secure New Helvetia and extend his power, Sutter set up an army of 150 Indian infantrymen and 50 native cavalry, who were supervised by several white officers. The troops wore Russian green-and-blue uniforms with red trim that came from Fort Ross, which Sutter purchased from the Russians in 1841. There was a cadet corps of young Indian boys that drilled every Sunday morning, wearing "blue drill pantaloons, white cotton shirts & red handkerchiefs tied around their heads." The army of Nisenans, Miwoks, and mission refugees kept military discipline at the fort with a guard of twelve or fifteen. During the night a soldier kept time with an hour glass, striking a bell and crying out "All is well" every half hour. The white officers commanded their Indian troops in German. In the 1840s this cosmopolitan army must have presented a colorful—if curious—sight in the isolated California interior.[38]

But Sutter's Indian army was more than a mere curiosity. Although it did not eliminate native resistance to Sutter, the army dominated the

36. Sutter, "Reminiscences"; Webfoot [William D. Phelps], *Fore and Aft: Or, Leaves from the Life of an Old Soldier* (Boston, 1871), 258; Sutter to William A. Leidesdorff, Aug. 8, 1844, MS 22, LC; and Sutter to Antonio Suñol, May 14 and June 13, 1842, SuC.

37. Sutter, "Reminiscences"; and alcalde to prefect, Mar. 18, 1841, in Cook, "Expeditions, 1820–40," 193.

38. Sutter, "Reminiscences."

southern Sacramento Valley. His correspondence was peppered with references to Indian wars. Besides, his Indian army made Sutter a powerful figure in Mexican California, as was shown during the revolt of 1845. In return for an additional land grant and a captain's commission, Sutter supported Alvarado's successor, Manuel Micheltorena, the last governor appointed by the Mexican central government. Micheltorena—and the ex-convict soldiers who accompanied him—so alienated the californios that they revolted under the leadership of Alvarado and José Castro. Sutter marched to southern California with his army to defend the beleaguered governor. After several inconclusive engagements Micheltorena capitulated and returned to Mexico. Castro and Alvarado captured and held Sutter briefly, but freed him after he promised to be loyal to the new government, whose leaders promptly reinstated his military rank, privileges, and property. Sutter was too valuable in the defense of the Indian frontier to be deposed. In the meantime, Sutter's disarmed Indian soldiers had been at the disposal of the people of Los Angeles, who made them work as burden carriers with no pay and little food. The californios must have been horrified when Sutter came marching to the coast with an army composed partly of former horse thieves dressed in garish Russian uniforms, armed and under military discipline. Still, all his troops were permitted to return to New Helvetia.[39]

When Sutter returned to the fort he found his labor force in disarray. During his absence some of them had fled from New Helvetia, so he spent much of the summer of 1845 rounding up and punishing runaway workers. To add to his difficulties, José Castro evidently regretted releasing him and incited the rebellion of a Muquelemne Miwok named Raphero, the son of Captain Maximo. When Sutter learned of the rebellion he captured Raphero, executed him, and displayed his head over the fort's gate. Rufino, a Muquelemne who was a lieutenant in Sutter's army, was so outraged that he killed his brother-in-law, a loyal member of the guard. A few months later Rufino was also captured and executed at Sutter's Fort. But that was not the end of the matter. Maximo, outraged at his son's execution, became the bitter foe of Sutter, who likewise regarded his former captain as an enemy.[40]

By 1845 Sutter was too well entrenched for disaffected Muquelemnes to dislodge him, and the Miwoks were divided on the issue. Some threat-

39. Ibid.; Zollinger, *Sutter*, 131, 134, 317–20; and Bancroft, *History of California* 4:455–56.

40. Sutter to Pierson B. Reading, Feb. 15, May 8, May 10, and May 11, 1845, RC; Sutter to Marsh, May 17, 1845, MC; Sutter, *Diary*, 32; Zollinger, *Sutter*, 158; Wilbur, *Pioneer at Sutter's Fort*, 3; Sutter et al., *New Helvetia Diary*, 2; and "An Aged Indian Chief," Sacramento *Daily Record Union*.

ened to drive whites out of the valley, but other Miwoks and Nisenans remained loyal. In June 1845, moreover, Sutter began negotiating with Miwok raiders south of the Mokelumne River, whose leaders declared that they would stop stealing horses if Sutter would pardon them. The following spring Sutter made an arrangement with the notorious José Jesus, the San José neophyte who had been raiding for more than a decade, and another Miwok raider named Pollo. Sutter hoped to send out these new allies to "ketch" the horse thieves "in their holes," as he informed General Castro in an effort to prove his allegiance and demonstrate his influence with the Indians. The master of New Helvetia wanted to teach Castro that Sutter would not be beaten at his own game.[41]

The Mexican War stalled Sutter's plans to stop Indian raiding, and meanwhile the growth of huge feral horse herds in the San Joaquin Valley testified to these unrelenting depredations. In 1844 Lieutenant John C. Frémont, who was reconnoitering for the United States, found numerous horses between the Stanislaus and Kings rivers. The herds were principally on the west bank of the San Joaquin, where the plains were "alive with immense droves of wild horses." The mountain Indians, Frémont declared, made "frequent descents upon the settlements west of the Coast Range, which they keep constantly swept of horses; among them are many . . . refugees from the Spanish missions." Since wild horses had little value, Indian raiders rode past them to risk their lives stealing from the californios. Two years after Frémont's visit, William Robert Garner reported "forty thousand wild horses and mares" in the San Joaquin Valley, which was a "complete nursery of horses for California." At the end of the Mexican era, rancheros who wanted to replenish their herds would ride to the valley to round up the progeny of their own stolen horses.[42]

Indian livestock raiders dealt to Mexican California a crippling blow, but not a mortal one. Rancheros may have lost thousands of horses, but during the Mexican era the californio population doubled and the total white population more than tripled, while the number of Indians dropped sharply, though they still substantially outnumbered whites.[43]

The years of Mexican rule brought momentous changes to the interior

41. Sutter to Suñol, June 14, 1845, SuC; and Sutter to Marsh, Apr. 3, 1846, MC.

42. Donald Jackson and Mary Lee Spence, eds., *The Expeditions of John Charles Frémont*, 3 vols. (Urbana, Ill., 1970–73), 1:661–63; and William Robert Garner, *Letters from California, 1846–1847*, ed. Donald Munro Craig (Berkeley, 1970), 104.

43. See Heizer and Almquist, *The Other Californians*, 16; Cook, "The Physical and Demographic Reaction of the Nonmission Indians," 30–36; and Bancroft, *History of California*, 2:393, 5:524–25, 643.

and the Indians who lived there. Once an isolated Indian country that Hispanic people visited only rarely, the interior became part of an international fur trading system. Mountain men provided a market for stolen horses and so presented new opportunities to the Indians. But mountain men heeded their own interests first. They were not powerful new allies helping the Indians against the Mexicans; at best they were neutral and sometimes they sided with the californios. Unintentionally, fur traders imported malaria and other infectious diseases. Trade, whether for pelts or horses, made the interior Indians dependent on the outside world for their livelihood. Whatever time and energy Indians devoted to these new pursuits had to be taken from traditional subsistence activities. Elsewhere in the American West trapping significantly reduced rich wetlands as the beaver ponds dried up. But California's golden beaver do not ordinarily build dams, so the riverine landscape was not significantly affected as the beaver disappeared. Nevertheless, the fur trade impoverished the environment because the formerly bountiful wetlands harbored the malaria-carrying anopheles mosquito. Previously a rich source of food for Indians, the lowlands had become a perilous place. Thus, Indian resources became less productive because Indians abandoned them and because native people who continued to use lowlands were physically debilitated. Finally, raiding, trading, and native labor linked California's resources and the interior Indians to outside forces—nationalist ambitions, imperial rivalries, and an expansive market economy—that they did not understand.[44]

Sutter fit neatly into an Indian world that he helped to rearrange not merely because the weakened Indian population had become passive. Quite the contrary, some Indians fought Sutter and other whites. Simultaneously, Miwoks and Nisenans chose to provide labor to build his colony and to protect it with military strength because Sutter supplemented their subsistence and provided protection for cooperative Indians. In a country that was becoming increasingly dangerous and where food was becoming more scarce, Sutter seemed to offer the promise of survival. Unfortunately for the Indians, the bargain was not what it appeared to be. Although the Indians were superior in numbers and

---

44. David J. Wishart, *The Fur Trade of the American West, 1807–1840* (Lincoln, 1979). According to Wishart, Indians were reliant on one or more closed ecosystems, but fur traders depended on a much broader source of subsistence, a biosphere. After the trader had skimmed off the best of Indian resources, he left seeking new territory that could be incorporated into the biosphere. The Indian remained, with his ecosystem—and hence his ability to survive—significantly weakened (p. 215). See also Elna Bakker, *An Island Called California: An Ecological Introduction to Its Natural Communities* (Berkeley, 1971), 133; and Raymond F. Dasmann, *The Destruction of California* (New York, 1965), 46, 48.

willing to resist whites when it seemed necessary, permanent white settlement irrevocably changed the conditions of native survival. Under
Sutter the Indians became a labor pool that he made available to other
white frontier entrepreneurs. Indeed, the very value of their labor put
Indian survival at risk. Thus, Indians became dependent and vulnerable
to a new set of dangers in a primitive frontier economy.

3

"Saved so Much as Possible for Labour:" New Helvetia's Indian Work Force

Indian labor, long established on the Hispanic frontier, was a fact of life in Mexican California. Sutter used Indian labor much as Mexicans did, but he modified Hispanic practices to suit his needs. With his model before them, Anglo-Americans who settled the interior quickly adapted Indian labor. They had to. Before the Mexican War there were only a few hundred whites in the Sacramento Valley and more than twenty thousand Indians who were not only potential laborers but a threat to white life and property, as well. Sutter understood this when he advised his overseer, Pierson B. Reading, to give Feather River livestock thieves a "severe punishment" but to avoid driving the Indians away. It was preferable "for those who have land," he explained, that the Indians were "saved so much as possible for labour." He had no illusions about how these two goals could be accomplished. Native people had to be kept "strictly under fear" or it would "be no good."[1]

According to Sutter, whites who employed Indians had to be vigilant, flexible, and willing to use force. Anglo-Americans who possessed these characteristics used native labor to make the interior productive according to white standards. By so doing, they changed the landscape that Indians had relied on, making it less useful and accessible to them. The conversion of Indian country to an agricultural frontier required a labor force that was disciplined to work according to whites' needs and on a schedule that fit the white clock and calendar. This sense of discipline pervades John Bidwell's reminiscence of Sutter's Indian grain harvesters. "Imagine," he asks us, "three or four hundred wild Indians in a grain field . . . with sickles . . . butcher-knives" and "pieces of hoop iron roughly fashioned into shapes like sickles." Many used their bare hands until they grew sore and then "resorted to dry willow sticks, which

---

1. Sutter to Reading, May 11, 1845, RC; and J. A. Sutter, "Statistics of the District East of the San Joaquin & Sacramento Rivers," Dec. 20, 1847, MS 28–29, MKP.

were split to sever the straw." Indian reapers carried the wheat to a large corral, where they drove wild horses through the ripened grain to thresh it. Then they drew shovels full of grain high into the air so the wind would blow away the chaff. Finally, Indian hands bagged, stored, and ground the wheat into flour.[2]

The New Helvetia wheat harvest was a long and arduous undertaking. In 1847 it began on June 14 and was not finished until November 28. One reason it took so long was that Sutter had difficulty in keeping his labor force at work. Through the summer they came and went, and Sutter repeatedly sent for workers from surrounding communities. Indians were reluctant to stay at New Helvetia partly because an illness sickened and killed many of them, and partly because Sutter's harvest conflicted with their own. Since Indian harvesters depended on manifold natural resources, they returned home to hunt and gather traditional foods when they were abundant. Sutter's work schedule happened to overlap with the acorn season, the fall salmon run, and the time of ripe seeds. Agricultural employment kept Indians from hunting deer, elk, and antelope and snaring wild birds. Sutter's seasonal work provided Indians with trade goods and temporary subsistence, but it did not replace wild foods that were stored for the winter. Thus, the new seasonal round of plowing, planting, and harvesting had to fit into the Indian food cycle or native people would suffer. This simple fact was often lost on whites, who believed that traditional Indian subsistence patterns were inherently slothful and inefficient and that agriculture was a better way to use California's resources. Indian and white economies both produced surpluses, but agricultural abundance was destined for the commercial marketplace, not for hungry Indians in lean times. Nevertheless, whites were forced to maintain agricultural production with native labor, whatever the consequences for the Indians.[3]

The employment of Indians led to cultural as well as physical conflicts, which were invariably resolved in favor of the white settlers' needs. One priority was to make the European clock and calendar paramount and to compel Indians to abandon their sense of time and concomitant seasonal demands. John Yates, a seaman who piloted Sutter's launch, was impressed by the orderliness and punctuality of the Indians who worked at New Helvetia in 1842. At Sutter's Hock Farm Yates "was surprised

2. Sutter, "Reminiscences"; Milo Milton Quaife, ed., *Echoes from the Past, by General John Bidwell; In Camp and Cabin by Rev. John Steele* (Chicago, 1928), 82–83; and William Cronon, *Changes in the Land: Indians, Colonists, and the Ecology of New England* (New York, 1983), 34–53.

3. Sutter et al., *New Helvetia Diary*, 50–96; Heizer and Elsasser, *Natural World of the California Indians*, 28–113.

by the ringing of a very large bell which was used . . . to call the natives to work" in the morning. He had seen the "habits and customs of natives in other countries" and was gratified to see twenty Indians answer the signal. After they received instructions, the bell was rung again and the Indians "promptly & willingly set about the making of Adobes" for Sutter's new house. Yates toured the farm and "found that much had been done and learnt that all was the achievement of the natives."[4]

Sutter's bell heralded the arrival of a modern sense of time in the Sacramento Valley. While he could impose rigid schedules on Indians only when they were under his direct control, Sutter's concept of "time-thriftiness," as the historian Richard D. Brown calls it, starkly contrasted with the Indians' sense of time. Before Sutter, native people had heeded the cycle of the seasons, time was infinite, and life's rhythms were unchanging. Now, for at least part of their lives, some Indians were wedded to a concept that proclaimed that time was limited and that it had economic value. The clang of Sutter's bell announced that time was money, that it marched onward, and that it waited for no man, including Indians in the 1840s. Necessarily, the arrival of the modern sense of time coincided with the establishment of market agriculture, which in turn was linked with an international economic network. Sutter and other whites were enmeshed in a web of debt, credit, and trade that encumbered them and, by extension, their Indian workers as well. By answering the bell, Indians stepped into a world that was modernizing at a pace that whites and Indians could scarcely comprehend.[5]

Working for whites also meant that Indians personally encountered other modern economic conventions, namely, the use of money and credit. The simple metal currency necklaces that Sutter's Indians wore were emblematic of these innovations. The perforated disks were symbols of Indian time and labor that had been turned to Sutter's account. And by issuing credit at his trading house, Sutter obtained a claim to Indian time and labor in the future. Thus, labor, time, and money tended to pull Indians away from their communities and closer to New Helvetia.

Even though the system worked in Sutter's favor, he did not use it consistently. If credit and trade goods were not sufficient inducements to attract workers, Sutter forced Indians to work for him. According to an Indian oral account, when Sutter was short of Indian labor, he sent his army to the foothills to capture additional Nisenan men for the

4. Yates, "Sketch of a Journey in the Year 1842 from Sacramento California through the Valley by John Yates of Yatestown," MS, Bancroft Library, Berkeley, Calif. (hereafter cited as Yates, "Sketch").

5. Richard D. Brown, *Modernization: The Transformation of American Life, 1600–1865* (New York, 1976), 33, 60–61.

harvest. Armed Indian guards kept them in a high corral at night and Sutter fed them poorly. After the harvest he paid them off with a small string of beads.[6]

As was customary, Sutter provided food and sometimes shelter for his farm laborers. Efficiency was needed to feed a work force of hundreds, so he fed them in long communal troughs, a practice that reminded Sutter's overseer, Heinrich Lienhard, of feeding pigs. According to a Nisenan account the Indians ate a mixture of boiled beef and wheat in a device "like a hog's feeding trough." This arrangement made eating a competitive affair. Sometimes an Indian would reach over one of his fellows at the trough to get a bone that "dripped and burned" the others' backs.[7]

Housing conditions among Sutter's Indian workers varied considerably. Those who lived close to the fort probably slept in their own houses even when they were employed. Others temporarily moved to the fort. When John C. Frémont entered California in 1844, he encountered a Nisenan ranchería about ten miles from the fort and found "a large Indian village, where the people looked clean, and wore cotton shirts and other articles of dress." When he asked about Sutter, a well-dressed Indian addressed him in Spanish. "I am a vaquero . . . in the service of Capt. Sutter," he said, "and the people of this *rancheria* work for him." Indian workers whom Sutter did not trust were confined within the fort's walls at night. Lienhard was responsible for locking Indian men and women together in a large room, where the inmates had to sleep on the bare floor. He recalled that when he opened the door in the morning, "the odor that greeted me was overwhelming, for no sanitary arrangements had been provided." These conditions, he believed, caused large-scale desertions during the day.[8]

Sutter tried to make sure that his Indian workers were clothed with at least cotton shirts, but his goal was not always met. In 1845 Sutter wrote to William Leidesdorff requesting some brown manta cloth for his "boys and girls of the house, about 100, who are nearly all in rags and naked." He was concerned because "when strangers come here it

6. This account was attributed to the late Lizzie Enos, a prominent Maidu woman, by Bernice Pate of Auburn, Calif. For stories by and about Enos, see Richard Simpson, *Ooti: A Maidu Legacy* (Millbrae, Calif., 1977).

7. Wilbur, *Pioneer at Sutter's Fort*, 68; and Hans Jørgen Uldall and William Shipley, *Nisenan Texts and Dictionary*, University of California Publications in Linguistics, vol. 46 (Berkeley, 1966), 67.

8. Jackson and Spence, *Expeditions of Frémont*, 1:652; and Wilbur, *Pioneer at Sutter's Fort*, 68.

looks very bad." Eventually Sutter wanted to provide blankets to cut down on the expense for manta cloth.[9]

Food, shelter, and clothing were all badges of allegiance to Sutter and signs of submission to white discipline, but New Helvetia could not be maintained by voluntary Indian service alone. To keep the Indians under control Sutter whipped, jailed, and executed recalcitrants and rebels. His army apprehended runaways and discouraged malcontents from taking rash actions. When necessary, Sutter banished incorrigibles to distant ranchos. Indians who freely cooperated with Sutter could expect rewards; uncooperative Indians were roughly handled.[10]

The utility of interior Indian labor extended far beyond the borders of New Helvetia, for Sutter supplied workers to other settlers as well. Indeed, Sutter's role as an Indian labor supplier was an integral part of his effort to escape debt. For example, beginning in 1839 Sutter purchased goods from Antonio Suñol, partially paying him with beaver pelts, branding irons, brandy, deer tallow, and wheat. In June 1844 he still owed Suñol and agreed to provide him with thirteen Indian workers. The terms of their agreement are not known, but Suñol probably reduced Sutter's account in return for three months of the Indians' service. The next year Sutter promised to send Suñol thirty Indians by way of John Marsh's farm. "I shall send you some young Indians," he added, "after our campaign against the horse-thieves." A few weeks later Marsh told Suñol that the Indians arrived "as usual, dying of hunger." According to Sutter, these Indians were "among the best we have, and work with a good will." They had never been associated with the mission Indians, so they were "perfectly guileless."[11]

Sutter sent Indian workers to many whites in northern California, including Suñol, Marsh, Henry Delano Fitch, Charles Weber, Vicente Peralta, John Coppinger, and William Leidesdorff. The surviving financial details of these transactions are sparse, but among the manuscripts in the Leidesdorff Collection at the Huntington Library is a statement of Sutter's financial dealings with Leidesdorff from August 1844 to January 1846, showing that he owed Leidesdorff $2,198.10. To help pay his debt, Sutter charged Leidesdorff for Indian labor as well as other goods and services. After giving himself credit for all these

9. Sutter to Leidesdorff, July 31, 1845, MS 58, LC.

10. Sutter to Reading, May 10 and 11, 1845, RC; and Sutter to Marsh, May 17, 1845, MC.

11. See Sutter's correspondence with Ignacio Martinez, Aug. 14, Sept. 25, and Oct. 28, 1839, SuC; Sutter to Suñol, June 18 and Aug. 30, 1844, and May 19 and June 14, 1845, SuC; and Marsh to Suñol, June 16, 1845, MC.

TABLE 3.1.   *Credit Provided to John A. Sutter by William Leidesdorff Between August 1, 1844, and January 27, 1846*

Services rendered	Rate charged per Indian	Subtotal
Passage of two Indian children to New Helvetia	$ 5.00 @	$ 10.00
Two Indian boys for 3 days	2.00/day	12.00
Services of two Indians, 4 months, 21 days	8.00/mo	76.92
Four vaqueros and eight horses, 13 days	3.00/day	144.00
"Services of Mobe (Ind)," 2½ months	8.00/mo.	20.00
"6 months and 19 days service of two Indians"	8.00/mo.	106.13
"6 months service of Sula"	9.00/mo.	56.00
"5 months & 7 days of 6 Ind who ran away on 16 September"	8.00/mo.	251.00
"2 months Service of Manl." [Manuel?]	20.00/mo.	40.00
	TOTAL	$716.05

Source: Account of W. A. Leidesdorff, Aug. 1, 1844, to Jan. 27, 1846, MS 32, LC.

items, Sutter reckoned he owed only $114.90. By Sutter's figures, $716.05 of his charges to the merchant were for Indian labor and associated expenses (see table 3.1). In other words, Sutter was able to liquidate nearly one third of his debt by supplying Leidesdorff with Indian workers.[12]

The account shows that the value of Indian workers varied according to their skills and that Sutter charged higher rates for short terms of service. For example, he received two dollars per day apiece (or the equivalent of sixty dollars per month) for Indian boys kept for only three days. On the other hand, Sutter received eight to ten dollars per month for Indians whom he sent to Leidesdorff for two months or more. A vaquero equipped with two horses returned three dollars per day. This account also indicates some dissatisfaction among the Indians who went to Leidesdorff, since six of them ran away. Two others "left previous" to the date that the document was executed, but no reason was reported.[13]

The Sutter-Leidesdorff correspondence reveals other characteristics of the traffic in Indian people. In the spring of 1846 Leidesdorff requested nine Indians, including a girl, but Sutter could not supply them

12. The following documents include references to various rancheros in California who asked Sutter to supply them with Indians: Sutter to Suñol, June 18 and 29, 1844, SuC; Sutter to Henry Delano Fitch, April 17, 1846, MS 391, FP; Sutter to Leidesdorff, May 11, 1846, MS 129, LC; Sutter to Marsh, May 17, 1845, MC; and Sutter, "Account of W. A. Leidesdorff," Aug. 1, 1844, to Jan. 27, 1846, MS 32, LC.

13. Sutter, "Account of W. A. Leidesdorff," Aug. 1, 1844, to Jan. 27, 1846, MS 32, LC.

because he did not have enough workers for his own rancho. Several weeks later Sutter begged off again, claiming he only had a few new hands from the mountains. He promised to send the merchant ten or twelve "selected Indians . . . which will be of some service to you," as well as "6 new hands for Vicente Peralta, and five Sawyers and Shingel makers to Denis Martin." In the meantime he sent Leidesdorff "two Indian Girls, of which you will take which you like best, the other is for Mr. Ridley whom I promised one longer as two year's ago." Sutter added, "As this shall never be considered an article of trade [I] make you a present with the Girl." For reasons of his own, Sutter made a distinction between Indian girls that he sent to Leidesdorff and Ridley and the other Indians whose services were obviously an article of trade. Moreover, Sutter's blacksmith, John Chamberlain, reported that it was "customary for Capt Sutter to buy and sell Indian boys and girls at New Helvetia." Evidently, Sutter did not commit to writing some details of the New Helvetia Indian trade.[14]

In any case, Leidesdorff not only accepted the Indian girls from Sutter but gave one of them to Mrs. William G. Rae, widow of the Hudson's Bay Company representative in California. Since William Buzzell, Leidesdorff's Sacramento Valley rancho overseer, occasionally sent Indian children to Yerba Buena, he also participated in the trade in native services.[15]

The employment of valley Indians at New Helvetia and elsewhere made rancherías vulnerable to attack. In the fall of 1840 several Mission San José Indians arrived at Sutter's Fort with a pass to visit their relatives at the Sakayakumne Miwok ranchería on the Mokelumne River in order to trade for feathers, baskets, and women. Julian, one of Sutter's Indian workers, asked for permission to accompany the Christians to Sakayakumne. Sutter complied, but insisted that no woman should be taken away from her ranchería against her will. The Indians departed, but instead of going to Sakayakumne they went to the Yalisumni Nisenan ranchería on the American River. Julian must have known that all the able-bodied Yalisumni men were then assisting Sutter with the harvest. They attacked the defenseless ranchería, killed five men, and kidnapped the women and children, whom they intended to sell to rancheros. According to a Nisenan account, an old man escaped and went to Sutter's place to alert the Yalisumni men. The next morning Sutter took a force

14. Sutter to Leidesdorff, Apr. 17, 1846, MS 122, and May 11, 1846, MS 129, LC; and John Chamberlain, "Memoirs of California Since 1840," MS, Bancroft Library, Berkeley, California.

15. Sutter to Leidesdorff, June 1, 1846, MS 137, LC; and "Contract between Leidesdorff and William Buzzell," Apr. 12, 1845, MS 43, LC.

of "twenty men and a lot of Indians," captured the assailants about thirty miles south of the fort on the Sacramento River, and executed Julian along with several of his accomplices.

Afterwards Sutter wrote to José de Jesus Vallejo, secular administrator of the Mission San José and brother of the powerful Mariano, explaining that he wanted no more mission Indians in his territory because they frightened his workers and made them flee to their rancherías. Sutter thus served notice to the Vallejos that his turf was off limits for them and that they could not raid there for Indian workers. If Sutter was to cement Indian alliances and control labor in the interior, he had to assure native people that he would keep intruders out, but he could not always do so. As late as June 1846 Sutter complained that he could not supply Leidesdorff with Indians, explaining that they "all remain at home to protect their family's" because they feared a Muquelemne Miwok uprising.[16]

Plainly, New Helvetia threatened Indian communities by draining off able-bodied men, but Sutter also interfered directly in traditional marriage customs and disrupted Indian family life. Before Sutter's arrival, the Miwok and Nisenan practiced polygyny, a custom that permitted a few powerful men to have several wives, although most had only one. Sutter decided to restrict polygyny among the Indians because "the chiefs had so many wives that the young men complained they could have none." To change this situation, Sutter instituted a new system of marriage. He lined up the Indian men and women in rows facing each other. "Then I told the women one after another," Sutter recalled, "to come forward and select for a husband the man they wanted." Afterwards, Sutter forbade the chiefs to have "more than one or two wives each."[17]

Sutter did not name the Indian communities where he restricted polygyny, but probably they were the ones that were closest to his fort, where his influence was greatest. While young Indian men without wives may have supported Sutter's interference in ranchería social arrangements, the choice of mates was left to women. This betrothal method

16. Sutter to José de Jesus Vallejo, Oct. 15, 1840, SuC; and Sutter to Leidesdorff, June 1, 1846, MS 137, LC. This conflict is one of the few during the early frontier period for which an Indian version survives. In 1930 the linguist Hans Jørgen Uldall interviewed an elderly Nisenan man, William Joseph, at the ranchería near Auburn, Calif. William Joseph was born in the 1850s and was thoroughly familiar with Nisenan oral history. His account of the mission Indians' attack on the Yalisumni ranchería conforms closely to the account provided in the Sutter documents, although some of the details appear to be allegorical. His account is in Uldall and Shipley, *Nisenan Texts and Dictionary*, 69.

17. A. L. Kroeber, *Handbook of the Indians of California*, 402; and Sutter, "Reminiscences."

was a radical departure from the usual practice, in which the suitor arranged marriage with the woman's father (see fig. 4). Moreover, Sutter did not entirely eliminate polygyny, but restricted it to chiefs—or captains, as he often called them. Since Sutter sometimes appointed the captains, one honor that cooperative Indian leaders received was the privilege of having two wives. Sutter's meddling exacerbated trends already inherent in Indian society. California Indians often married out of their home rancherías in order to avoid marrying people who were related within three to five generations. Because suitors paid a bride-price and marriage was an important economic and political alliance, affluent and powerful men had an advantage in the marriage market. Furthermore, since the Indians were patrilocal, women moved to their husbands' rancherías. With Indian population already declining, these traditions tended to take women away from small, poor rancherías. Sutter's captains and white settlers became highly eligible bachelors and as a result attracted women from their rancherías and into the orbit of New Helvetia.[18]

At New Helvetia the highest-ranking captain was John Sutter, who cohabited with several women as befit his high status. His wife was Annette Dübeld, who remained in Switzerland until 1850, when she joined Sutter in California. In the meantime he lived with Manaiki, a Hawaiian woman who came with Sutter from the Sandwich Islands in 1839. Eventually, Sutter permitted her to marry Kanaka Harry, also a Hawaiian, and gave the couple a small plot of land on the American River in return for their faithful service. Manaiki was Sutter's favorite California consort, but according to Lienhard, he was intimately involved with Indian women too. Lienhard claimed that at the fort there was a special room next to Sutter's chambers where a "large number of Indian girls . . . were constantly at his beck and call." The overseer, who was not one of Sutter's admirers, claimed that Sutter had sexual relations with girls as young as ten, who became ill and died of neglect after he banished them from the fort. One of these unions allegedly produced a child who later died. Although Lienhard's unflattering description of Sutter's sexual relationships may have been exaggerated, an 1846 statistical statement shows ten mixed-blood children at New Helvetia, whose fathers were not identified.[19]

Whatever Sutter's sexual arrangements may have been, white men

18. Kroeber, *Handbook of the Indians of California*, 401–02; Bean and Blackburn, *Native Californians*, 106–08; and Wilbur, *Pioneer at Sutter's Fort*, 68.

19. Zollinger, *Sutter*, 10; Wilbur, *Pioneer at Sutter's Fort*, 76–78; and Sutter, "Statistics of the District East of San Joaquin & Sacramento Rivers," Jan. 8, 1848, MSS 28–29, MKP.

FIG. 4. Mike Clenso and Bride. Clenso, a Nisenan Indian who had worked for John Sutter at New Helvetia, was obviously a man of enough means to buy nice clothes for himself and his unidentified bride. And he could afford the cost of a photographer to mark the occasion of his wedding in the 1850s. Subject to Sutter's regulation of Indian marriage in the 1840s, Clenso evidently took some Victorian marriage practices to heart, but we do not know how these two people actually determined to mate. Did they rely on traditional Indian courtship practices, or did they woo according to the new customs of the country?

customarily had Indian wives in the California interior and some of these relationships were polygynous. Yates recalled that Nicholaus Allgeier, a German emigrant who worked for Sutter, had an "adopted wife (a California native)" who called him "Nicholassee." He also reported that Sutter's Irish blacksmith, John Chamberlain, was "much given to gazing at the native females." Yates learned that Chamberlain "had been married nineteen times to native women & to my own certain knowledge ... wedded ... an American girl of thirteen." Yates also enjoyed the company of two Indian women. Later he married a sixteen-year-old English girl, but the marriage soon broke up because the Indian women refused to give up their white husband, a development that Yates found quite agreeable.[20]

Michael C. Nye, another of Sutter's employees, also lived with two Indian women. In 1847 he married Harriet Pike, a sister of one of the Donner Party women. Apparently Nye was willing to dissolve his relationship with his Indian mates, but he was upset when one of them took his infant daughter to Sutter's Fort since he feared the child would sicken and die there. Eventually she agreed to live with an Indian vaquero at a rancho near Nye, an arrangement that seemed satisfactory, but nonetheless their little girl soon died.[21]

The emotional strength of Indian-white unions is difficult to judge. For men like Sutter, Nye, and Chamberlain, the acquisition of an Indian wife was merely a temporary arrangement, to be abandoned when eligible white women arrived in the region. The sentiments of the Indian women are harder to know because of the lack of sources, but marriage to a white man probably provided some security, prosperity, and status at New Helvetia.

If the motives of Indians and whites differed, frontier circumstances in the Sacramento Valley created a pattern of sexual relations and marriage that undermined native communities and their values. Formerly women moved from one ranchería to another, helping each group to maintain an adequate population level. But under Sutter's administration, some women left Indian communities for white husbands. Others married Indian men who were closely associated with Sutter and became concentrated in a few communities.

Fortunately, some statistical evidence helps explain the demographic effects of white intervention in Indian culture. In 1846 Sutter had an employee take a census of Indians living in the country between the Mokelumne and Feather rivers (see table 3.2). Although this document

20. Yates, "Sketch"; and Wilbur, *Pioneer at Sutter's Fort*, 61–62.
21. Wilbur, *Pioneer at Sutter's Fort*, 53–55.

TABLE 3.2 *A Census of Indians at New Helvetia in 1846*

Village name	Current spelling (if different)[a]	Tribe (if known)	Males	Females	Total
Tame or Neophyte Indians					
Sakisimne	—	—	28	16	44
Shonomes	—	—	11	6	17
Tawalemnes	—	—	25	21	46
Seywamenes	Seguamne	Miwok	21	24	45
Mukelemnes	Muquelemne	Miwok	45	36	81
Cosumne	Cosomne	Miwok	34	25	59
Subtotal			164	128	292
Wild or Gentile Indians					
Sagayacumne	Sakayakumne	Miwok	27	20	47
Locklomnes	Locolomne	Miwok	43	45	88
Olonutchamné	—	—	31	23	54
Newatchumne	Newachumne	Miwok	31	30	61
Yumagatock	—	—	21	15	36
Shalachmushumne	—	Miwok	32	18	50
Omutchamne	Amuchamne	Miwok	18	9	27
Yusumne	—	—	35	49	84
Yaleyumne	—	—	124	113	237
Yamlock-lock	—	—	40	27	67
Sapototot	—	—	45	29	74
Yalesumne	Yalisumni	Nisenan	228	257	485
Wapoomne	Wapumni	Nisenan	75	67	142
Kisky	Kishkish	Nisenan	48	45	93
Secumne	Sekumni	Nisenan	23	26	49
Pushune	Pusune	Nisenan	43	40	83
Oioksecumne	—	—	16	19	35
Nemshau	—	—	29	21	50
Palanshau	—	—	17	18	35
Ustu	—	—	25	14	39
Olash	Ollash	Nisenan	30	22	52
Yukulme	—	Nisenan	12	11	23
Hock	Hok	Nisenan	39	40	79
Sishu	Sisum	Nisenan	54	49	103
Mimal	—	Nisenan	22	16	38
Yubu	Yupu	Nisenan	56	65	121
Bubu	—	—	19	16	35
Honcut	Honkut	Nisenan	41	45	86
Subtotal			1,224	1,149	2,373
Tame Indians Employed by Sutter			85	18	103
TOTAL			1,473	1,295	2,768

Sources: Adapted from [McKinstry], Nov. 1846, [Population Enumeration of the Sacramento Valley], MSS 12–13, MKP; and Sutter, "Estimate of Indian Population," Dec. 20, 1847, MSS 14–15, MKP.

[a]Current spellings and tribes are from Heizer, *Handbook*, 370, 388, 399.

TABLE 3.3.   *Sex Ratios for Indians at New Helvetia in 1846*

Major subgroups	Males	Females	Total	Sex ratio (males per 100 females)
1. Wild or gentile Indians	1,224	1,149	2,373	106.5
2. Tame or neophyte Indians	164	128	292	128.1
3. Tame Indians employed by Sutter	85	18	103	472.2
4. All tame Indians (2 + 3)	249	146	395	170.6
5. Total Indian population (1 + 2 + 3)	1,473	1,295	2,768	113.8

Sources: Adapted from [McKinstry], Nov. 1846, [Population Enumeration of the Sacramento Valley], MSS 12–13, MKP; and Sutter "Estimate of Indian Population," Dec. 20, 1847, MSS 14–15, MKP.

lacks sufficient data for a thorough demographic analysis, it is the most detailed Indian census for the period. According to this source, there were altogether 2,768 Indians in thirty-four rancherías and at New Helvetia. The total Indian population was slightly imbalanced sexually, with 1,473 males outnumbering 1,295 females. The census and a later amendment to it indicated that there were only 218 white males, 71 white females, 1 Negro man, and 5 Hawaiians, one of whom was a woman. Males outnumbered females in all ethnic groups and white women were in short supply. While Indian men outnumbered Indian women, the margin of difference varied from ranchería to ranchería. Overall, the sex ratio for Indians was 113.8 (males per 100 females); but the census showed that the aggregates for "tame" Indians had significantly higher sex ratios than the aggregates for those communities designated as "wild" Indians (see table 3.3). Sutter described the tame Indians as "Christian Indians and those that have been civilized since the settlement of the valley by the whites and are employed in the shops of the fort and as Baqueros and working men on the different farms." Wild Indians lived in rancherías and came "into the settlements at Harvest time [to] assist in gathering the crops." Thus, all Indians in the census worked for whites, but those who were most closely associated with them had the highest sex ratios.[22]

22. [George McKinstry], Nov. 1846, [Population Enumeration of the Sacramento Valley], MSS 12, 13, MKP. Apparently McKinstry made this census at Sutter's behest. The following year Lt. Henry Halleck, a U.S. Army officer serving on the staff of the American military governor, requested that a census be made of all persons in California. Sutter submitted McKinstry's census with the addition of John Bidwell's very rough estimate of Indian population in the valley north of the Feather River. McKinstry's original census appears to have been a careful enumeration of the communities between the Feather and Mokelumne rivers, and from the Sacramento and San Joaquin rivers on the west to the Sierra foothills on the east. Under the circumstances it was not possible to extend the

Table 3.3 shows that the wild Indian aggregate had a sex ratio within the normal range (about 105), although some rancherías closely allied with Sutter had an extraordinary abundance of women. The Yalisumni, Hock, Yupu, and Honcut villages all had more women than men. It is likely that New Helvetia had created more eligible bachelors for the women in these rancherías. On the other hand, the sex ratio for all tame Indians appears to be abnormally high. The least normal sex ratio is found in the small tame Indian population employed by Sutter. As a general rule, populations with a deficiency of fertile females have difficulty maintaining a healthy birthrate and their numbers decline; but without a knowledge of age distribution it is not possible to state with precision the reproductive potential of each ranchería and the aggregate populations. Moreover, imbalanced sex ratios can occur randomly in human populations. We also lack information about the rate of intermarriage between Indian groups, a practice that may have improved the native reproductive potential. Nevertheless, it seems probable that New Helvetia affected rancherías' prosperity unevenly and that women tended to marry into communities with men who were well-off.[23]

The census is suggestive, but could it also indicate an overabundance of Indian men imported from outside the reporting area, a dearth of women who had been exported from New Helvetia, or a higher mortality rate for women who were associated with whites? These explanations are also plausible. Sherburne F. Cook found similar sex ratios among mission Indian populations. He attributed sexual imbalances to the recruitment of more males into the missions and diseases, especially syphilis, that killed more females than males. At the missions the spread of

---

census farther because, according to Sutter, "the western side of the California [Sierra Nevada] Mountains is thickly settled with wild Indians who are generally at war with the numerous small tribes at the base and do not visit the Valley. Their number I am not able to give" (Sutter to Halleck, Dec. 20, 1847, MSS 50–51; MKP). See also Bidwell to Sutter, Dec. 21, 1847, MSS 16–19, MKP, containing Bidwell's population estimate, figures that he apparently first communicated to Sutter orally (Halleck, "Circular," Sept. 18, 1847, MS 29a, MKP). For Sutter's spelling corrections to McKinstry's original, see his letter of Dec. 20, 1847, MSS 14–15, MKP; and the census that was finally sent to Halleck on Jan. 8, 1847, MSS 28–29, MKP. MSS 12–13 MKP was published in Robert F. Heizer and Thomas R. Hester, "Names and Locations of Some Ethnographic Patwin and Maidu Villages," *University of California Archaeological Research Facility Contributions* 9, no. 5 (1970):96. See also Sutter, Dec. 20, 1847, MS 28–29, MKP; and Sutter to Halleck, Dec. 20, 1847, MSS 50–51, MKP.

23. Michael S. Teitelbaum, "Factors Associated with the Sex Ratio in Human Populations," in *The Structure of Human Populations*, ed. G. A. Harrison and A. J. Boyce (Oxford, England, 1972), 90–109; and Carl W. Meister, "Methods for Evaluating the Accuracy of Ethnohistorical Demographic Data on North American Indians: A Brief Assessment," *Ethnohistory* 27 (Spring 1980):153–69.

diseases was accelerated by sexual relations between the races, the aggregation of the Indians, increased communication between widely separated areas, poor sanitation, and a new diet. Similar social conditions were present at New Helvetia. Although there is no direct evidence of syphilis, it was very common in the nineteenth-century white population, and, as previously indicated, epidemic diseases that killed thousands of Indians periodically erupted in the Sacramento Valley.[24]

As the census indicates, comparatively few Indians worked full-time for Sutter. Most were male seasonal laborers, fitting into the rhythms of frontier agriculture with its periodic demands for sowers, reapers, and gleaners. From the Indian perspective, New Helvetia provided one among several seasonal resources that they relied on. While men substituted farm work for hunting, most women continued to gather native plant foods and carried on with traditional female work.

Force alone did not inspire native people to work for Sutter; he could usually depend on some Indians to work a few weeks at a time in return for his trade goods. These workers incorporated New Helvetia into their seasonal round. Indians who neglected traditional pursuits to work primarily in the new cash and trade economy—like Sutter's soldiers—became more dependent on whites. When voluntarism failed, Sutter used force, and Indians living at the fort, or who were in debt, no doubt had little choice about meeting Sutter's demands. Indian labor, therefore, defies simple characterization. It was a complex combination of slavery, peonage, and free labor, defined by white and Indian perceptions and needs. Some Indians, especially Nisenans, accommodated to Sutter by providing him with labor. Others, like many Miwoks, adjusted differently to this new condition by raiding Sutter and resisting his influence. For Miwoks, raiding Sutter's herds may have been a convenient alternative to making a foray to the coast. New Helvetia was a new resource for them, too.

But New Helvetia had social as well as economic effects on interior Indians. When whites exported Indian workers, family and community bonds were weakened and the absence of working men made rancherías vulnerable. Simultaneously, the marriage patterns of some Indians shifted as women married whites and other powerful men, a subtle change that was important because of the overall shortage of women.

24. Cook, "The Indian Versus the Spanish Mission," 28–34. Accounts of epidemics and their effects on Indian communities during the 1830s and 1840s are found in Sutter et al., *New Helvetia Diary*, 28–101; Wilbur, *Pioneer at Sutter's Fort*, 99; Cook, "The Epidemic of 1830–1833," 303–26; and Maloney, *John Work's California Expedition*. On syphilis statistics, see Mark Thomas Connelly, *The Progressive Response to Prostitution in the Progressive Era* (Chapel Hill, N.C., 1980), 69–70, 74–75, 89.

On the whole, Indian population was declining, but some groups were especially hard hit. The Shonome and Amuchamne Miwok and the Yukulme and Buku Nisenan were disappearing. Depopulation was the hidden cost for Indians who responded to the work bell that tolled at New Helvetia. Far from preparing the natives for a future of harmonious relations and gainful employment in white society, their enlistment in the work force hampered the ability of native communities to survive while it gave strength to the white minority. Some native people, it is fair to say, benefited from Sutter's immediate presence since they received trade goods, food, protection, and power from their association with him. But these benefits were short-lived and must be seen against the background of a declining native population dominated by a white minority.

The Anglo version of Indian-white labor relations in the interior produced many of the same consequences that Indians had faced in Mexican California—depopulation, intermarriage, and the weakening of tribal bonds on individuals. On the other hand, California's Anglo society displayed few of the influences that ameliorated Indian life among Hispanic people. Hispanic culture and history conditioned Mexicans to think of Indians as a permanent part of their society. True, Mexican abuse of Indians was common, but at least the Mexican government and the Catholic Church expressed an interest in their welfare. Even rebellious Indians like Estanislao could sometimes expect Franciscan missionaries to protect them. Likewise, even though they finally failed to help Indians, Mexican governors had instituted secularization as a reform to benefit neophytes as well as Mexicans. In the interior Indians could not turn to the governor or priests for help, but relied exclusively on the goodwill of men like Sutter. Moreover, in adapting Hispanic Indian labor practices, Anglos did not necessarily abandon their own heritage that taught them to despise Indians as dangerous exotics who should be kept away from civilized society. Anglos who easily took up alien institutions as a matter of convenience could easily forsake them when convenience dictated. Like unwanted Indian wives, Anglos could renounce Indian labor when a more desirable alternative became available.

Indians were "saved so much as possible for labour" because of their temporary utility to a frontier landholding elite that gave little thought to the long-term consequences for workers. Indian labor was not an end in itself, but part of a larger process. Neither Indians nor whites may have clearly understood it, but they participated in the thoroughgoing changes in work habits that accompanied modernization throughout the world. The British labor historian Sidney Pollard has said of the British peasants, laborers, and craftsmen who became factory workers: "There was a whole new culture to be absorbed and an old one to be traduced and spurned; there were new surroundings, often in a new part of the country, new relations with employers and new uncertainties of livelihood, new friends and neighbors, new marriage patterns and behavior patterns of children and adults within the family and without." Pollard's summary statement describes the Indians at New Helvetia as well as the incipient British proletariat. Like British workers, California Indians had to change as their homelands were transformed. The introduction of new conditions of life, however, did not produce uniform results for Indians any more than for British workers. Nor were the reactions of native people identical or predictable. Indians, as we shall see, tried to shape their futures and thus made their own histories.[25]

25. Sidney Pollard, *The Genesis of Modern Management: A Study of the Industrial Revolution in Great Britain* (Cambridge, Mass., 1965), 162. See also Herbert G. Gutman, *Work, Culture, and Society in Industrializing America: Essays in American Working-Class and Social History* (New York, 1977), 3–78.

4

Indians in the Service of Manifest Destiny

The growth of New Helvetia and the Anglo farms that surrounded it increased Indian reliance on white employers while reducing the resources available for hunting and gathering. Nevertheless, large parts of the interior — much of the San Joaquin Valley, the Sierra Nevada range, and the far northern reaches of the state — remained in Indian control. Indians there were autonomous and could flee from Sutter's system. Within the orbit of Sutter's Fort, white influence on Indian life was pervasive but not absolute. When the new system seemed onerous, Indians rebelled and retired to places where Sutter's army did not hold sway. Moreover, in the interior, Indians could exert some measure of influence over white settlers through raiding, trading, and working for whites. In 1846 Indian survival still depended on choices that Indians made as well as the actions of whites who depended on them for labor. Soon, however, California's Indian affairs would become the business of people who were unfamiliar with conditions in the interior, and whites who had been in charge would be replaced by strangers to the Indians who lived there.

California had long attracted the attention of United States policy makers who wanted to expand the North American republic to Pacific shores and beyond. Anglo-American expansionist designs were carried out by a host of supporting characters: merchants and ship captains in Monterey, fur traders and Sutter in the interior, and the growing tide of overland emigration from the United States. During the 1840s Anglo-Americans in California publicized the virtues of the Mexican province to encourage more emigration from the United States. Not surprisingly, they commented favorably on the Indian labor that made California lands productive. The image of California Indians as unthreatening, docile drudges helped to achieve the aims of Manifest Destiny before the Mexican War. During the war some native people would become even more useful to the Anglo-American cause, but for far different reasons.[1]

1. Albert K. Weinberg, *Manifest Destiny: A Study of Nationalist Expansionism in*

In 1845 Thomas O. Larkin, the American consul at Monterey, encouraged Anglo settlers to write to newspapers and friends to stimulate immigration that would lead to American acquisition of the country. The Anglo ranchero John Marsh, who had impressive credentials in Indian affairs, responded to Larkin's call. Before settling in California, Marsh had been a United States Indian subagent to the Sioux and the Sac and Fox, compiled a Sioux language dictionary, and served as a commissioner at the Black Hawk War treaty negotiations. Well known in the United States, Marsh found that potential immigrants eagerly sought his opinions on California. In 1843, for example, Richard Fulton of Sparta, Missouri, wrote to him asking about the prospects for Americans in California. What kind of land, soil, and timber did California have? What kind of artisans did California need? Were doctors and lawyers in demand? Was the only church Catholic? Did Californians have a representative government? Finally, Fulton asked a question that was becoming increasingly important in the decades preceding the Civil War: "Is California a slave state and could our citizens bring their slaves with them?"[2]

In several letters to newspapers and friends Marsh answered Fulton's questions, explaining that California had its own peculiar labor arrangements, even though the Mexican constitution had outlawed slavery. In a letter to the New Orleans *Picayune*, Marsh explained that he estimated the population of California to be comprised of about eight thousand non-Indian people, including about nine hundred Americans, English, Irish, Scots, French, Germans, and Italians. There were about ten thousand "civilized or rather domesticated Indians," and perhaps one or two million "wild Indians." Marsh emphasized the agricultural possibilities of the magnificent Sacramento and San Joaquin valleys, which were "capable of supporting a nation" and "abounded with vast herds of wild horses, elk & antelope." Domestic grains that were accidentally dropped

American History (Baltimore, 1935); Frederick Merk, *Manifest Destiny and Mission in American History: A Reinterpretation* (New York, 1963); John A. Hawgood, "Patterns of Yankee Infiltration in Mexican Alta California," *Pacific Historical Review* 27 (February 1958):27–38; Ray A. Billington, "Books that Won the West," *American West* 4 (August 1967):25–32, 72–74; and John D. Unruh, Jr., *The Plains Across: The Overland Emigrants and the Trans-Mississippi West, 1840–1860* (Urbana, Ill., 1979), esp. 338–42.

2. Fulton to Marsh, June 12, 1843, MC; and George D. Lyman, *John Marsh, Pioneer: The Life Story of a Trail-blazer on Six Frontiers* (New York, 1930), 3–180. Larkin encouraged John Marsh to write to American newspapers stating what sort of products California soil would produce. The American consul told Marsh to "write everything you can regarding California, and I will have it published in New York papers...." Larkin is quoted in "Letter of Dr. John Marsh to Hon. Lewis Cass," *California Historical Society Quarterly* 22 (Dec. 1943):315–22.

on the fertile soil, Marsh declared, sprouted spontaneously and spread quickly across the plains. Some settlers were beginning to raise cotton, which promised "to succeed very well." Other crops that southern farmers cultivated with slave labor were well suited to California too. "Hemp, flax & tobacco have been cultivated on a small scale, & succeed very well."[3]

Marsh sent a similar letter to his old friend and benefactor, Senator Lewis Cass of Michigan, who as territorial governor and Andrew Jackson's secretary of war had become well versed about the Indian frontier. Marsh told Cass that the California Indians were timid and stupid people who reminded him of Cass's remark that "Indians were only grown up children." If true, Marsh continued, he believed the California Indians to be "a real race of infants" who could easily be taught all the occupations necessary to run a farm, especially "when caught young." Marsh knew many whites who established farms near Indian communities and soon had "the whole tribe for willing serfs." They submitted to "flagellation with more humility than negroes." An Indian customarily declared what punishment he deserved; then another Indian applied the specified number of lashes to the offender, who accepted his punishment "without the least sign of resentment or discontent." Marsh claimed that he would not have believed the docility with which the Indians received corporal punishment if he had not seen it himself. He added that they were the "principal laborers," and without them "the business of the country could not be carried on." Although Marsh did not mar his effusive description with disquieting information about livestock raiding, a few days after writing to Cass he complained that one of Sutter's Indians was killing his cattle, forcing him to maintain a "constant Guard" over them. "It would be disagreeable to kill any of your Indians," he warned Sutter.[4]

Marsh exaggerated in his description of spontaneously sprouting crops that were harvested by Indians who virtually enslaved themselves. Wild horses were plentiful, but he did not mention the Indian horse raiding that created them. Instead he portrayed California as an appealing paradise for northern and southern farmers.

The interior was no peaceable kingdom, even though some Anglos insisted that the Indians were utterly inoffensive. In 1844 Pierson B. Reading, a Sutter employee who had once been a New Orleans cotton broker, described the advantages of native labor to Phillip P. Green.

3. Essex [John Marsh] to the editor of the *Picayune*, February 1846, MC. Larkin had suggested that Marsh discuss the possibilities of raising cotton and hemp as well as other products when writing for American newspapers ("Letter of Dr. John Marsh," 315).

4. *Dictionary of American Biography* (hereafter *DAB*), s.v. "Cass, Lewis"; "Letter of Dr. John Marsh," 315–22; and Marsh quoted in Sutter to Reading, Jan. 29, 1846, RC.

"The Indians of California make as obedient and humble slaves as the negroes in the south," he wrote, "for a mere trifle you can secure their services for life." They were "mild and inoffensive in their manners and easily taught the duties of the farm." On Reading's Rancho Buenaventura, the northernmost farm in the Sacramento valley, there were two rancherías, he pointed out, each with about 150 inhabitants. Reading was confident that if he treated the Indians kindly, he could "easily convert them into useful subjects, and at the same time improve their conditions as human beings." Two years later, Indians killed Reading's caretaker, burned his house, and stole his livestock. Perhaps a bit more circumspect, he continued to use Indian labor and built one of the most successful ranchos of the 1850s.[5]

Another promoter of American immigration was Lansford W. Hastings, a young Ohio lawyer who had visited California in 1842 and 1843 and published his famous *Emigrant's Guide* in 1845. Hastings visited New Helvetia and saw Sutter's Indian army, but did not mention its role in suppressing livestock raiding and drafting Indian labor. Indian labor also reminded Hastings of slavery, but he thought it was a great advantage because labor was scarce and whites' wages were high. While he acknowledged that slavery was prohibited in Mexico, he described the position of native workers as "absolute vassalage, even more degrading, and more oppressive than that of our slaves in the south." Nevertheless, the repugnant custom would "for many years, be as little expensive to the farmers of that country, as slave labor, being procured for a mere nominal consideration." Hastings thought that with the help of Indian labor California's commerce eventually would grow to exceed "any other country of the same extent and population in any portion of the known world.[6]

Perhaps the most widely read book on California was Captain John C. Frémont's *Report of the Exploring Expedition to Oregon and North California in the Years 1843–44*. He described Sutter's Indian workers, who were "by the occasional exercise of well-timed authority" converted into a "peaceful and industrious people" and who received "a very

5. Reading to Green, Feb. 7, 1844, RC; and Gertrude Steger, "A Chronology of the Life of Pierson B. Reading," *California Historical Society Quarterly* 22 (Dec. 1943):365–71.

6. *Emigrant's Guide*, 103, 132–33. Hastings's observations of California were hastily written and contain numerous errors, including the assertion that Sutter was a Swede. His description of native labor, however, agrees with reliable sources. The importance of Hastings's views is that they were widely disseminated. His *Emigrant's Guide* was published in several versions that influenced a generation of overland travelers. For a favorable assessment of Hastings's book, see Thomas F. Andrews, "The Controversial Hastings Overland Guide: A Reassessment," *Pacific Historical Review* 37 (February 1968):21–34.

moderate compensation—principally in shirts, blankets, and other articles of clothing." When Sutter needed labor he gave clothing to the "chief of the village [and] . . . readily obtained as many boys and girls as he has any use for." Frémont saw "a number of girls at the fort, in training for a future woolen factory." The fort was guarded by a force "of 40 Indians, in uniform—one of whom was always found on duty at the gate." He also reported that Indians in the mountains made several raids on Mexican settlements while he was in the valley, a disclosure that may have given pause to thoughtful readers.[7]

From the writings of Frémont, Marsh, Hastings, and others, people interested in California could gain basic information. They learned that Indians comprised the labor force; that native people worked cheaply; that they were docile; that they could be easily controlled with corporal punishment; that Indian labor was plentiful; and that white labor was scarce and expensive. Many observers compared Indian labor relations in California to slavery in the South and referred to Indian serfdom and vassalage. These allusions served to emphasize a point. The Indian majority was not a barrier to settlement; rather, native people were willing workers who helped to make California's resources useful to whites.

Between 1843 and 1848 some of California's nearly three thousand overland immigrants may have been encouraged by these partially accurate descriptions of the Indians. While Anglos ordinarily wanted to rid a country of Indians before settlement, in California the presence of native people seemed a positive benefit. Only the best informed could know that Indian labor was a double-edged sword. Occasionally workers rebelled, colluded with horse thieves, stole stock, and killed whites. Insofar as they were slaves, they were troublesome property. They were pliant and docile when compared to racist white images of eastern Indians as frontier terrorists; but taken on their own terms and viewed in historical context, they frequently resisted white encroachment, as Anglo and Mexican Californians knew well. If Indians were like black slaves, then demographically California resembled Africa more than South Carolina.[8]

California's publicists presented Indians as virtual pacifists in the belief that their apparent meekness would appeal to prospective settlers who could imagine the ease with which Indians could be broken to the yoke of agricultural labor. Perhaps the writers correctly estimated the immediate psychological and economic needs of emigrants, but Indian

7. Jackson and Spence, *Expeditions of Frémont*, 1:xix–xx, 654–55, 664.
8. Unruh, *The Plains Across*, 119. Cf. Rawls, *Indians of California*, 69–80.

military skill and courage had frequently been used to foster Anglo frontier interests in the past. In the colonial era, Anglo-Americans had customarily enlisted Indian allies in wars against their French and Indian rivals. Not only were Indians willing to fight their traditional native enemies, they were also enmeshed in the web of European trade and did not want to alienate their British trading partners. This pattern held true on the trans-Appalachian frontier in the early years of the nineteenth century. Even the peaceful Lewis and Clark Expedition enlisted Mandan warriors to make war on Teton Sioux who stole some American horses. During the War of 1812 thousands of Indians fought on the British side in the Old Northwest and Southwest, while comparatively few helped Andrew Jackson's Tennesseans defeat the Creeks. The vast majority, heeding the anti-American messages of the Shawnees Tenskwatawa and Tecumseh, fought with the British in the vain hope that they could halt the relentless westward movement of the American frontier. When it became clear that Americans were not going to be driven off, some tribesmen opted to aid the United States Army as scouts and auxiliaries, fighting alongside white troops in the western campaigns of the nineteenth century.[9]

The military utility of Indians was well known to Lieutenant Frémont, who took two Delawares on his 1843–44 California trip. When Frémont returned in 1845, he brought nine Delawares, a Chinook, an Indian whose tribe was not given, and two California Indian boys who had gone East with Frémont in 1844. In all, Indians comprised 25 percent of Frémont's expedition when he left the Missouri border. When the Mexican War erupted his need for Indian assistance would grow rapidly.

In the summer of 1846, Frémont and other American officers needed fighting men, not the tame Indian serfs that Californians had advertised. Under the Polk administration, relations with Mexico steadily worsened until April 1846, when fighting on the Texas border resulted in a declaration of war. On July 7, Commodore John Sloat demanded California's surrender, marking the beginning of official United States occupation. Shortly thereafter Sloat turned over command in California to Commodore Robert Field Stockton. In the meantime, Anglo settlers and Frémont had acted on their own authority. Frémont's second ex-

9. Axtell, *The European and the Indian*, 42, 262–64; Francis Jennings, *The Invasion of America: Indians, Colonialism, and the Cant of Conquest* (Chapel Hill, 1975), 146–70; James P. Ronda, *Lewis and Clark among the Indians* (Lincoln, 1984), 108–09; Reginald Horsman, *The Frontier in the Formative Years* (New York, 1970), 182–83; R. David Edmunds, *The Shawnee Prophet* (Lincoln, 1983), 117–42; Robert M. Utley, *The Indian Frontier of the American West, 1846–1890* (Albuquerque, 1984), 157–58, 166, 168, 191, 197–201.

pedition had arrived in the interior in January. Understandably suspicious, the californio government ordered him to leave. Instead Frémont took up a defensive position near San José, but withdrew after General José Castro raised a substantial californio force. Not knowing that war with Mexico was imminent, Frémont started for Oregon. While heading up the Sacramento Valley, Peter Lassen and other settlers complained about livestock thieves, so Frémont obligingly attacked the Indians for them. In southern Oregon Lieutenant Archibald Gillespie, a messenger from Washington, caught up with Frémont and evidently convinced him to return to California. That night Klamath Indians killed three of his party, and the incensed Frémont took his revenge by attacking unoffending rancherías as he marched back to California. Unaware that Congress had declared war on Mexico, he camped north of Sutter's Fort, where his presence encouraged Anglos to rebel under the banner of the Bear Flag and declare California independent of Mexico. Frémont resigned his U.S. commission to become the commander of the Bear Flag rebels, augmenting their numbers with his own well-armed expeditionary force. When word of war finally arrived, the Bear Flaggers joined the United States Army as a volunteer force called the California Battalion.[10]

In a theater of operations where manpower and supplies were scarce, the acquisition of Indian allies was a matter of some importance. Under the Bear Flag, Frémont took command of Sutter's Fort and its Indian garrison. He replaced Sutter with Lieutenant Edward Kern, the exploring party's artist, and renamed the post Fort Sacramento (see fig. 5). Commodore Stockton retained this arrangement, and fifty of Sutter's native soldiers enlisted as volunteers in the United States Army. According to naval instructions the Indian soldiers were to be governed by the "militia laws of the US" and were entitled to "the pay & subsistence of Troops of the regular army." Thirty Indians were needed for a permanent guard at the fort, but several hundred soldiers would be needed to defend the place if it was attacked. Lieutenant John S. Missroon, one of Commodore Stockton's officers, authorized Kern to call to his aid "as many of the civilized indians in the employ of Captain Sutter as can be mustered, all of who[m] . . . are expert in the use of fire arms. Under Lieutenant Kern, Sutter was appointed lieutenant of the

10. Jackson and Spence, *Expeditions of Frémont*, 1:428, 2:124–25 n., 137–39, 174–77, 487–89, 2:xxvii; and Neal Harlow, *California Conquered: War and Peace on the Pacific, 1846–1850* (Berkeley, 1982), 61–114. Historians still debate exactly what transpired between Gillespie and Frémont in Oregon. According to Spence and Jackson, evidence of an attack on California Indians prior to Frémont's return from Oregon is unclear.

FIG. 5. Fort Sacramento. Sutter's Fort, renamed Fort Sacramento during the Mexican War, was the military core of New Helvetia. This view shows Indian soldiers drilling in front of the fort's gate. John Sutter's Indian army had helped him subdue the Indians in the interior. During the war, John C. Frémont enlisted them in the U.S. Army to help conquer California.

Indian force and given responsibility for "drilling and exercising the soldiers." In addition to the Indian guard, U.S. authorities enlisted twenty native cavalrymen. These recruits were first referred to as hunters, but when their final payroll was prepared they were identified as "Cavalry troops [enlisted] August 8—1846."[11]

The demoted Lieutenant Sutter and the Indian troops at Fort Sacramento soon had an opportunity to prove themselves. Early in September reports arrived that one thousand Walla Walla warriors from Oregon Territory were on their way south to attack the fort. Rumors greatly exaggerated the size of the Indian party and misrepresented their intentions. The previous year some Walla Walla, Cayuse, and Spokane

11. Lt. Kern arrived in California in 1845 as an artist with Frémont (Robert V. Hine, *In the Shadow of Frémont: Edward Kern and the Art of Exploration*, 2d ed. [Norman, Okla., 1982], 25–47). Missroon to Kern, Aug. 8, 1846, MS 27, and Aug. 16, 1846, MS 28; John B. Montgomery to Kern, Aug. 26, 1846, MS 63, FSP. Cf. "List of Clothing Sent to E. M. Kern for Men at Fort Sacramento", Aug. 2, 1846, MS 87, FSP. The payroll certified by E. M. Kern, Feb. 26, 1847 (MSS 20, 21, 22, 23, MKP) included Lt. Sutter and Indian cavalry privates Olimpio, Celestina, Clemente, Nannook, Ajeas, Dushuma, Sula, Nieronemu, Youti, Tokatchi, Wisha, Nutchumnie, Yuieko, Osa, Nusha, Sapne, Nugishe, Witash, Lisha, Hella, and infantry privates Homobono, Augustine, Francisco, Leandro, Eulatario, Juan, Pascasio, Carlos, Bassilio, Pompeya, Andreas, Burtola, Butchi, Laquela, Valentia, Nuut, Fabian, Augustine, Wokna, Wolahuck, Walabackse, Sixte, Wesidario, Juan, Kilog, Gasto, Jesus, Nipolita, Wolahucke, and Brunno.

Indians had come to the Sacramento Valley to trade horses, beaver pelts, and deer and elk hides for cattle. Trading was friendly until the Walla Wallas fought with some California Indian horse raiders. The Oregon Indians prevailed and took a herd of horses and a mule that had been stolen from whites. When New Helvetia whites discovered that the Walla Wallas had recovered their animals, they demanded their return; but the Indians refused. Grove Cook, who was particularly incensed because they had his mule, vehemently insisted that his animal be returned. But Elijah Hedding, a Walla Walla man who had been educated at a Protestant mission in Oregon, claimed that since the animals had been recovered at the peril of the Indians' lives, they should be able to keep them, following the Oregon custom. Not persuaded, Cook killed Elijah in fit of rage at Sutter's Fort. The other Indians then fled to Oregon, leaving their stock behind them.[12]

The death of Elijah caused a great commotion among the various Oregon tribes. Elijah White, the United Sates Indian subagent in Oregon, was particularly concerned that the event would cause a war. The American consul Larkin attempted to contain the consequences of Cook's rash act by instructing Sutter to give White a full account and to take up a collection of cattle "to make up the compliment lost by friends of the Deceased." At the same time Larkin asked White to tell Elijah's father, Pio-pio-mox-mox—also known as Yellow Serpent—that Cook would be brought to justice and to issue a passport so the Indians would "come direct to Captain Sutter . . . for their cattle" and legal retribution. Larkin requested that White try to restrict the number of California-bound Indians to "only enough men . . . to protect themselves on the road, and to drive the Cattle away." Too many Walla Walla Indians would "cause mistrust here."[13]

As Larkin suggested, Pio-pio-mox-mox led a small party of Walla Wallas and other Oregon Indians to California in the fall of 1846. The group included a few dozen men, women, and children seeking justice and the cattle that Sutter was supposed to be keeping for them. Their arrival caused a panic among Anglos, who assumed these invaders wanted bloody revenge. Commander John B. Montgomery of the U.S.S. *Portsmouth* ordered forces from San José, Sonoma, and Monterey—

12. Elijah White's version of these events and their consequences is in the *Californian*, Sept. 17, 1846, 1–4.

13. Larkin to Sutter, Nov. 1, 1845, MS 74, LC. This letter is not published in Hammond's edition of the *Larkin Papers* or in John A. Hawgood, ed., *First and Last Consul: Thomas Oliver Larkin and the Americanization of California*, 2d ed., (Palo Alto, 1970), 36–37. Cf. Larkin to White, Nov. 1, 1845, MS 74, LC; and Hawgood, *First and Last Consul*, 36–37.

altogether about "100 mounted men"—to reinforce Fort Sacramento. Montgomery ordered Kern to hold out with the Indian garrison until his provisions were exhausted. "In the meantime," Montgomery advised Kern, "be prudent and watchful." Preparations for war against the Walla Wallas continued until Pio-pio-mox-mox rode to the fort and assured the military authorities that he sought only peaceful trade and justice on behalf of his murdered son. This turn of events apparently disgusted some of the white volunteers, who wanted an Indian war and suggested that their force should chastise the California Indians in the mountains. Kern stopped short of initiating a California Indian war, but marched the volunteers northward to the Sutter Buttes to discourage native live-stock raiding.[14]

Not one to let opportunity slip away, Lieutenant Sutter decided to sign up the Walla Walla men for the California Battalion, which would soon head south to fight californios in rebellion against the new American regime. Besides providing much needed reinforcements, this adroit tactic removed the Walla Wallas from the valley, where chagrined whites wanted to fight the Oregon natives. Promising that they would be paid for their service, Sutter organized the Walla Wallas as a company under François Gendreau, a Canadian with a Walla Walla wife. These new soldiers left their families at Fort Sacramento, where Frémont directed Kern to supply them "with beef and flour regularly; and to give regular rations to Jeandrois' [Gendreau's] family."[15]

Simultaneously, Sutter convinced the inveterate raider José Jesus and other Miwoks to volunteer for the California Battalion. They were "old horse-thieves now reformed" he said, "under Jose Jesus, a christianized indian." Sutter remained at Fort Sacramento and sent Edwin Bryant with some American volunteers to take charge of as many Indians as Bryant deemed "safe to accompany us" to join the California Battalion. At the Mokelumne River, Bryant met "Antonio, an Indian chief, with twelve warriors," and the next day José Jesus, Felipe, Rimondo, and Carlos, whom he identified as "chiefs," with thirteen "warriors." The Miwoks formed the California Battalion's Company H, under the com-

14. Montgomery to Kern, Sept. 10, 1847, MS 65, FSP. A detailed account of the military preparations during the Walla Walla incident is provided in John Adam Hussey and George Walcott Ames, Jr., "California Preparations to Meet the Walla Walla Invasion, 1846," *California Historical Society Quarterly* 21 (March 1942):9–21. Hussey and Ames did not examine the role of the Walla Walla Indians as soldiers in the California Battalion and were apparently unaware of Larkin's role in the affair. Robert F. Heizer's brief history of the Walla Wallas in California from 1844 to 1847, "Walla Walla Indian Expeditions to the Sacramento Valley," *California Historical Society Quarterly* 21 (1942):1–7, includes some information about Walla Walla activities in the Mexican War.

15. Sutter, "Reminiscences"; and Jackson and Spence, *Expeditions of Frémont*, 2:230.

mand of Bryant. Armed with bows, "the chiefs and some of the warriors
. . . were partially clothed, but most of them were naked, except a small
garment around their loins," Bryant later recalled. After six Indian
swimmers had towed rafts across the rain-swollen San Joaquin River,
he noticed that they "trembled as if attacked with ague." They may
have suffered from malaria, a legacy of the 1833 epidemic. With or
without malarial chills, José Jesus and the men of Company H had fought
the californios for decades, a wealth of experience that the newcomer
Bryant could not have fully appreciated.[16]

The names of thirty-three California Indians are inscribed in the
records of the California Battalion, and perhaps ten or twelve Walla
Wallas whose names were not recorded also fought. Frémont wrote
later that the Indians camped without fires up to three miles in advance
and to the rear of the battalion, "so that no traveller on the road escaped
falling into our hands." On November 20 the Walla Wallas fought at
the battle of Natividad, with results that inspired Frémont to commend
their bravery. Besides providing guards and fighting, the Indian troops
raided the herds of the enemy. Control of the horse herds was vital and
the battalion resolutely plundered California's *caballadas*. José Jesus no
doubt pitched in. In grudging recognition of their wartime adventures,
the californios called Company H the "forty thieves."[17]

Hostilities ended on January 13, 1847, when californio officers signed
articles of capitulation at Cahuenga Pass. On February 18 Company H
disbanded, but nineteen California Indian servants remained in the employ of battalion officers. The officers claimed that the United States
owed them for servants' hire in the amounts of $6.00 per month pay,
$6.00 per month rations, and $2.50 per month for clothing for each
Indian retainer as provided for by law. Pierson Reading, the battalion

16. Sutter, "Reminiscences"; proposal signed by Bryant and others, Oct. 28, 1846, MS
51, FSP; and Bryant, *What I Saw in California* (1848; reprint, Berkeley, 1985), 359–60.

17. "Muster Roll of Company H," Feb. 18, 1847, T135, reel 2. Besides Bryant, Company
H included Sergeant Oliver P. Paulson, privates John Sly, Solomon Sly, William M.
Ritchey, Henry Peterman, Thomas Towson, John Lennon, and Indian privates Antonio,
Santiago, Masua, Kusbu, Tocoso, Nonela, Michell, Weala, Arkell, Koluss, Hesll, Casiano,
Estephan, José Jesus, Feleipe, Kuliganio, Onofariu, Francisco, Feliciano, Pablo, San
Antonio, Polinario, Rimondo, Carlos, Nicolas, Graciano, Salnordio, Ramero, Eusebio,
Gregorio, Bruno, and Juan. Edwin Bryant listed only thirty-one Indian names in *What I
Saw in California*, p. 359. Three names that Bryant gives—Huligario, Bonefasio, and
Merikeeldo—do not appear in T135. Six names appear on the muster roll that did not
appear on Bryant's list: Kuliganio, Onofariu, Eusebio, Gregorio, Bruno, and Juan. Jack-
son and Spence, *Expeditions of Frémont*, 2:235, 302; and Bancroft, *History of California*,
5:358–63.

paymaster, reckoned that the government owed him $328.64 for two Indian servants.[18]

Battalion records do not show how much the officers actually paid their servants, but it seems doubtful they would have given them the full $14.50 per month in pay, rations, and clothing. It is more likely that they traded old clothing and other items, following the custom of the country that Sutter, Reading, and other old California hands taught the newcomers. For example, Sutter loaned Lieutenant Missroon an Indian in August 1846. Missroon later sent Sutter "a Couple pair of half worn pantaloons," items that the sailor learned were "the most Suitable article of exchange for Indian Curiosities." Missroon was seeking some bows and arrows "to send home for Specimens to a public Institution."[19]

Instead of standard volunteer army pay, the Fort Sacramento Indian troops received only clothing and other trade goods. Early in their term of service, naval authorities decided to pay thirty Indian guards $6.00 per month in clothing rather than in cash, so Lieutenant Kern requisitioned blankets, blue flannel shirts, duck frocks, trousers, and combs to compensate the troops. The navy was short of these goods and his request was not in the proper form, so Kern had to submit a new requisition. Montgomery acknowledged that delays would cause "embarrassment in the settling of . . . accounts since there are no experienced officers who understand US bookkeeping procedures." Among the embarrassed were the fort's Indian guards, who were never paid in full because of supply shortages and the vicissitudes of frontier warfare. The twenty Indian cavalrymen fared a little better. Mounted troops were supposed to be paid $12.50 per month, but the Indians got supplies instead. Each trooper received one pound of tobacco worth $0.25, one blue shirt at $2.31, two pairs of duck trousers costing $0.72, and one duck frock valued at $0.93—a bargain for the U.S. government.[20]

18. "Approval of Servant Hire for Officers of the California Battalion by John Charles Frémont," Apr. 1847; and The United States to P.B. Reading, n.d., T135. Reading requested $8 per month pay for each servant hired. He described the two servants as being 5 feet 10 inches tall, both having coffee-colored complexions, dark hair, and dark eyes.

19. Missroon to Kern, Aug. 19, 1846, MS 30; and Missroon to Kern, [no day or month] 1846, MS 29, FSP.

20. Joseph W. Revere to Kern, Sept. 16, 1846, MS 43, FSP. Besides paying the Indian troops in clothing, naval authorities decided that Indians should not receive tea, sugar, or tobacco as part of their regular issue of rations (Missroon to Kern, Aug. 16, 1846, MS 29, FSP). Payment of volunteers in clothing did not conform to the law that was then in force, which provided that volunteers were to receive the same pay and allowances as regular troops, except that they were supposed to receive pay in lieu of a clothing issue.

José Jesus and the other Indians in the California Battalion were entitled to the same pay as whites, $25.00 per month, but none of the volunteers was paid immediately. Indians and whites alike were given receipts, which could be redeemed for cash when Congress appropriated funds. When the Indians mustered out of the battalion, each made "his mark" beside his name indicating that he had taken a receipt for three months' service. Payment for volunteer service was part of the California claims that Congress did not settle until 1858. After eleven years the Indians' receipts had probably been sold to speculators at a discount, so the amount of money that the California Indian volunteers actually received cannot be determined. Lacking immediate payment, José Jesus and his Indian allies returned to raiding livestock herds on the coast.[21]

The Walla Wallas took their pay in horses and plunder. Sutter reported that the Oregon Indians "brought back much spoils, trophies, clothing of the Mexicans they had killed." With this evidence of their service to the United States in hand, the Walla Wallas were angry because they were not paid immediately and accused Sutter of deceiving them. To keep the peace, Frémont gave them "a lot of old broken down government horses, stamped U.S. which were roaming about the fort." Pio-pio-mox-mox did not even get to see his son's murderer brought to justice, for Grove Cook was never punished for his crime. Deeply dissatisfied, the Walla Wallas raided Indian rancherías and white livestock herds as they headed back to Oregon, impoverishing the valley tribes and forcing them to steal livestock from whites. In November 1847 the bad California experiences of Cayuse and Walla Walla Indians were among the complaints against Americans that led them to kill Protestant missionaries Marcus and Narcissa Whitman in Oregon. As late as 1855 Pio-pio-mox-mox complained bitterly to federal officials about his son's murder.[22]

In addition, each mounted volunteer was supposed to receive forty cents per day for the use of his horse (*U.S. Statutes at Large*, 9:9–10). The rate of pay was fixed at $7 per month for privates, $1 of which was retained by the United States towards retirement. Thus, volunteers received only $6. See *U.S. Statutes at Large*, 5:308; draft for articles for men in garrison at Fort Sacramento, Oct. 14, 1846, MS 85; Montgomery to Kern, Aug. 26, Sept. 17, Sept. 26, and Oct. 13, 1846, MSS 63, 66, 67, and 69; and accounts of men in garrison at Fort Sacramento for month ending Sept. 7, 1846 [unsigned draft], MS 94, FSP. Problems were exacerbated when a launch sent to Fort Sacramento with payment for troops was lost with all hands (Montgomery to Kern, Dec. 3, 1846, MS 75, FSP). Sutter also stated that the United States did not pay the Indian troops at Fort Sacramento ("Reminiscences").

21. Montgomery to Kern, Aug. 26, 1846, MS 63, FSP; and "Muster Roll, Company H," T135; and *California Star* Apr. 10, 1847, 4.

22. Sutter, in his "Reminiscences," claims that he gave the horses to the Walla Wallas, but in his daily journal he indicated that Frémont actually ordered that the horses be

There were few short-term benefits for Indians who helped the United States to acquire California, yet they provided assistance in several ways. Before the war, whites eager to encourage Anglo immigration promoted Indians as servile agricultural labor, virtual slaves who could be used for practically nothing. But American commanders found California a less pacific place than Californians had advertised. Short on men and material, they relied on the enlistment of the Indian auxiliaries, a time-honored frontier practice. Officers did not enlist natives because they were docile, but because of their experience as soldiers and raiders. With hindsight, it is reasonably certain that the United States could have conquered California without Indian assistance, but Stockton, Frémont, Kern, and other officers did not know that to be the case. In their haste to assemble an effective volunteer force, they made promises to Indians that they could not keep. Indian volunteers who gave up their hunting, gathering, and raiding time to the California Battalion could not clothe and feed their families with promises of future payment. Consequently, discharged California and Walla Walla Indians turned to raiding, an unintended consequence of their volunteer services.

Because the war impoverished Indians, their first encounter with the American government was not auspicious. Army ineptitude and frontier exigencies foreshadowed difficulties that would ensue when the federal government assumed control over Indian affairs. In the meantime, many Indians looked to the livestock herds for survival, much as they had for several decades. Unfortunately for all concerned, the war had consumed much of California's pastoral wealth, making raiding less profitable for Indians and more devastating to rancheros. Indian livestock raiding would not last for many more years, but neither Indians nor whites could foresee the future as Miwok, Yokuts, and Nisenan raiders fanned out across the central valleys heading for interior and coastal ranches. After Mexican California was subdued, military governors devoted their resources to this problem, giving it their serious attention until the gold rush.

---

given to them (Sutter et al., *New Helvetia Diary*, 51; Kern to his commander, March 30, 1847, MS 83, FSP; Christopher L. Miller, *Prophetic Worlds: Indians and Whites on the Columbia Plateau* (New Brunswick, N.J., 1985), 104, 113. Frémont did not deliver the horses to the Walla Wallas until June, so apparently the Walla Wallas left in several groups over a period of months.

5

"Conciliate the Inhabitants:"
Federal Indian Administration
during the Mexican War

Between 1846 and 1849, American military governors were responsible for Indian affairs. They faced problems peculiar to California with broad authority but no clear instructions from Washington. The usual federal laws governing Indian-white relations hardly seemed to be a useful model, for they were established with the idea that Indians and whites lived in separate communities and that racial separation should be maintained. In California, Indians and whites were mutually dependent and deeply involved in one anothers' daily lives. Cognizant of these novel conditions, the military governors developed an Indian policy adapted to the needs of California's Mexican and American residents. This policy, shaped by local exigencies, provided an assurance to Mexicans and Anglo-Americans that United States authorities would protect white interests, control the Indian majority, and maintain the established pattern of race relations in California. It was intended to permit landowners to use Indian labor while safeguarding a thinly settled frontier against the raids of Indian forces.[1]

For their part, Indian raiders assailed Anglo and Hispanic herds because the Mexican War had increased their poverty. Indian volunteers who were not promptly paid stole stock because Indian life depended on taking a variety of resources when they were available. The war had eliminated a season of natural harvests and opportunities for agricultural labor from the round of economic activities that had supported Indian society for years. Warfare had even depleted the livestock herds that raiders depended on. Even though a comparatively small number of Indians participated in the war, they ordinarily helped to feed their families in their home rancherías, so the effects of the war extended beyond the number of Indians who had enlisted. Moreover, unpaid soldiers resorted to raiding not only whites' livestock herds but native

---

1. Prucha, *Great Father*, 1:5–314, passim.

communities as well, impoverishing noncombatants and forcing them to raid also. Thus, the impact of the war on native people was widespread.

At first the Indians' reasons for raiding were of little concern to military governors, who were preoccupied with pacifying Mexican California. Typically, military men attempted to quell Indian livestock raiding rather than eliminate its causes. In July 1846 the first military governor, Commodore John D. Sloat, authorized a force of mounted volunteers to pursue raiders and prescribed punishment for captured Indians, but Sloat departed a few days later, leaving the development of a comprehensive policy to his successors. The second governor, Commodore Robert F. Stockton, also recognized the need to take action against Indian raiders. In July Consul Larkin advised Stockton that California could not be secured from Mexico or protected from Indians without a "force of horsemen, who are accustomed to the Rifle and the Saddle." In March he estimated that 920 cavalrymen were needed for Indian defense, but only 720 would be necessary to guard against Mexican rebellion. In 1846 Stockton did not have so many men to deploy against Indians, but he sent a few of his troops to pursue Indians who were harassing Santa Clara's ranchers. On August 15 the *Californian* editorialized on the necessity of "interior defenses sufficient to protect the property of our citizens from the depredations of wild indians." Two days later Commodore Stockton issued a proclamation declaring California "free of Mexico" and announcing that "as soon as circumstances" permitted the country would be governed by laws similar to those of other U.S. territories. Recognizing the importance of stopping Indian forays, Stockton agreed to use the California Battalion to "prevent and punish any aggression by the Indians or any other persons upon the property of Individuals, or the peace of the Territory." Captured thieves were to be put to labor at public works until they had made restitution for stolen property.[2]

If Stockton had wished to expand his Indian policy, the opportunity faded when rebellious Mexican forces compelled him to direct the California Battalion to operations in the south. Subsequent political controversy diverted the military governor's attention, resulting in the neglect of Indian affairs for months. Shortly after the Mexican Californians capitulated, Commodore Stockton appointed Frémont military governor and left California. Meanwhile, General Stephen Watts

2. Sloat to John Montgomery, July 12 1846, in *Message from the President . . . to the Two Houses of Congress*, Sen. Ex. Doc. 1, 30th Cong., 2d sess., ser. 537, 1,023–24; Larkin to Stockton, July 24, 1846, *Larkin Papers*, 5:159–60; Larkin to Kearny, March 6, 1847, ibid. 6:41; *The Californian*, Aug. 15, 1846, 1–2; and "To the People of California," *The Californian*, Sept. 5, 1846, 2.

Kearny had arrived in California by way of New Mexico, carrying orders from Secretary of War William L. Marcy to assume the governorship and set up a "temporary civil government" under military control. Marcy thought it best for Kearny to "act in such a manner as best to conciliate the inhabitants, and render them friendly to the United States," and suggested that it might be necessary to procure some goods for Indian gifts. The rest he left to Kearny's discretion. On the authority of these orders General Kearny and his successor, Colonel Richard B. Mason, proceeded to develop a settled policy for Indian affairs that conformed to the interests of California's substantial ranchers and other large landholders.[3]

For a few months General Kearny was distracted from his duties by the controversy with Frémont; but by April 1847 Kearny's command was supreme and Frémont would soon be on his way east to court-martial proceedings. Although the California Battalion refused to serve under Kearny's orders for the pay that federal law allowed, Kearny commanded enough forces to establish firm control of the governorship.[4]

The early disorder of American military government had allowed Indian raiding to go unchecked, while victimized ranchers demanded the army's protection. Fifteen Sacramento Valley ranchers expressed their distress in a February 28, 1847, petition to Lieutenant Kern, who was still in command at Fort Sacramento. The Indians of the valley, they claimed, were uniting with those of the mountains. If a military force was not soon forthcoming, the petitioners warned, "we will be forced to abandon our farms and leave our property to the Murcy of the Indians [or] purhaps something worse." Similar reports came to Governor Kearny from Sonoma, Monterey, Los Angeles, San Luis Obispo, and San Diego. Raiders had made traveling dangerous, threatened livestock herds everywhere, and killed whites who challenged them. Larkin, who was not an alarmist, informed Secretary of State James Buchanan that "strong and efficient measures" were needed to stop livestock raiding so that farming could advance. Kearny told the sec-

3. Kearny, a career soldier since the War of 1812, marched into California in late 1846 commanding a small contingent of the Army of the West. After assisting in pacification of California, he became embroiled in a dispute over his claim to the military governorship. Kearny was eventually vindicated, and—after Frémont's court-martial—he was appointed civil governor of Vera Cruz. See *DAB*, s.v. "Kearny, Stephen," and Marcy to Kearny, June 3, 1846, in *Message of the President of the United States Containing the Proceedings of the Court Martial of Lieutenant John C. Frémont*, Sen. Ex. Doc. 18, 30th Cong., 1st sess., ser. 507, 28–31.

4. For some of the details of the controversy between Frémont and Kearny (and Kearny's representative, Mason), see Jackson and Spence, *Expeditions of Frémont*, 2:368–69, 375; and Harlow, *California Conquered*, 193–278.

retary of war that "wild Indians" were driving off California's stock. The so-called wild Indians "as well as the Christian Indians have been badly treated by most of the Californians; they think they are entitled to what they can steal and rob from them." Kearny recommended that some presents be sent out for the Indians, hoping that some timely gifts would curtail raiding.[5]

Some white informants, however, grossly misrepresented the threat of Indian and white hostilities. Lieutenant G. W. Harrison, commander of the U.S. Marine force at Sonoma, reported that the Indians were about to attack local ranches. Harrison requested twenty more men to reinforce his garrison, then discovered he had been misled. In fact, whites had stormed an Indian "village and attempted to take some of them into servitude—were resisted and lost one of their number, not however without killing four of their opponents." Harrison urged Kearny to station a military force at Sonoma to protect both Indians and whites.[6]

George McKinstry, recently appointed sheriff of the Sacramento district, also reported his views on Indian affairs to military headquarters. McKinstry noted that a U.S. force, including the "best men in garrison with carbines and lances," had departed for a "disturbed district" north of Fort Sacramento. He insisted that a strong force was a "great necessity" to protect both the Sacramento and San Joaquin valleys. "The latter valley," he declared, was "inhabited by a brave band of Indians known by the title of 'Horse thieves' and unless properly managed may be troublesome to the inhabitants in that part of the country." Before the Mexican War, McKinstry explained to American authorities, Captain Sutter's Indian soldiers had controlled native people in both valleys. McKinstry pointedly added that the native soldiers could be "employed at one half the expense that white men can and are far preferable for the service," if the government would retain them. The sheriff also recommended that the proper authority issue an order prohibiting the sale of liquor to Indians to prevent unscrupulous white traders from supplying the Indian soldiers with alcohol at exhorbitant prices. Kern also recommended the retention of the Indian soldiers, but they were

5. Daniel Sill et al. to the commander of U.S. forces at New Helvetia [Edward Kern], Feb. 28, 1847, MS 82, FSP; *California Star*, March 13, 1847, 1; Apr. 10, 4, Apr. 17, 2; John Nash to S. F. Dupont, March 1, 1847, M210; Larkin to Edwin Bryant, Apr. 7, 1847, *Larkin Papers*, 7:87–88; Larkin to Buchanan, Aug. 25, 1847, ibid., 6:291–92; J. D. Stevenson to Kearny, May 15, 1847, vol. 63, CA; Richard B. Mason to José Salazar and Enrique Ayala, Apr. 10, 1847, CA; J. J. Warner to Kearny, Apr. 19, 1847, CA; Kearny to Marcy, Apr. 28, 1847, Sen. Ex. Doc. 18, 31st Cong., 1st sess., ser. 557, 274–76.
6. Harrison to Dupont, March 16, 17, 1847, M210.

not kept beyond their term of enlistment. In 1847 Sutter would again be responsible for keeping up his private army, but only briefly. The days of Indian soldiers guarding the interior were on the wane.[7]

The urgent necessity of attending to California Indian affairs had been amply demonstrated to the military government. In April General Kearny appointed Sutter the first federal Indian subagent in California, describing his territorial limits as the "Sacramento and San Joakin Rivers." With the appointment Kearny sent a letter that illustrated his understanding of the subagent's duties and proper Indian behavior. First he reminded Sutter that the Indians had given great trouble by driving off livestock and attacking isolated ranches. "This conduct on the part of the Indians must cease," wrote Kearny, "& I am in hopes that by good advice & prudent council which your perfect acquaintance with them will enable you to give, they will be induced to abstain from giving further cause for complaint against them." Otherwise, Kearny warned, they would "most assuredly be punished by an armed force which I will send among them & which I wish to inform them of." He directed Sutter to tell the Indians of the change from Mexican to United States sovereignty and to explain that Anglo and Mexican Californians were "now one People & any offenses which they commit against the latter will be punished in the same way as if committed against the former." Kearny advised his subagent that he would try to obtain "Indian goods" to be given to chiefs who conducted themselves "peaceably & honestly." The governor closed his letter by ordering Sutter to report any occurrence which he deemed worthy of attention, set his pay at $750 per year, and enjoined him not to contract any debts against the United States or the territory of California. One week later Kearny appointed a second subagent, Mariano G. Vallejo, who was responsible for the Indians north of San Francisco Bay, "including cash [Cache] Creek and [Clear] Lakes." His instructions were identical to those of Sutter.[8]

7. McKinstry to Hale, March 13, 1847, M210. The force commander, Lt. Kern, reported that his soldiers attacked three native communities and killed ten people (Kern to his commander, March 30, 1847, MS 83, FSP). The Indian soldiers were six-month volunteers whose enlistment ended in February 1847.

8. The duties of the subagent were not clearly distinguishable from the duties of the Indian agent. Agents and subagents were enjoined to uphold federal Indian laws, but subagents were appointed by the president without the advice and consent of the Senate, which was required for the appointment of agents. The major difference between the two agent and subagents was their rate of pay. Agents received $1,500 per year, while subagents received only $750 (*U.S. Statutes at Large*, 4:736–37). On June 1, 1837, Secretary of War Joel Poinsett issued detailed instructions defining the duties of superintendents, agents, subagents, and other department employees, in "Revised Regulation no. III," Sen. Doc.

Governor Kearny's first appointments reveal a basic design for his Indian policy. By giving commissions to Vallejo and Sutter, he followed Secretary Marcy's instructions to conciliate the people of California. Both men had extensive experience with Indian affairs on the northern frontier of Mexican California. Both were important landowners, former officials of the Mexican government, and well-known to the native people in their respective districts. Sutter and Vallejo had each proved useful to the American commanders during the hostilities with Mexican Californians. The governor's instructions to the subagents showed an almost wholly punitive attitude towards the Indians, placing the burden of guilt on them for any difficulties that arose. The only hint that Indians would have redress for their grievances was contained in Kearny's vague poetic allusion to a "Great Father" taking "good care of his good children." Indians he defined as "good" when they did not give "cause for complaint against them." If there were complaints, Indians would be "punished by an armed force." Kearny's measures showed no consideration for the immediate needs of the Indian people or the long-term problems they would face as more territory was taken by incoming settlers.[9]

Kearny left California in June 1847, but his successor, Colonel Mason, retained Sutter and Vallejo in his administration. Over a period of months he substantially expanded the military government's Indian policy. Governor Mason first turned his attention to the southern region, which was also subject to Indian livestock raiding. Attempts to end raiding with small patrols of soldiers and volunteers proved inadequate. In the spring of 1847 Indian raiders near Los Angeles had defeated a force of twelve dragoons and a number of ranchers, killing a civilian and wounding two soldiers. To take direct charge of the southern district, Governor Mason in early August appointed Jesse B. Hunter, a member of the Mormon Battalion that had marched overland to California, as the third Indian subagent under federal authority. Mason gave Hunter special instructions to protect the Mission San Luis Rey and to "reclaim the old mission Indians to habits of industry, and . . . the wild ones too," making sure to "protect them in their lives and true interests" while preventing them "from encroaching in any way upon the peaceable inhabitants of the land." To these ends, Mason required Hunter to

1, 25th Cong., 2d sess., ser. 314, 615–26. See also Kearny to Sutter, Apr. 7, 1847, M182; and Kearny to Vallejo, Apr. 14, 1847, M182.

9. Kearny to Sutter, Apr. 7, 1847, M182; Kern to his commander, March 30, 1847, MS 83, FSP. See also Agricola, "Letter to the Editor," *California Star*, Apr. 10, 1847, 4; and Mason to R. Jones, June 18, 1847, Sen. Ex. Doc. 8, 30th Cong., 1st sess., ser. 515, 518–19.

prevent Indians from "going about in crowds" and to issue passports to those who wished "to go any distance from their houses or rancherias." In the administration of mission affairs and property, Mason directed Hunter to defer to any priest who arrived. The southern Indian subagent, unlike his northern counterparts, was bound to obey the instructions of the district military commander, Colonel Jonathan D. Stevenson.[10]

Hunter's jurisdiction included all of southern California, but Mason stressed that the new agent should pay special attention to the Mission San Luis Rey as a means to control the surrounding Indian population. The governor's desire to reestablish a form of mission rule over southern California Indians was something of an experiment, an attempt to rely on an old California institution. The governor saw the mission as a kind of Indian reformatory that would restrain and rehabilitate Indians. Governor Mason went beyond Kearny's attempt to stop livestock raiding by restricting Indian's freedom of movement whether or not they were allied with "horse thieves."

Over the next few months Mason extended these regulations over all Indians, including the Indian labor force that was so important to pastoral California. The measures prohibiting native crowds and regulating Indian travel with passports had a precedent not only in Mexican California, but in the southern United States, where similar laws controlled the large southern slave labor force, as Virginia-born Mason must have known. As in the South, Mason and other Anglo-Americans deemed it necessary to assert control over numerous nonwhite people whose economic, social, and political places were racially defined.[11]

The military government, however, would find that in some respects California's Indian labor relations differed from southern slavery. In the first place, no statutory or military authority existed for the enslavement of Indians who had not been convicted of a crime, and the nefarious

10. Richard Barnes Mason, of the prominent Virginia Masons, was born near Mount Vernon in 1797. He joined the army in 1817 as a second lieutenant, quickly advanced to the rank of captain during the Black Hawk Indian War, and by 1846 had become a colonel. He arrived in California in February 1847 with orders from Washington reinforcing Kearny's claim to the governorship and ordering Mason to assume that office once U.S. control was firmly established. See *DAB*, s.v. "Mason, Richard Barnes," and Archibald Gillespie to Larkin, Apr. 7, 1847, *Larkin Papers*, 6:87–88. Jesse D. Hunter arrived in California in 1847 as captain of Company B of the Mormon Battalion. Hunter was a native of Kentucky who found California to his liking and remained until his death in 1877. See Bancroft, *History of California*, 3:791; William T. Sherman to Hunter, Aug. 1, 1847, in *Message from the President . . . Communicating Information Called for by . . . the Senate . . . Relating to California and New Mexico*, Sen Ex. Doc. 18, 31st Cong., 1st sess., ser. 557, 339; and Mason to Hunter, Aug. 2, 1847, in ibid.

11. For an analysis of slave codes and other methods for controlling a coerced labor force, see Wood, *Black Majority*, 271–84.

practice of kidnapping Indians for use as laborers and servants begged to be addressed. Speaking to this issue, Commander John B. Montgomery published a proclamation in February 1847 condemning forced Indian labor in the District of San Francisco. He ordered the release of all Indians held against their will. They should "not be regarded in the light of slaves, but it is deemed necessary that the Indians within the Settlement shall have employment with the right of choosing their own master and employer," with whom a written contract was to be executed. A worker under contract "must abide by it" unless he could obtain his employer's written release. The government would annul contracts for just cause, but the released worker had to obtain new employment immediately. Indians who were "idle and dissolute" would be liable to arrest and punishment by "labor on the Public Works." Although not slaves, Indians in Montgomery's view had considerably less freedom than whites inasmuch as his restrictive order made working for whites the only legitimate Indian activity in settled areas. Montgomery's proclamation illustrated the difficulty of reconciling white's needs with the rights of Indians as free men, prefiguring subsequent military government regulations.[12]

Some whites did not make fine distinctions between Indian freedom and slavery. On July 12, 1847, Sutter reported that Antonio Armijo, Robert "Growling" Smith, and John Eggar, residents of Sonoma, had attacked a ranchería sixty miles north of Fort Sacramento, killed thirteen people, and taken thirty-seven "as slaves." Governor Mason, fearing that this outrage might provoke an Indian war, ordered Sutter to make every exertion to bring the culprits to justice. "The safety of the frontier shall not be put at hazard for a few lawless villains," wrote the governor. He gave Sutter authority to employ military assistance, assuring the subagent that he would "organize a tribunal for their trial" and carry out a sentence of death if it were passed. The editor of the *California Star*, also fearing an Indian rebellion, asked the government to take measures to prevent Indian revenge and to bring those responsible for the crime to justice.[13]

By August 13 army officers had arrested the three men and Governor Mason ordered a "full fair and impartial trial" to be held at Fort Sacramento, with Sutter and Vallejo presiding as judges. Then Mason granted a change of venue to the defendants' home district of Sonoma

12. *California Star*, Feb. 20, 1847, 4.
13. Sutter to Mason, July 12, 1847, in *Message from the President... Communicating Information Called for by... the Senate... Relating to California and New Mexico*, Sen. Ex. Doc. 18, 31st Cong., 1st sess., ser. 557, 351; Mason to Sutter, July 21, 1847, M182; and "The Indians Again," *California Star*, July 24, 1847, 2.

and appointed Sonoma alcalde Lilburn W. Boggs as a third judge. In the end only Boggs and Vallejo presided, since Sutter claimed he was too ill to attend the trial. On October 25 and 26, a twelve-man jury acquitted Armijo, Smith, and Eggar of murder and enslavement charges. The two prominent Sonomans, Boggs and Vallejo, blamed the acquittal on the absent Sutter, claiming he had not obtained a proper affidavit against the men charged. The cost of the trial—more than $1,700—was exorbitant and one of the defendants demanded to be reimbursed for money he lost because of it.[14]

The prosecution of Indian kidnappers had not produced any gratifying results for Indians or those who would protect them. On the contrary, it showed that the military government could do little about it. The judges might not have been as concerned about Indian welfare as their official correspondence showed, for Sutter and Vallejo had both used Indian forced labor and might not have been enthusiastic about prosecuting kidnappers. In any event, it was the last trial of kidnappers under military rule.

While the wrangling over the trial went on, Governor Mason and his secretary of state, Lieutenant Henry W. Halleck, issued a series of amendments and additions to Kearny's original instructions to the Indian subagents. Taken together these orders, set forth between August 16 and November 29, constituted a comprehensive code of Indian regulations for California. Halleck restated stringent penalties for livestock raiders, recommending that Indians caught in the act of stealing cattle or horses be shot on sight, or at least vigorously pursued by local ranchers. Indian grievances would be redressed if they were duly reported to the subagents and local alcaldes were to prosecute white offenders for "ordinary offenses" against the Indians. In the case of "extraordinary offenses" (presumably like the Smith, Eggar, and Armijo affair), the authorities were to hold the offenders until instructions were received from the governor. Secretary Halleck authorized the subagents to call on the military commanders for assistance in bringing both white and Indian offenders to justice. He also expanded the jurisdiction of the subagents to include not only "gentiles or wild Indians; but . . . neophytes, or tame Indians of the missions and Ranchos." Indian laborers

14. Mason to Vallejo and Sutter, Aug. 19, 1847, M182; Halleck to Vallejo, Sept. 10, 1847, M182; and Boggs to Vallejo and Mason, Oct. 30, 1846, CA. Lilburn W. Boggs, a native of Kentucky, for many years lived in Missouri, where he was elected governor in 1836. He emigrated to California in 1846 and was appointed alcalde of Sonoma in 1847, a post that he held until 1849. He was elected as a representative to the California Constitutional Convention in 1849, but did not attend the meetings (Bancroft, *History of California*, 2:722).

were made subject to the municipal regulations of the local alcaldes and "all regulations you [subagents] may deem proper to establish for the government of these Indians," contingent on the governor's approval. The subagents were also given the responsibility to protect Indians against abuse from their employers, with a recommendation that they prosecute offenders before an alcalde. To enable whites to distinguish between laboring Indians and suspected horse thieves, all persons hiring Indians were required to issue certificates of employment to their native workers, and Indians who wished to visit a town for trading purposes had to procure a passport from the subagent in their district. Any Indian without a pass was "liable to arrest as a horse thief; and . . . subject to trial and punishment." The subagents and other officials were urged to bring to justice all white and Indian violators. To these regulations Governor Mason added a prohibition against the sale of alcohol to Indians, apparently based on Secretary of War Marcy's regulation of April 13, 1847.[15]

The amendments to Kearny's instructions show how far military authorities in California were willing to go in shaping an Indian policy that would be useful to local interests. Governor Mason, recognizing that many Indian people worked for ranchers, committed federal authority to the regulation of native labor in addition to the protection of ranch owners from Indian livestock raiding. Indeed, Indians who did not work for ranchers, or who did not have an official passport, could expect to be tried and punished. Worse, an Indian might be shot on the pretext that he was a horse thief. The governor's prohibition of liquor sales to Indians was congruent with federal antiliquor regulations that the United States had applied to Indian country since 1802. Because the federal government had not yet determined the status and extent of California Indian lands, the governor simply applied the regulation to all California Indians. The prohibition of Indian drinking may have been in the best interests of Indians and whites, but the benefits of sobriety were imposed on native people who had no choice in the matter. These new regulations, like Governor Mason's earlier vagrancy code, resembled the re-

15. Halleck to Sutter and Halleck to Vallejo, Aug. 16, 1847, M182; Sherman to John Burton, Sept. 6, 1847, in *Message from the President . . . Communicating Information Called for by . . . the Senate . . . Relating to California and New Mexico*, 31st Cong., 1st sess., Sen. Ex. Doc. 18, ser. 557, 347–48; and "Circular to Indian Agents and Others," Sept. 6, 1847, M182. See also Mason, "Proclamation," Nov. 29, 1847, M182. The antiliquor law then in effect, passed March 3, 1847, stipulated a two-year prison sentence for violators. Although the penalties for violation of liquor laws in California were less stringent—three to six months in jail—Mason's anti-alcohol proclamation was based on Marcy's regulation in *Message of the President . . . to the Two Houses of Congress . . .* , 1847, H. Ex. Doc. 8, 30th Cong., 1st sess., ser. 515, 767.

strictive southern black codes. The similarity of the two systems, however, should not be construed to mean that federal authorities—perhaps a cabal of southern officers—sought to impose a system of chattel slavery in newly conquered California, since most of the new regulations were based on California customs. Rather it should be understood that California and the antebellum South faced similar problems of controlling large racially and culturally distinct work forces that were potentially dangerous to the white population.[16]

Mason, understandably concerned about depredations on white property and the unpalatable prospect of frontier warfare, issued orders that were obviously biased against Indians, but at least he delineated an official channel through which Indians could petition the government. Unfortunately for California's Indian people, the governor depended on the goodwill and judgment of the Indian agents, two of whom were large-scale employers of Indians. Consequently, Governor Mason's Indian administration was burdened with a built-in conflict of interest that became abundantly apparent when an epidemic of measles broke out in the Sacramento Valley in the summer of 1847. Subagent Sutter, concerned about getting his wheat harvested, hired a physician whose ministrations to the Indians produced little improvement, and many native workers died. To replace his dead and dying work force, Sutter used armed force to compel "wild" Indians to work in his fields. The disease swept the valley for six full months, affecting many of Sutter's most loyal workers and allies. The seriousness of the disease apparently led to an increase in Nisenan ceremonies that were meant to cure the sickness. Indian workers conducted the dances at night near Fort Sacramento and Sutter felt that they disrupted the New Helvetia work schedule; he ordered them stopped. When the Indians continued to dance, Sutter burned down their dance house, an action scarcely in keeping with his instructions to protect the Indians from employers' ill-treatment.[17]

In the meantime, Governor Mason's experiment at the Mission San Luis Rey was not faring well. The local alcalde quarreled with subagent Hunter and the military commanders over their proper duties and respective authority. Finally the alcalde resigned. While this interdepart-

16. Felix S. Cohen provides an outline of liquor legislation applied to Indians in *Handbook of Federal Indian Law* (1942; reprint, Albuquerque, n.d.), 352–57.

17. Sutter et al., *New Helvetia Diary*, 58–101. The reference to Sutter burning the dance house is on p. 123. Williams to Larkin, July 28, 1847, *Larkin Papers*, 6:241; Halleck to Sutter, Aug. 1847, M182. On the measles epidemic, see Heizer, "Walla Walla Expeditions," 4.

mental bickering went on, Indian livestock raiding continued in the south. In December Mason ordered Hunter to speak with the Indians concerning livestock theft. "In your interview with them," the governor directed, say "that it is the wish of the United States to take all Red people by the hand and treat them as friend &c. &c"; but if they continued to raid "we shall treat them as enemies." If the peaceful mission experiment failed, Mason was prepared to use force.[18]

There is virtually no evidence that the military government achieved any success in California Indian affairs. Still, given enough time the army may have succeeded in stopping Indian raiding. Perhaps American officials may have eventually perceived the reasons for Indian unrest and devised a workable policy for California's unique problems. But that would have required a period of relative stability, and California was about to enter an era of social, economic, and political upheaval that could not have been foreseen. The discovery of gold at Captain Sutter's half finished sawmill on the American River in 1848 introduced this new turmoil. As had so often been the case with other innovations in Indian life, the gold rush began with one of Sutter's schemes. Sutter had concluded an agreement with the Koloma Nisenan to build a mill in their territory, but when gold was discovered he realized that this agreement would be insufficient to insure his exclusive right to mine the precious metal. In his capacity as Indian subagent, Sutter drew up a treaty to secure from the Koloma people a lease to their gold-rich territory. This document he submitted to Mason for official approval one month after the first gold discovery. On March 5 the governor refused to endorse the agreement, explaining that the United States did not recognize Indian rights to sell or lease land to private individuals. He added that the federal government likely would acquire the land from the Indians after the war, and then private claims like Sutter's "certainly would not be recognized, for as soon as Indian title may be extinguished," former Indian lands would become "at once part of the public domain."[19]

Neither Sutter nor the Koloma Nisenan were destined to gain wealth from the gold strike on Indian land. Within a week of the discovery Mexico and the United States negotiated the Treaty of Guadalupe Hidalgo, which guaranteed californios the right to retain their Mexican citizenship or to become U.S. citizens. Because Indians were citizens under the 1824 Mexican constitution, California Indians theoretically

18. John Foster to Mason, Dec. 3, 1847, CA; and Mason to Hunter, Dec. 1, 1847, M182.

19. Mason to Sutter, March 5, 1848, M182; and *U.S. Statutes at Large*, 9:922–43.

acquired U.S. citizenship; but the military government continue to treat them as a separate class.[20]

In 1849 Secretary of War George W. Crawford informed General Bennet Riley, the new military governor, that the federal Indian trade and intercourse acts, which governed native people in Indian country, were in effect in California. He further asserted that "all laws existing and of force in California at the period of the conquest are still operative, with the limitation that they are not repugnant to the constitution and the laws of the United States." In his opinion, "these continued the whole code of laws now in force in California." Local communities could make temporary laws to protect persons and property, the secretary averred, but they would be discarded when the federal government addressed California's special problems.[21]

Crawford's declaration was soon disputed by the new commissioner of Indian affairs, Orlando Brown. He asserted that the trade and intercourse laws were not in force and recommended the extension of those statutes to California so that a new superintendency could be formed there. Congress later refused to follow his recommendation. During the first year of the gold rush, California Indians were governed only by the regulations of military governors, who did not attempt to extend citizenship rights to them but treated native people as a distinct class, useful as laborers and dangerous as raiders.[22]

Military administration of Indian affairs during the Mexican War supported the customary framework of California Indian-white relations. The dual concerns of non-Indian landholders—regulating the Indian labor force and controlling livestock raiding—became the principal aims that shaped early United States Indian policy in this region. Moreover, the history of the military approach to policy making foreshadowed federal Indian policy in the 1850s, which would remain conciliatory towards white interest groups and give less attention to protecting native people. The Mexican War brought a rapid transition from Mexican to United States rule, but did not immediately change Indians' status in California. They could expect protection only if they remained passive and useful to California's non-Indian citizens.

But Indians would have to deal with a new and even more troubling

20. For an excellent discussion of interpretations of Indian rights under the Treaty of Guadalupe Hidalgo, see Ferdinand F. Fernandez, "Except a California Indian," *Southern California Quarterly* 50 (June 1968):161–75.

21. Crawford to Bennet Riley, June 26, 1849, in *Annual Report of the Commissioner of Indian Affairs*, 1849, Sen. Ex. Doc. 5, 31st Cong., 1st sess., ser. 569, 161.

22. Brown to Thomas Ewing, Nov. 30, 1849, in *Annual Report of the Secretary of the Interior*, 1849, Sen. Ex. Doc. 5, 31st Cong., 1st sess., ser. 570.

future than they could have guessed at. In February 1847 Sutter advertised for two machines capable of threshing forty thousand bushels of wheat. He looked forward to a time when he would be less dependent on Indian labor, an adjustment that Sutter hoped U.S. hegemony would make possible. With the close of the Mexican War, Sutter seemed to understand that the new era in California would bring rewards to those who would rapidly modernize, mechanize, and discard mass Indian labor. In the summer he began discharging his Indian cavalry, relying instead on the army to suppress raiders. The old Indian raider José Jesus also sensed that California was changing, but he adjusted to new conditions in a way that was based on old California customs. In 1848 he began capturing Indians in the mountains and taking them to San José, where they would be useful workers. He presented them to the town's alcalde as a token of his promise to give up horse raiding forever and be friendly to the new government. Evidently José Jesus understood that the days of Indian horse raiding were numbered. For him it was a logical choice to become a labor contractor, replacing his old nemesis Sutter, who had relinquished his native army and some of his former power in the interior. Sutter and José Jesus, who had adapted so well and so often to California's changing conditions, both looked forward to a new future. But the gold rush placed formidable obstacles in their paths to prosperity and survival.[23]

23. Sutter to Kearny, May 27, 1847, CA; Sutter, "Reminiscences"; Sutter et al., *New Helvetia Diary*, 53; Montgomery to Kern, Oct. 21, 1846, FSP; and Charles White to R. B. Mason, July 16, 1848, CA.

6

A Regional Perspective on
Indians in the Gold Rush

Before the gold rush, Indian-white relations had been governed by conditions and customs that were essentially Hispanic in character. Indian labor underpinned California society much as it had on other Hispanic frontiers since the time of Cortés. A few large landholders controlled the pastoral economy and required Indian workers to tend their herds and fields. Indians, who were not always willing to accept the subservient role in which they had been cast, nonetheless adjusted to the new situation that was thrust on them, trading, raiding, or working as conditions warranted.

The gold discovery alone would not necessarily have changed the Indians' place in California society, for the Spanish had customarily used Indian workers in mines as well as in the fields. Yet the gold rush forever altered the fundamental bases of Indian-white relations in California. Before the gold discovery, Indians had outnumbered whites by nearly ten to one. Their numerical preponderance enabled some native people—principally those in the northwest and in the Sierra foothills—to discourage white settlement and remain more or less autonomous. Indians could choose among several accommodation and resistance options to survive as best they could as an embattled majority. The gold rush changed this picture dramatically. By the early 1850s whites outnumbered Indians by perhaps two to one. From that time forward the white population steadily rose while the Indian population precipitously declined, reaching by 1880 a nadir of 23,000—perhaps 15 percent of the 1848 population.[1]

The new population profile in California reflected a redistribution of whites and Indians. In 1848 the richest gold-bearing regions in the state contained the most native people. Gold hunters consequently ventured directly into the territory of Indians who had previously been independent of white control. The United States Army, supposed to protect both white and Indian people, was severely weakened by desertion

1. Cook, *Population of the California Indians*, 65.

because the soldiers proved no more immune to "gold fever" than their civilian counterparts. Therefore, the mining districts became the scenes of boisterous disorder without sufficient police power to control Indian or white communities.[2]

Yet another new element in the social scheme tended to exacerbate the situation: the aims and attitudes of the incoming white population. Just as the gross racial proportions of the state shifted dramatically, so did the ethnic and cultural patterns of the non-Indian population. The Hispanic customs and institutions that had formerly influenced relations with the Indians melted away as Anglo immigration mounted, and the newcomers felt little need to defer to traditions that they regarded as alien. Thus, the Hispanic world-view that included Indians within society was replaced by the Anglo notion that Indians ought to be expelled from frontier areas. By and large, the gold rush immigrants were single, young males, most of whom wished to become wealthy quickly and return to their homes in the East. The new mining population had no long-term interest in California or its native people. The ranchers of Mexican California may not have had at heart the best interests of Indians, but since they depended on native labor, they did not want to eradicate the Indian population. Unconstrained by Hispanic historical, social, political, and economic traditions, the new majority imposed its will on the diminishing Indian minority.

The Central Mines

The gold rush rapidly spread to all auriferous areas in the state, but the various regions did not develop simultaneously or with the same results for Indians. In the central district Sutter's men made the first gold discovery on the American River (see map 3). From that nucleus mining spread farther north into the central district, then into the region drained by the San Joaquin River, comprising the southern district. In 1850 miners began to develop in earnest the gold resources of the north-western district along the Klamath and Trinity rivers. Since each of these districts was home to Indian peoples whose culture, language, and experience of whites differed, each area demands separate study to understand the changes in Indian-white relations during this critical period.[3]

Development of the central district began when Indian and white

2. Cook, "The Destruction of the California Indians," *California Monthly* 79 (December 1968):14–19; and James A. Hardie to William T. Sherman, May 28, 1848, M210.

3. Paul, *California Gold*, 92–93.

CALIFORNIA MINING REGIONS
IN THE 1850s

MAP 3. California Mining Regions in the 1850s

workers discovered gold while building Sutter's sawmill in Koloma Nisenan country. To start this project Sutter, who had recently been appointed federal Indian subagent, drafted an indenture with the Yalisumni Nisenan that ostensibly granted him and his partner, James Marshall, a twenty-year lease to the Nisenan property with the exclusive right to cultivate land, cut timber, and build a sawmill and "other necessary machinery for the purpose." Since the Yalisumnis lived twenty miles downstream from the Kolomas, it appears that Sutter was using his reliable Yalisumni workers to colonize the mountain country for New Helvetia. After gold was found, Sutter sent the indenture to Governor Mason for approval. Without mentioning gold, he claimed that the new settlement would teach the Yalisumni habits of industry and protect them from wild mountain Indians. Chiefs Pupule and Gesu, along with alcaldes Cahule and Sule, endorsed the document, which bound Sutter and Marshall to annually give the four Indian signatories $150 worth of clothing and farming utensils for the benefit of the tribe; but it did not explain how the four Indians would distribute the goods. This agreement, had it been honored, would not have benefitted the Kolomas at all.[4]

Mason refused to sanction the indenture, which in any case could not have kept other gold seekers from overwhelming the foothill Nisenan country that embraced the heart of the Mother Lode. Sutter, rebuffed in his attempt to control mineral land, decided then to mobilize Indian labor for the mines. Capitalizing on his experience in native labor procurement, he formed a partnership with Marshall and two others to whom he furnished "Indians, teams and provisions" and scoured northern California for Indian miners. When this venture, like so many of Sutter's schemes, failed to gain a profit, he left the partnership. Indeed, demand for Indian labor was so great that he was unable to harvest his own crops. As the gold rush spread, native laborers left New Helvetia because they were "impatient to run to the mines, [since] other Indians had informed them of gold and its value," Sutter recalled bitterly. New Helvetia lived by Indian labor and, when Indians caught gold fever and went to the mines, died for lack of it.[5]

Sutter's star was fading. He retired to his Feather River property, the Hock Farm, but his influence on whites who relied on Indian labor remained strong. In the early days of the gold rush, whites who were experienced in managing Indian labor skimmed the easy wealth from placer deposits. In August 1848 John Bidwell, George McKinstry, and William Dickey agreed to supply Edward Kemble and T. H. Rolfe with "as many Indians as convenient to work the machine for Washing Gold." The two parties were to split the profit and the cost of boarding the Indians. Kemble and Rolfe were enjoined to treat the Indians kindly, and Bidwell and his two partners were to retain "sole controul" of the native workers, who would become a source of wealth for the former Sutter employees.[6]

4. Sutter to Mason, Feb. 22, 1848, with enclosure [lease with the Yalisumni Indians], Jan. 1, 1848, Box 236, MKC.

5. Sutter, *Diary*, 45–46.

6. Agreement between William Dickey, John Bidwell, and George McKinstry, party of the first part, and Edward Kemble and T. H. Rolfe, party of the second part, Aug. 7, 1848, MKC.

In 1848 there was a high demand for native labor in the central mining district. That summer Governor Mason toured the central mines and reported about four thousand miners at work, "of whom more than half were Indians." The Indian miners, as Mason described the scene, used "pans or willow baskets, [to] gradually wash out the earth and separate the gravel by hand, leaving nothing but gold mixed with sand," which they cleaned so that only the gold remained. Suñol and Company employed about thirty Indians, who were paid in trade goods. These native miners washed out gold "in sufficient quantities to satisfy" their employers. Perry McCoon and William Daylor, former New Helvetia men, got easy profits with Indian labor. Mason reported that they had hired four white men and "about a hundred Indians" who in one week mined so much gold that the two promoters cleared a $10,000 profit. On the North Fork of the American River Mason found John Sinclair working fifty Indians who washed out $16,000 worth of gold for him in closely woven willow baskets. Seven whites from Monterey had employed fifty Indians for seven weeks and mined 273 pounds of gold. After they paid their expenses, each white received 37 pounds of gold, indicating that expenses were 2 pounds of gold each, or 14 pounds total. Using these raw figures and calculating the price of gold at $16 per ounce, the Indian labor cost the *montereños* about $40 per Indian per month, or about four times more than Sutter had charged for Indian labor in 1846 (table 3.1). Indians probably took their pay in trade goods purchased at inflated gold rush prices, and it is difficult to say that they gained more earning power than they had as farm workers. White profits, on the other hand, substantially increased, making Indian labor more valuable than it had ever been.[7]

Central district mining affected Indians far distant from the mines as whites brought in native labor to exploit their claims. Some avaricious miners tried to squeeze too much profit out of Indian labor and paid dearly for their greed. The so-called massacre of Andrew Kelsey and a man known only as Stone illustrates these points. Augustin, the head Indian vaquero for Stone and Kelsey, recounted the events that led to the killing of the two white men. In 1847 Stone and Kelsey purchased from Salvador Vallejo a herd of cattle together with the right to pasture the stock at Clear Lake, which is nestled in a valley in the Coast Range. To run their ranch the two men employed Lake Pomo Indians who had worked for Vallejo. Cruel masters, Stone and Kelsey imposed harsh

7. Mason to Brig. Gen. R. Jones, Aug. 17, 1848, in *Message from the President . . . to the Two Houses of Congress . . .* , Sen. Ex. Doc. 1, 30th Cong., 2nd sess., ser. 537, 56–64 (hereafter cited as "Mason's Report"). This report renders Suñol as "Linol" and Daylor as "Daly." On white miners' wages, see Paul, *California Gold*, 349–52.

discipline, whipped Indians for sport, appropriated Augustin's wife for themselves, and fed the laborers poorly. After the discovery of gold they took twenty-six Indians to the Feather River mines, where they worked for one month and amassed a "bag of gold as large as a man's arm." All returned safely and each Indian received "a pair of overalls, a hickory shirt and a red handkerchief for their summer's work."[8]

Encouraged by this success, Stone and Kelsey took some partners, purchased provisions, recruited more than one hundred Indians, and returned to the mines in the fall. Apparently Benjamin Kelsey, Andrew's brother, sold most of the company's provisions to other miners, so the partners could not adequately feed their Indians. To make matters worse, malaria struck the party, including Benjamin Kelsey, who was carried back to Clear Lake on a bed, leaving the sick Indians behind. Kelsey and Stone told the men's families that the workers would eventually return; but when only three survivors came home, the extent of the calamity was clear.

Stone and Kelsey next invested their mining profits in one thousand more cattle, which Augustin and eleven other vaqueros drove to Clear Lake. A total of two thousand cattle were now on the range, no doubt creating problems for the Pomos, who relied on grass seeds for food, as well as elk, deer, and antelope that now competed with cattle for forage. Moreover, Stone and Kelsey did not pay Indian vaqueros, so working Indians could not contribute to the native economy. Perhaps the food situation was one of the causes of Stone and Kelsey's attempt to get rid of Clear Lake's nonworking Indians. In 1849 they planned to send the unneeded Indians to Sutter's Fort, where they may have been intended to replenish Sutter's dwindling work force. The partners ordered their Indian servants to make ropes for binding any who were strong enough to fight during the journey.

Already abused and undernourished, Pomos objected to the removal plan and decided to kill Stone and Kelsey. On the night before the killing, Augustin's wife, who lived in the house with Stone and Kelsey, poured water down the barrels of their guns, making them useless. The Indians killed their tormentors the next morning, momentarily ridding Clear Lake of unwanted interlopers. Stone and Kelsey had gone too far when they ceased to provide any benefits for the Pomos; when they became an undeniable threat, the Pomos did away with them. But Stone and Kelsey only represented a larger world that impinged on the Pomos,

8. Lyman L. Palmer, *History of Napa and Lake Counties, California* (San Francisco, 1881), 49–62. The researchers who prepared this account interviewed participants, including the Indians, and printed their sometimes conflicting testimony with few attempts to settle discrepancies. Augustin's account is on pp. 58–62.

a world that included new gold rush demands for labor, beef for forty-niners, and farm workers for New Helvetia.[9]

The Stone and Kelsey killings may have satisfied the Pomos' sense of rectitude, but whites would also want to impose their ideas of frontier justice and discipline in the Clear Lake region. To avenge the deaths of Stone and Kelsey, the United States Army and white volunteers attacked the Clear Lake Pomos in 1850, killing sixty to one hundred Indians in the Bloody Island massacre. For the Pomos the lesson was clear: regardless of whether the Indian cause was just, white society would not permit white deaths to go unavenged.[10]

The several thousand Indians who were part of life in the central mines also generated capital for white traders. There are many accounts of Indians paying for trade goods with an equal weight in gold, but they soon learned to weigh gold to establish a fair rate of exchange. Traders responded by inventing the "Digger Ounce," a lead slug that substantially outweighed the legitimate weights that traders used to measure whites' gold. To protect their economic interests, Indians often traded in groups and tested the merchants' honesty by having several native people offer to purchase a particular item. Shrewd barterers, the Indians would not permit the traders to outwit them for long.[11]

The stereotype of the white trader who took every opportunity to exploit the Indians in mining districts was well deserved. Everyone had to buy goods at inflated gold rush prices as merchants strove for profits, but some businessmen offered important services to their customers, including Indians. The gold rush merchant Alonzo Delano set up his store among the Koncow Maidu Indians on the Feather River at Oleepa. Delano later claimed that he tended the native population near his store, washing a chronic skin eruption that seemed endemic among them. According to him, the Indians appreciated Delano and protected his store's inventory when he was away on business, although they did not get on so well with other traders in the vicinity. The relationship between Delano and the Koncow Maidu may have been extraordinary, but it is not unthinkable that a merchant would seek good relations with his customers, especially after they became knowledgeable about gold and trading became more competitive.[12]

9. Ibid.

10. Lyons to E. R. S. Canby, May 22, 1850, reprinted in Heizer, *Destruction of the California Indians*, 244–46. Lyons may have overestimated the number of Indians that his troops killed, since Augustin stated that only sixteen Indians were killed at the Bloody Island engagement (Palmer, *Napa and Lake Counties*, 62).

11. James Rawls, "Gold Diggers: Indian Miners in the California Gold Rush," *California Historical Quarterly* 55 (Spring 1976):28–45.

12. Delano published his experiences in *Life on the Plains and among the Diggings* (Auburn and Buffalo, N.Y., 1854), 293–320.

As Indians learned the value of gold and their labor, customary economic relationships were upset between natives and settlers. A white woman who had lived on the Bear River with her husband and daughter before the gold discovery claimed that until the arrival of the "emigrants," as she called them, the Nisenan Indians were friendly and reliable laborers. "When we begun to find gold on the Yuber [Yuba River], we could git 'em to work for us day in and day out, fur next to nothin'. We told 'em the gold was stuff to whitewash houses with, and give 'em a hankecher for a tin-cup full." Such a wonderful relationship could not last long, for "after the emigrants begun to come along and put all sorts of notions in their heads, there was no gettin' them to do nothin'." At least there was "no gettin' them to do nothin' " without being paid a reasonable wage for their labor.[13]

Indians, who formerly obtained trade goods by exchanging skins or arduous hours and days of labor, suddenly had access to specie, which they could readily trade for anything that was available in California. As Governor Mason put it, the Indians had abruptly "become consumers of the luxeries of life." This new consumer class required the shipment of large quantities of goods to the mines, where they were traded to the Indians for gold.[14]

That natives looked after their own interests in the mines should not be construed to create a new stereotype, a class of California Indian gold barons. During the gold rush Indians began as poor laborers; they remained poor laborers who were exploited because they were Indians, because they were poor, and because they were ignorant of the new order of things. But once they learned about the trade system, Indians were able to exert some control over new conditions by bargaining their gold for goods.

If they had continued to work as miners, more California Indians might have survived the gold rush, but this was not to be. As early as 1849 whites began driving native workers out of the central district labor force. Unaccustomed to an Indian work force, free white workers vehemently and brutally objected to competition from cheap Indian labor mostly controlled by California's ranchero class. Some whites brought with them a violent animosity towards Indians, as shown by a conflict near Coloma between the Nisenans and a party of Oregonians with fresh memories of the Whitman killings and the Cayuse War. Friction occurred at Coloma when some Oregonians raped native women. Subsequently the Indians—perhaps Kolomas who had been festering since Sutter's sawmill invasion—killed several Oregon men. In blind retal-

13. Bayard Taylor, *Eldorado: Or, Adventures in the Path of Empire*, 2 vols. (New York, 1850), 2:22.
14. "Mason's Report."

iation, the whites indiscriminately killed local ranchería Indians. This episode marked the beginning of the end of large-scale Indian labor in the central mines, but many Indians continued to live on the margins of mining camps and boomtowns (see fig. 6).[15]

Perhaps the memory of the Whitman murders caused recent arrivals from Oregon to kill Indians, but other whites without such hardening frontier experiences were also quick to resort to violence. In the summer of 1849 men of the Palmetto Mining Company of Charleston, South Carolina, came via Panama and set off for the Coloma mines. En route, two Carolinians armed with a rifle went after some water with a brass kettle. When they failed to return, their companions concluded that Indians had murdered them for the kettle and rifle. On the strength of this assumption, the bereaved party of South Carolina greenhorns resolved to "Sack and burn" the nearby "Indian Ranch." They were ready to embark on their grisly task when the two wanderers returned and put an end to talk of attacking the ranchería. It was fortunate for the Indians that the pair had not returned an hour later.[16]

Some immigrants expressed frank opinions about why they so quickly resorted to violence against the Indians. Charles Ferguson, an overlander who had fought against Nevada Indians, wrote that he did not believe in "wanton cruelty to the Indian, but when you are in a country where you know he is your enemy, and is not only waiting his chance but looking out for his opportunity, why not cut him down as he most surely will you?"[17]

Forty-niners resorted to violence against Indians because of past experiences, ignorance, the racist notions of the age, and because of real and imagined fears. But whites did not force Indians out of the mines overnight. Rather, they shunted them into the worst jobs or occasionally permitted them to work mine tailings. To feed their families, some women prostituted themselves, while others scavenged through dumps and slaughter pens for the leavings of white miners. A demographic sketch of Indians can be drawn from the 1852 state census that enumerated "domesticated Indians" who were not hostile, lived relatively close to whites, and sometimes worked for and traded with whites. Historians have been reluctant to use the state census because it is incomplete and inconsistent. Nevertheless, it recorded 32,529 Indians, approximately one fifth of whom lived in the central mines, where they

15. Rawls, "Gold Diggers," 38–39.

16. "Journal of a Passenger on the Palmetto Mining Company Voyage from Charleston, South Carolina," MS, California Room, State Library, Sacramento.

17. *The Experiences of a Forty-niner during Thirty-four Years Residence in California and Australia*, ed. Frederick T. Wallace (Cleveland, 1888), 105–06.

FIG. 6. Sam Pit, shown here striking a pose with pick and gold pan, was James Marshall's companion and spiritual guide. Like many other California Indians, Pit lived and worked in the gold fields. Marshall, John Sutter's partner in the saw mill where gold was found, employed Indians and bitterly condemned the brutal killing of Indians that became common during the gold rush.

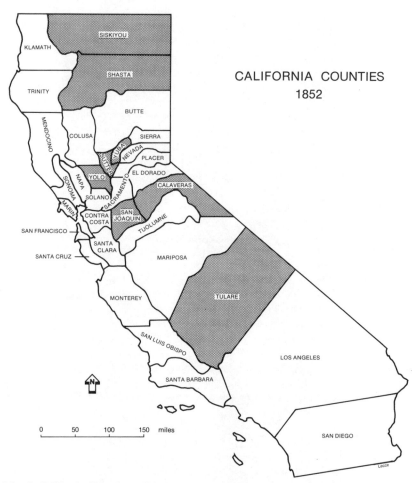

CALIFORNIA COUNTIES
1852

Map 4. California Counties, 1852. Shaded areas indicate counties with Indian populations analyzed in chapter 8.

constituted 4.1 percent of the population (see map 4). El Dorado
County, which included the Coloma site, reported only an undifferen-
tiated total population, although an Indian Office report estimated that
eight thousand Indians lived there. If El Dorado County's gross estimate
is thrown out, Indians constituted 5.4 percent of the total population
(see table 6.1). Nevada County, with more than three thousand Indians
constituting 15.1 percent of the population, reported more Indians than
any other central county, while Calaveras and Placer counties each
reported more than 6 percent. According to the census, 6,678 Indians

TABLE 6.1. *Domesticated Indians by Mining District and County in 1852*

County	Non-Indians	Indians	Indians as percentage of total population
Central District			
Butte	8,542	30	0.3
Calaveras	28,936	1,982	6.4
El Dorado*	40,000	—	—
Nevada	18,139	3,226	15.1
Placer	10,867	730	6.3
Sierra	4,808	0	0
Tuolumne	25,730	590	2.2
Yuba	20,593	120	0.6
Subtotal	157,615	6,678	4.1
Subtotal w/o El Dorado	117,615	6,678	5.4
Southern District			
Mariposa	4,231	4,533	51.7
Tulare	175	8,407	98.0
Subtotal	4,406	12,940	74.6
Northern District			
Klamath	523	0	0
Shasta	3,855	73	1.8
Siskiyou	2,214	26	1.2
Trinity	1,933	4	0.2
Subtotal	8,525	103	1.2
TOTAL	170,546	19,721	10.4
TOTAL w/o El Dorado	130,546	19,721	13.1

Source: 1852 California Special Census, California State Archives.

*El Dorado County returned a population estimate of 40,000 that was not broken down by age, race, or sex.

had found ways to survive around the edges of mining society. The 1852 Indian census figures vary greatly from county to county, indicating a great deal of turmoil and graphically showing that there were some places where Indians could not safely live.[18]

18. An excellent description of Indians in the central mining district is found in W. P. Crenshaw to Thomas J. Henley, Dec. 16, 1854, M234:33. The El Dorado County Indian population estimate is in E. A. Stevenson to Thomas J. Henley, Dec. 31, 1853, quoted in Heizer, *Destruction of the California Indians*, 13–16. On the strengths and weaknesses of the 1852 state census, see Dennis Harris, "The California Census of 1852: A Note of Caution and Encouragement," *The Pacific Historian* 28 (Summer 1984):59–64.

The Southern Mines

The central mining district was the nucleus from which the southern mining district evolved, but relations between Indians and whites in the two contiguous regions developed quite differently. The native people in the two districts, culturally and linguistically related, had been in contact with Europeans for decades, but Miwok and Yokuts raiders made whites wary of the southern district. Before the gold rush there' had been little white settlement in the adjacent San Joaquin Valley. Except at its northern end, the southern district was not as rich in gold as the central district, so mining development and settlement generally came later and remained less intense.

Indian miners were among the first to exploit the southern district. Charles M. Weber, an old California hand and founder of Stockton, contracted with the recently reformed raider José Jesus through the intercession of John Sutter. José Jesus supplied Indian workers who washed gold for Weber on Weber Creek and then went to the Stanislaus to open gold mining in that region. In 1849 a Chilean miner described an Indian miners' community on Weber Creek that may have been associated with José Jesus. The Indians worked according to a division of labor in which "the men dug and gave the mud to the children, who then carried it in baskets to the women," who lined up on the stream and washed the gold "in grass baskets of the most perfect construction" (see fig. 7). The Indians then tied up the gold in rags, "in amounts more or less equal," using them "to trade with just as if they were money." José Jesus not only recruited Indian miners but took surplus workers to the coast, where labor was increasingly scarce. Thus, Miwok miners who had adandoned raiding helped to open the southern mines.[19]

James Savage was the best-known employer of Indians in the southern district. He had arrived in California from Illinois in 1846 and joined the California Battalion. After mustering out of service, he worked for Sutter at New Helvetia, where he gained experience with native labor. According to his business partner, Savage went south after the gold discovery, "keeping in advance of the white Emigration as far as possible, and making Treaties of peace with the different Tribes of Indians as he came to them." By the winter of 1849 Savage had reached the Fresno River, where he made a treaty with the local Yokuts Indians.[20]

19. Bancroft, *History of California*, 6:75–76; Edwin A. Beilharz and Carlos U. López, trans. and ed., *We Were 49ers! Chilean Accounts of the California Gold Rush* (Pasadena, Calif., 1976), 52; and Charles White to R. B. Mason, July 16, 1848, CA.

20. L. D. V. Haler to G. W. Patten, Sept. 20, 1852, GWP. See also Annie R. Mitchell, "Major James D. Savage and the Tularenos," *California Historical Society Quarterly* 28

Fig. 7. Indian Woman Panning Out Gold. Indian women commonly panned gold in the mining regions. They used shallow baskets of their own manufacture until iron pans became more widely available. Sometimes whole communities—including children—helped with the task of gathering gold. Evidently this woman did not intend to remain long at the task, for she did not remove her carrying basket. Perhaps she panned as part of a larger daily gathering routine that required her to keep the carrying basket close at hand. Or perhaps white animosity towards Indian miners meant that she had to be prepared to quickly leave the diggings should her furtive mining be discovered.

Savage's success as an Indian trader along the San Joaquin River and in the foothills became legendary as he quickly amassed a fortune by employing and trading with native miners. One year after opening his

(December 1949):323–41; Lafayette Haughton Bunnell, *Discovery of Yosemite and the Indian War of 1851 which Led to that Event*, 4th ed. (Los Angeles, 1911), 2–16.

Fresno River store, the trader build a second trading post on the Mariposa River and divided his time between the two places. To secure his commercial position and influence among the Indians, Savage married native women from the tribes he traded with. Like Sutter and other whites on isolated frontiers, Savage learned that it was provident to use marriage as a diplomatic and economic tool. By so doing, they adapted the Indians' time-honored view of marriage as a powerful way to link distinct communities.[21]

Impressed by Savage's success with the Indians, contemporary observers and historians have attributed great skill to the trader and complimented him extravagantly for his wise and humane treatment of the Indians; but he made some mistakes. In 1850, for example, he took the Indian José Juarez to San Francisco to demonstrate the power of white civilization. Both got drunk, Savage gambled away the gold that Indians had entrusted to him and then hit Juarez for complaining about it. This episode convinced some Indians that the white trader had to go. Luckily for him, Savage was absent in December 1850, when Indians attacked his Fresno River post, killing three white employees—an event that led to the Mariposa War and the incidental discovery of the Yosemite Valley. Savage overtook the attackers and negotiated with the leaders, who offered to mine for Savage if he would take their side in a war against the whites. He refused and instead joined the volunteer force that defeated the Indians. In May 1851 he interpreted for the federal commissioners who were negotiating treaties with the California tribes, an episode that will be discussed more fully in the next chapter. Subsequently, the commissioners licensed him as an Indian trader. He then repaired his friendship with the Indians and once again became an important trader among them.[22]

Savage, like other white traders, was dedicated to making a profit in his dealings with the Indians. To keep their confidence he provided rudimentary medical treatment and other services. His partner even claimed that Savage taught the Indians the alphabet and how to read sheet music well enough to sing parlor songs, an impressive achievement for a mountain man with little formal education. Savage wanted customer loyalty, but he put his own interests before theirs. When, for example, he distributed government beef to the Indians, Savage made

21. Haler to Patten, Sept. 20, 1852, GWP.
22. Ibid. Major Patten claimed that he "had the pleasure of hearing from female— (*Fresno*) *lips parlor stanzas*, Sung with an expression of sentiment which hardly could be expected from a people whose richest covering was a Blanket whose homestead was thatched with brambles and enclosed by mud (adobe) Walls."

certain that the cattle did not reach native hands and were illicitly sold to white gold miners.[23]

Savage's role in Indian affairs eventually led to his death. In the summer of 1852 Yokuts Indians warned whites to vacate a trading post and ferry on the Kings River because the federal treaty they had signed in May reserved that part of the country for the Indians. Savage supported the Indians, but Walter Harvey, a Tulare County judge and a competing Indian trader, took white volunteers to the Indian ranchería. A fight resulted in which one white man was wounded and twenty-seven Indians were killed and wounded. Savage reportedly "expressed his dissatisfaction of the course pursued by Major Harvey and his fellows in terms of high indignation." Savage's remarks got back to Harvey, who threatened to kill him. The attack had alarmed Indians as far away as the Fresno, where the Chowchilla Yokuts chief Tomquit assumed that whites would exterminate all of the Indians. Pasqual, the principal Yokuts chief on Kings River, had displayed an American flag before his door as a symbol of his faith in the treaty. Now he tore it down, declaring that the flag was stained with blood.[24]

Whites in the region were also thoroughly alarmed, fearing the outbreak of general Indian war. The Yokuts decided to meet in a grand council at Four Creeks to determine whether to defend their treaty lands or retire to the mountains and fight from there. When Major G. W. Patten, commander of Fort Miller on the Fresno, heard of the Indian council, he was so concerned that he requested reinforcements and attended the gathering in force. Responding to Patten's request for assistance, Savage drew a map of the route to Four Creeks and agreed to accompany the expedition; but because he had business to attend to, he would have to catch up to the command. The army was going to camp at Kings River after the first day's march, and Savage wanted to catch up with it before it left the next day because it was rumored that his enemies had threatened to kill him if he crossed the river.

Patten and his command reached the Kings River camp without incident, but Savage did not appear. On the next morning Patten marched without Savage. When he reached Four Creeks he encountered Harvey, who said that Savage had made ungentlemanly remarks about him. Harvey was anxious to confront Savage before witnesses at Four Creeks and said that he would attend the Indian meeting. Patten waited for Savage "with no little anxiety" as several Indian leaders began to visit

23. On Savage's cattle dealing, see E. F. Beale to Luke Lea, Sept. 30, 1852, M234:32.
24. Patten to Gardner, Sept. 26, 1852, GWP.

his camp. While he was waiting a courier rode up hurriedly and informed Patten that Harvey had killed Savage at the Kings River trading post. When Savage arrived at Kings River he found Harvey waiting, and as Patten said, there was an "angry argument, which from words proceeded to blows." In the melee Savage lost his pistol. After their friends separated the two men, Harvey drew a revolver and shot Savage several times.[25]

Shaken by this news, and worried about the increasing number of armed Indians who were arriving at Four Creeks, Patten had the unenviable task of informing the Yokuts that their worst enemy had killed their best friend. Fearing the worst, Patten asked the council to assemble, implored the Indians to remain peaceful, and assured Pasqual that Indian treaty rights would be observed. Finally he asked Pasqual—whom Patten described as a "haughty chief"—to send a peace message to surrounding tribes. After receiving an assurance that the United States would officially investigate the attack on the ranchería, Pasqual sent the message, reestablished the flag on a standard in front of his house, and the war scare was over. Even Wa-ta-ka, chief of the ranchería that had been attacked, seemed reassured, although he asked permission to move the survivors to the powerful Pasqual's ranchería, where they would be safe from further attacks.

In the end, Savage was killed in a disagreement that began as a dispute over how to deal with Indians. He wanted to preserve the Indians on their treaty lands, where they benefited him as a licensed trader. Others, like Harvey, must have envied Savage's access to Indian resources. In a county where fewer than two hundred whites lived among eight thousand Indians, a share in the Indian trade was an important matter (see table 6.1). In the tradition of Sutter, Savage profited from the labor and trade of the Indian majority, and others wished to do likewise. However opportunistic Savage may have been, Indians in the southern mines deeply mourned his passing. Hundreds attended his funeral and asked for this coffin to be opened so they could see him again.

Because Indians outnumbered whites, they could occasionally assert claims to resources that whites also coveted. In 1852 whites near Fort Miller employed Chowchilla Indians and also permitted them to mine independently upstream from their wing dam, marking off the boundary with a rope stretched across the river. When two Chowchillas crossed the line, a white fired a pistol shot to intimidate them. All the Indians left, returning three days later with Tomquit leading a crowd of Chowchillas. Completely naked and armed with an old sabre, Tomquit de-

25. Ibid.

clared that he wanted the *pistolero* turned over to him and increased mining privileges for his people. After both demands were denied, Tomquit declared peace and the Chowchillas returned to work as before.[26]

At first glance, Tomquit's foray can hardly be heralded as a major diplomatic or military achievement, but it is important to recognize that he was not automatically cowed by white power. Why should he have been? Whites may have wanted to exterminate Indians in the southern mines, but they lacked sufficient numbers to do it. Moreover, the soldiers at Fort Miller had promised to protect Indians. Instead, attrition caused by disease, gradual displacement, and only occasional fighting eventually would make the south a white man's country.

Even after the U.S. Senate refused to ratify their treaties, southern Indians stood their ground and remained at peace with the white minority. Remarkably, most of them quickly gave up horse raiding. In 1853 Captain H. W. Wessells, the new commander at Fort Miller, knew of only one band of raiders, and they hid out in the mountain fastness of the Yosemite country. Perhaps growing white settlement made raiding impossible, or perhaps the Indians had decided to keep the peace as Pasqual had urged. Except for those at Yosemite, Indians no longer had any horses, but we do not know why they gave them up. Whatever the reasons, the abandonment of horse raiding surely marked a watershed in the history of Indian-white relations along the banks of the San Joaquin and once again demonstrates the flexibility of California Indians seeking survival.[27]

The Northwestern Mines

The northwestern mining district, composed of Klamath, Trinity, Shasta, and Siskiyou counties, was the largest and poorest gold region, with rugged mountains cloaked in redwood and fir as well as a forbidding stretch of seacoast that extended from Humboldt Bay northward to the Oregon border. The native people, who spoke languages from three distinct linguistic groups, shared many northwest coast cultural values and lifeways. The Tolowa, Yurok, and Wiyot tribes resided near the coast, while the Shasta, Hupa, Karok, Whilkut, and Chimariko lived farther inland. The historical experience of the northwest Indians dif-

26. Lilbourne Alsip Winchell, *History of Fresno County and the San Joaquin Valley* (Fresno, 1933), 27–28.

27. Wessells to E. D. Townsend, Aug. 2, 1853, "Reports Relating to Indian Customs," RG 393; and Kelsey, "California Indian Treaty Myth," 225–38.

fered markedly from their central California counterparts. Beginning in 1829 they established relations with the Hudson's Bay Company, soon acquiring a reputation as shrewd traders and fierce protectors of their country. They believed that every transgression had a particular value, and they required restitution for each wrong committed.[28]

The gold rush into the northwest began in 1848, when Pierson B. Reading entered the region along the Trinity River with a band of Indian workers from his ranch at the head of the Sacramento Valley. Reading and New Helvetia Indians had trapped the headwaters of the Trinity in 1845, so he was familiar with the area. In 1848 Reading and his Indian companions took about eighty thousand dollars' worth of gold dust out of the Trinity before Oregonians drove Reading out because they objected to Indian labor. The region was not extensively exploited until 1850, when a sea route eased the problems of transportation, supply, and local Indian resistance to mining.[29]

As soon as whites appeared in force in the northwestern district, Indians began to trade and work with them. In 1851 John Carr and some other miners hired Yuroks to ferry them across the Klamath River at the Weitchpec ranchería. "The Indians would not take gold for their pay," Carr remembered, "silver was their currency." Instead, Carr and his associates traded their mule and "got some money to boot." Apparently the Weitchpec Yuroks protected their financial interests by insisting on payment in silver specie rather than unminted gold. Since they had acquired a surplus of coins by 1851, the Yuroks must have been shrewd traders indeed.[30]

However, relations between natives and whites in the northern district were not characterized by peaceful trading. While Yurok ferrymen took Carr across the Klamath in 1851, Karoks killed three white miners farther upriver that same year. When federal Indian agent Redick McKee arrived in the fall to negotiate a treaty, Indian headmen from the Klamath River tribes showed him a bone marked with twenty-six notches representing white deaths and twenty-seven for Indians. Moreover, whites had burned several rancherías and the Indians insisted that the United States pay damages for the unavenged death and property losses. McKee agreed to make resititution and, according to the expedition interpreter George Gibbs, the United States was bound to give

28. Paul, *California Gold*, 93; Heizer, *Handbook* (see chapters for each tribe); and Heizer, "The California Indians," 6.
29. Reading, "Account Book," 1845, RC; Paul, *California Gold*, 93; and Rawls, *Indians of California*, 126–27.
30. Arnold Pilling, "Yurok," in Heizer, *Handbook*, 140; and Carr, *Pioneer Days in California* (Eureka, Calif., 1891), 104.

"sixteen pairs of blankets for the extra Indian, and a squaw and a child not enumerated," plus four dozen axes to rebuild the rancherías. In addition, the Indians were supposed to retain a large tract of land for a reservation; but these stipulations became moot when the U.S. Senate failed to ratify the treaty in 1852.[31]

With no federal treaty to regulate matters, Indian affairs in the northern mines continued on a violent course. In May 1852 whites suspected that Karok Indians had killed a miner on the Salmon River. Twenty or thirty miners went to the nearest ranchería to seize the killers, but the Salmon River Karoks insisted that the murderers belonged to other rancherías. The miners nevertheless told the Indians that if the murderers were not turned over within two days "their ranches would be destroyed and their men shot." Two days later four headmen from friendly rancherías protested the injustice of being held responsible for the acts of persons over whom they had no control. They promised to deliver up the culprits if the whites would not attack their rancherías. George Gibbs reported that "a minority of our people inclining to mercy, and believing them sincere, these terms were granted and not a shot was fired or a plank burnt."[32]

During the reprieve, the miners adopted some resolutions for "the better regulation of our Indian relations . . . to prevent hasty and inconsiderate revenge on the one hand, and to secure adequate punishment on the other." The miners' code of Indian relations merits quotation at length because it illustrates the argonauts' concept of justice towards Indian people. It held:

> That in all cases of crime committed by Indians, unless the party should be taken in the act, no revenge should be allowed until an investigation by the neighborhood should take place; that the delivery of the aggressors should be demanded of the nearest ranches, and after a reasonable time given punishment should be inflicted as follows: for murder by the destruction of the ranch to which the criminal belonged and its inhabitants if known. If not known, by that of those nearest the spot. For theft, by destruction of the ranch or such lighter punishment as should be awarded, but life not to be taken except for stealing horses or in preventing robbery. The punishment of a thief when taken to be in other cases whipping, not to exceed 39 lashes; and cutting the hair. Offenses of whites against Indians, whether

31. A. J. Bledsoe, *History [of] Del Norte County, California, with a Business Directory and Traveler's Guide* (Eureka, Calif, 1881), 8; and Robert F. Heizer, ed., *George Gibbs' Journal of Redick McKee's Expedition through Northwestern California in 1851* (Berkeley, 1972), 47.

32. George Gibbs, J. A. Whaley, C. Woodford, J. W. Holt, Chas. Liscom, R. Wiley, and Edw. Kingwood to the governor of California, June 27, 1852, IWP.

by killing without cause, burning ranches or otherwise, to be punished [at]
... the discretion of a jury, as also the sale of firearms and ammunition to
the Indians.

Despite the obvious double standard of justice embodied in this code,
its authors proclaimed that it was the "general wish of the community
to protect Indians from maltreatment and to preserve peace with
them."[33]

The code was distributed among the Klamath River camps, serving
notice that the white community sanctioned drastic measures against
whole Indian communities for transgressions by Indian individuals. Soon
the code was put into practice. Late in June two whites visited a Karok
ranchería on the Klamath River above the Salmon River, where they
discussed the previous month's unpunished murders. As the Karoks
began to quarrel, one of them pointed out the alleged murderers and
told the whites to take them. The two accused men "immediately seized
their arms" and with their friends stood off the crowd. The miners
decided that it would be best to leave while they still could. Making
their exit, they were approached by one of the four headmen who had
promised in May to turn over the killers. He told the miners that besides
the two accused murderers who had just been identified, three others
were involved. The Karoks had revealed the two killers because several
old men feared the consequences of harboring fugitives from white
vengeance.[34]

The Karok informant may have been trying to comply with the miners'
code of Indian relations, hoping that if the guilty parties were turned
over to the whites the destruction of his people could be averted. The
Indians immediately began to remove their women and property in
preparation for a white attack. The next day a Karok leader arrived "in
great haste and apparent alarm" at Orleans Bar, where he told the
miners that the Indians had made prisoners of the two accused men and
agreed to deliver them to a small group of whites. The miners went
along with the Karok plan, although they suspected that it was an elaborate ruse "intended to throw responsibility off the shoulders of the
Indians upon that of the whites." When miners arrived at the ranchería
to take the two men into custody, they later reported, the Karoks
claimed that "the murderers had just escaped and it was attempted to
stampede the [white] party in pursuit." Instead the miners prepared to
destroy the ranchería. Seventy-five men under "efficient leaders" went
by night over a "very difficult and dangerous trail" to the mouth of the

33. Ibid.
34. Ibid.

Salmon River, attacked two rancherías, and destroyed the houses, but were able to kill only one Indian and wound two others because the Karoks had fled to the mountains.[35]

After reflection, some miners believed they were in greater danger than before. They informed the governor that "the greatest excitement" existed among the Indians on Klamath River and that the situation had become "really dangerous" for the small white communities in the district. Peace could not easily be restored because "the nominal chiefs of these ranches have in reality little power or control over their men and their promises, even if made in sincerity are of doubtful fulfillment." For their part, the miners believed that they had behaved with "extraordinary moderation and humanity," not resorting to "violent redress" until it became clear that it was "vain to hope for sincerity on the part of the Indians." The miners wondered why they had to protect themselves even though they paid taxes to the state. While the miners complained to the governor about ineffectual state government, the Karok and other river Indians were moving to the mountains, where they could find better defensive positions.[36]

Miners' protestations about their humane attitudes were self-serving and incredible, but their fear of the Indians was understandable. In 1852, according to the state census, there were only about five hundred non-Indians and no enumerated domesticated Indians in the northern district (see table 6.1). If the census had been taken before the Indian exodus, perhaps some domesticated Indians would have been recorded, but probably no more than a few dozen, judging by the other northern counties. In Klamath County, warfare had driven virtually all Indians out of the work force, yet the Karok alone probably numbered about two thousand, and the total county Indian population may have been four or five times larger, with commensurate numbers in the rest of the district.

Independent Indians were a majority in the northern mining country, and fewer domesticated Indians could be found there than in any other district, partly because Indians had less need to work for whites. Since they had been the most isolated tribes, having the least contact with whites before 1848, their land and resources were substantially unaltered. Their concept of equity and justice held that whites who used their resources must pay for them, so they shared very little common ground with whites who did not heed Indians' sense of fairness. To make matters worse, arable land was scarce in the northern mountains, most

35. Ibid.
36. Ibid.

of it being found around the rancherías. Thus, a few white miners and farmers could put intense pressure on the Indian resource base. Not surprisingly, the California Indian War Papers show that the north country became the most strife-ridden region in the state. Time and again, volunteer units went after the Karoks, Hupas, Shastas, and their neighbors. Because northern Indians retaliated against whites who encroached on native resources and attacked rancherías, the U.S. Army regarded most northern tribes as warlike.[37]

Not all northern Indians resisted the advance of the mining frontier. Around Humboldt Bay about eight hundred Wiyots remained in their rancherías. At Fort Humboldt, Colonel Robert Buchanan attributed their peacefulness to laziness. In truth, they had no place to go because the mountain Indians were their enemies. The Wiyots had to take their chances with whites. In 1860 many of them were living on an island in Humboldt Bay. White ranchers, apparently exasperated by Indian raids on their herds, assaulted this harmless native settlement and butchered fifty-five inhabitants, mostly women and children. At the same time, whites killed more than 130 Wiyots in other unoffending settlements nearby. Flight and resistance seemed to be the only plausible route to survival in the north country.[38]

A Regional Comparison

In just a few years the gold rush radically altered the foundations of Indian-white relations in the California mining districts, where Indians had previously been a relatively independent majority. In all the major mining regions change began in the same way. Whites experienced in dealing with Indian laborers, many of whom had worked for Sutter, opened new mining regions, traded with and employed the natives, and quickly exploited the placer deposits. At first Indian miners could rely on traditional native foods, but they became increasingly scarce as placer mining silted the rivers and ruined the salmon runs, and as whites expropriated land and barred Indians from using it. In the central mines, whites quickly overwhelmed Indian resistance and limited their place in the work force, but some Indians continued to be a part of the Mother

37. Cook, *Population of the California Indians*, 1–7; and Col. G. Wright to E. D. Townsend, Aug. 1, 1853, in "Reports Relating to Indian Customs," RG 393. On the frequency and location of the state volunteer expeditions, see the Indian War Papers, State Archives, Sacramento.

38. Robert C. Buchanan to E. D. Townsend, Aug. 1, 1853, in "Reports Relating to Indian Customs," RG 393; Heizer, *Destruction of the California Indians*, 255–63.

Lode scene, eking out a living near the mining camps. In the southern mines the Indian majority sometimes worked for whites while continuing to hunt and gather. With only a few exceptions, they remained at peace and gave up horse raiding. In the north, Indians and whites fought bitterly until the Civil War.[39]

Indian and white violence erupted everywhere, but it was not evenly distributed in frequency or intensity. Why were the northwestern and southern mines, both of which had Indian majorities, so different? The answer lies in the perceptions and choices made by whites and Indians. The Miwoks and Yokuts had a long history with whites, from the missions to the mines. Witnessing changes in white society, they made adjustments in their own. Well traveled through raiding and trading, they could readily grasp the significance of the gold rush and the changes that came with it, so most of them opted for peaceful accommodation with whites. There were exceptions; but compared to the north, resistance was rare. Northern Indians did not have the same experience as the southerners. They maintained unchallenged control over their own country until the gold rush, when the sparse white occupation forced them from their lands and impoverished them. Not recognizing that the rules of the game had irrevocably changed, these Indians tried to uphold their own standards of justice. When that failed and they attempted to compromise, as in the case of the Karok, they were met with white aggression that led to brutal rounds of retaliation. During the 1850s the north became California's dark and bloody ground.

The gold rush was a complicated series of events that brought complex changes to California Indians. Coping with them, nearly twenty thousand natives found ways to survive in the mining counties in 1852, according to the state census. But survival did not necessarily mean a long and prosperous life. Everywhere Indians were impoverished. And everywhere they risked infection with diseases that brought increased mortality rates for decades. Survival was a dangerous and tricky occupation, as the life of José Jesus shows. He had adapted to successive changes in white society, and he seemed to accomodate to the gold rush as well. Yet he did not sign any treaties in 1851, nor does his name appear on the 1852 manuscript census rolls. Did he hold out in Yosemite, or quietly retire to some camp where the census takers recorded him merely as an unidentified Indian? Or was he one of the tens of thousands of gold rush casualties for whom there were no epitaphs? Though we may never learn his fate, the record of his life is a fitting monument to the Indians who survived the gold rush. Indians were victimized; but

---

39. Carranco and Beard, *Genocide and Vendetta*, 101–56.

they were not merely victims. They made choices about their futures based on their sense of history and their standards of justice. Accommodating, working, fighting, hiding out—in a word, surviving—they were the seed for today's California Indians.

7

"Extermination or Domestication:" The Dilemma of California Indian Policy

The gold rush created unparalleled difficulties not only for California's Indians, but for white policy makers who tried to master the situation, for acquisition of the Mexican province put the federal government squarely on a collision course with California customs and local interests. Before 1848 the Indian situation had been intractable but relatively easy to understand in broad scope. Indians sought survival through raiding, labor, and trading, while whites wanted to suppress the former as they gained advantage from the latter. Neither whites nor Indians could consistently predominate because the whites' advantage in technology and organization was offset by the Indians' superior numbers. Both sides used violence when it suited them, and diplomatic relations were based largely on personal—indeed, intimate—relations between whites and Indians. If Sutter could work out an arrangement with José Jesus, then New Helvetia's herds would be safe from Muquelemne Miwoks; otherwise the bones of Sutter's livestock would litter the banks of the Mokelumne River. Similar agreements, even marriages, helped to determine the availability of Indian labor to white ranchers, at least in times of relative calm. In brief, following Hispanic traditions Anglos sought to integrate some of the Indians into white society, if only for economic reasons, and Indians accepted this arrangement for reasons of their own.

Patterns of race relations in the California interior can hardly be said to be a matter of Mexican policy. After 1839 the authority of the Mexican government was seldom felt in the interior, except insofar as Sutter represented official interests. But he and other Anglos persisted in the interior because of personal relations with Indians, not through official regulations carried out by government functionaries. These well-understood patterns would be substantially challenged after 1848 as state, federal, civilian, and military bureaucracies largely replaced individual initiatives with the Indians, thus overlaying California's customs with a confusing maze of treaties, laws, and administrative orders that added a hitherto unknown level of complexity to the Indian quest for survival.

The origins of federal difficulties in California may be traced in the history of policies that aimed to segregate Indians from whites. The Constitution gave the United States government supreme authority over Indians and the power to negotiate treaties that allowed Indians to keep some lands while ceding others to the nation in return for cash, goods, and services. Indian reservation boundaries formed a frontier line that amounted to a racial barrier, which whites and Indians could cross only with federal permission. Humanitarians wanted to educate Indians to white cultural norms, but this ordinarily occurred only in Indian communities segregated from the mass of white society. After the Louisiana Purchase, the government hoped to convince eastern tribes to remove west of the Mississippi. Facing a growing white population and increasing pressure on diminishing native resources, some tribesmen chose to go west. During President Jackson's administration, the government grew more insistent, and under duress most Indians who remained in the East signed treaties that traded their old lands for new homes in the West. Theoretically, federal administration permitted orderly white expansion while Indian rights were protected in Indian country, which the federal government would hold in trust for the Indians. Ceded lands became part of the public domain to be surveyed, classified, mapped, and sold at public auctions. Indian country was closed to unauthorized white entry, and the United States was supposed to prevent illegal incursions. Indians were expected to govern and support themselves on traditional subsistence, annuities, and government-regulated trade. After the Mexican War the new continental scope of the republic made the removal policy illogical and unworkable. The spread of settlement to the Far West and consequent border warfare caused Indian service administrators to respond by establishing reservations, where they could assert more direct control over the Indians.[1]

Federal Indian policy was largely incompatible with California's local interests, which demanded access to Indian labor—a practice that in effect integrated some Indians into white society. Furthermore, the Treaty of Guadalupe Hidalgo provided that Indians in the Mexican cession could obtain U.S. citizenship—a provision that Congress ultimately chose to ignore. The orderly transition from Mexican to United States rule that the treaty anticipated was knocked aside in the hurly-burly of the gold rush. Thousands of miners occupied Indian lands before

1. Prucha, *American Indian Policy in the Formative Years*, 57–60; Prucha, *Great Father*, 1:5–436, passim; and Trennert, *Alternative to Extinction*, 40–42.

the federal government could intervene; then its agents had to consider how policy might be made to fit reality. In the meantime, the state leaped into the breach and initiated its own policies, complicating the federal task of asserting supremacy in the midst of local actions. The resulting conflict and consensus of state and federal governments importantly affected native people, who under American sovereignty had little chance to retain their independence, their land, and life itself.[2]

At first federal officials in Washington did not perceive the magnitude of California's Indian problems. In March 1849 the Office of Indian Affairs was occupied with the impending move from the War Department to the new Department of the Interior, and it was expedient to continue the system of Indian subagents that General Kearny had inaugurated. Thomas Ewing, President Taylor's new interior secretary, reappointed Captain Sutter subagent for the territory embraced by the Sacramento River and its tributaries, and named subagent Adam Johnston for the territory along the San Joaquin River. There were no new instructions for the subagents; during the first half of 1849 none seemed necessary because California was still under military rule.[3]

By 1850, however, California had become a state, and it would not do to maintain subagents acting on the instructions of the defunct military regime. The government's inadequacy was made clear by critics like Sylvester Woodbridge, pastor of the Presbyterian Church in Benecia, who informed President Taylor that miners were ruthlessly driving the Indians high into the Sierras, where there was not enough food. Starvation forced them to steal immigrant stock, and whites then retaliated by killing Indian men, women, and children in "cold blood." A new arrangement was needed. Woodbridge suggested that Indians be gathered "into ranches of their own, separate from the white community," perhaps at Clear Lake and the Kings River, where "good men

2. Chauncy Shafter Goodrich, "The Legal Status of the California Indian: Introductory," *California Law Review* 14 (January 1926):81–100; Ellison, "Federal Indian Policy in California," 35–67; Hoopes, *Indian Affairs and Their Administration*, 35–67; Kelsey, "California Indian Treaty Myth," 273–94; and Rawls, *Indians of California*, 137–60. A complete history of the California Indian wars has yet to be written, but Carranco and Beard, *Genocide and Vendetta*, covers most of the important northern California conflicts, and Joseph Ellison discusses the California Indian War debt in *California and the Nation, 1850–1869: A Study of the Relations of a Frontier Community with the Federal Government* (Berkeley, 1927), 97–102. The main body of documentation for the state Indian wars is found in IWP.

3. D. C. Goddard to A. S. Loughery, Mar. 22, 1849, and T. Ewing to Orlando Brown, Nov. 17, 1849, M234:32; and George Crawford to Bennet Riley, Aug 24, 1849, *Annual Report of the Commissioner of Indian Affairs*, 1849, Sen. Ex. Doc. 5, 31st Cong., 2d sess., ser. 569, 166; and Bennet Riley to R. Jones, Aug. 30, 1849, ibid., 170–71.

farmers, teachers, &c" could guide them. Woodbridge further suggested that Christian missionaries be sent among the native people to help with their education.[4]

If complaints were not sufficient to prod Washington to action, the resignation of one California subagent must have underscored the need to reassess the situation. In May Sutter quit citing "old age & the decline of life" as well as pressing business matters, and suggested that subagent Johnston could handle both positions. Salaries and expenses should be increased, he explained, because the tribes were scattered over a huge territory, making any future treaty negotiations an expensive business.[5]

The critics and the press of circumstances had their effect. Commissioner of Indian Affairs Orlando Brown asked the state's U.S. senator-elect, John C. Frémont, for his ideas about Indian affairs. In June 1850 Senator Frémont issued suggestions that were not revolutionary, but based on long-established practices in Indian administration as well as his personal observations of California. The state contained, he conservatively estimated, forty thousand Indians living in "very numerous small tribes [and] speaking many different languages and dialects," making it impossible to assign agents to particular tribes. He thought the country should be divided into three jurisdictions with an agent in charge of each, all under the supervision of a state superintendent who should live at Sacramento. He suggested that one "agent be stationed at or near 'Reading's Rancho,' " to control the Sacramento Valley and the country west of the Sierra Nevada Mountains. Another agent should be near the Kings River, to take charge of the San Joaquin Valley and the surrounding country. The third agent should live in Los Angeles and preside over southern California. Each agent would oversee several subagents, with one stationed at Sonoma to take care of the north coast. He suggested that since the Indians were "generally docile . . . [and] disposed by missionary teaching" and subsisted on "agricultural labor," clothing, seeds, stock, and implements would be suitable presents for them. Frémont even volunteered a suggestion regarding the salary each employee ought to receive. "For his services the Superintendent should receive three thousand dollars," he wrote, "each agent two thousand and upwards, and each sub-agent fifteen hundred dollars," double the salary then allowed by law.[6]

While the Indian Office considered these suggestions and cautiously moved towards a serviceable policy, the new state government quickly

4. Woodbridge to Taylor, Jan. 23, 1850, M234:32.
5. Sutter to the secretary of the interior, May 23, 1850, M234:32.
6. Frémont to Brown, June 17, 1850, M234:32; Prucha, *Great Father*, 1:159–63; and *U.S. Statutes at Large* 4:736–37.

codified the old patterns of Indian relations. In March 1850 the first state legislature considered Indian legislation, first hearing a bill by state Senator John Bidwell, Sutter's friend and former employee. Bidwell's bill, An Act Relative to the Protection, Punishment, and Government of the Indians, provided for the subdivision of counties into as many as ten Indian districts, each with a "Justice of the Peace for Indians," to be elected by the qualified voters—including "male Indians of the district"—who were at least eighteen years old. The bill defined Indian crimes, punishments, and rights to be adjudicated by the Indian justice. Limited Indian suffrage was the most striking feature of Bidwell's proposal. A justice of the peace for Indians would have all the powers of a regular justice of the peace and could fine anyone who abused an Indian, although Indian testimony alone could not convict a white defendant. Whites could take Indian children to raise and retain the proceeds of their labor, but the parents would have to appear before the justice of the peace for Indians to prove that they consented to adoption. When indentured Indians reached their majority, they were to receive fifty dollars and "two good suits of clothes" from their former masters. Indians were not required to work for whites, but if they did, employer and employee had to execute a contract ratified by the Indian justice. Indians living in rancherías on white-owned or U.S. lands were not to be molested and could come and go as they pleased. Anyone convicted of forcing Indians to work in the mines could be fined as much as five hundred dollars.[7]

Only the most credulous readers would believe that paper guarantees could have protected Indians caught in the maw of the gold rush. Even so, these mild safeguards were too much for the legislature. Bidwell's bill was read twice and tabled when the assembly passed an Act for the Government and Protection of the Indians, which the senate eventually passed and the governor signed into law on April 22, 1850. The measure included many of the features of Bidwell's bill, but omitted provisions for Indian justices of the peace and Indian suffrage. Instead, the regular county justices of the peace had authority in "all cases by, for, or against Indians, in their respective jurisdictions." Indians were permitted to remain in "homes and villages" that they had occupied "for a number of years," but the "white person or proprietor" could apply to have "sufficient" land set aside for the Indians, who could appeal to the county court. Native people would remain on this designated land until "otherwise provided for." The law left out Bidwell's language that specifically

7. Old Bill File, California State Archives, Sacramento; *California State Senate Journal*, 1850, 217, 224, 228–29, 257, 337–38, 343, 366, 369, 384–87; and Goodrich, "Legal Status of the California Indian," 89–93.

protected Indian hunting, fishing, and gathering sites, and eliminated the phrase "from time immemorial" in reference to their tenure at rancherías. References to the rights of Indian descendants also disappeared. Gone were requirements to set off Indian land "in a body" and to require a minimum of one acre per resident Indian. The law looked forward to a federal solution to the problem of Indian lands; but in the interim, the Indians' land use would be curtailed and they would be hemmed into small rancherías.[8]

The law also dealt with Indian labor. The act allowed native children to be indentured with the consent of their parents, or if they were orphans. Boys were to be kept until they were eighteen; girls would be released at fifteen. White custodians were required to treat indentured Indians well and to clothe and feed them properly; violators could be fined not less than ten dollars and the child transferred to the keeping of a more suitable person with the "same rights and liabilities" of the former master. Masters were not required to give money or clothing to servants when they were released.[9]

The justice of the peace had to approve all labor contracts between Indians and whites. Any person who forced an Indian from his home or compelled him to labor against his will could be fined not less than fifty dollars. The law virtually compelled Indians to work because any Indian found "loitering or strolling about" was subject to arrest on the complaint of any white citizen, whereupon the court was required within twenty-four hours to hire out arrestees to the highest bidder for up to four months. Setting fire to the prairie and livestock theft were considered to be special Indian crimes, so the legislators included punishments for these acts in the Indian indenture law. For untold generations Indians had periodically fired the landscape to encourage the growth of wild plants, but ripe wheat fields and luckless livestock were increasingly at risk as settlement proliferated. Consequently, the legislature deemed this act an Indian crime. Unlawful burning was punishable by fine or other punishment that the "Court may adjudge proper," while theft of livestock or "any valuable thing" could be punished with a maximum fine of two hundred dollars or up to twenty-five lashes. For Indians unable to pay fines, "any white person" could pay the fine or give bond for the native, then compel him to work for a specified period. Indians could complain to a justice of ill-treatment, "but in no case" could "a white man be convicted of any offense upon the testimony of an Indian."[10]

8. *Statutes of California*, 1850, Chapter 1033.
9. Ibid.
10. Ibid.

Understandably, white ranchers wanted to stop livestock theft and wildfires, yet the law may have inadvertently encouraged rustling. The prohibition of burning compelled Indians to forgo a resource management strategy that enhanced the productivity of the environment. Indians, forced onto small tracts of land, were not permitted to use their meagre resources in the most productive ways they knew. Thus, they had to work, steal, or starve.

This first state Indian law served agricultural interests by providing a legal process that enabled white ranchers to procure Indian workers and Indian land. Penalties could be levied on Indians for the crimes that ranchers feared most, livestock theft and firing the grasslands, while Indians received some consideration under sections that allowed land to be set aside for their use. Humane treatment of the Indians was made mandatory, even though convictions of whites would be difficult to obtain without Indian testimony. Overall, it may be said that the 1850 Act for the Government and Protection of the Indians protected them very little and governed them quite a lot. Furthermore, the deletions from Bidwell's bill show that the state legislature was concerned to mute language that imputed any extensive Indian land rights and removed statements about "Spanish or Mexican grant[s] or . . . United States lands." By so doing, the legislature pointedly ignored Indian and Mexican land rights, making Anglo occupation its paramount consideration. California's leaders recognized that Indian labor was useless without access to Indian resources, so according to state law conflicts over land tenure would be resolved in favor of whites—preferably Anglos.

While local forces were molding California Indian affairs, the sectional debates that resulted in the Compromise of 1850 claimed the attention of Congress. In the meantime, Secretary Ewing hastily reorganized the Office of Indian Affairs so as to provide Indian administrators for New Mexico and Utah. Indian affairs throughout the new western territories forced Congress to address unresolved problems of frontier warfare, land tenure, and jurisdiction. California, Texas, and Oregon each received federal Indian commissions. Only the Oregon commission had authority to make treaties of land cession. The Texas commission was merely supposed to collect information about the tribes, and lack of congressional support and local opposition ultimately prohibited the accomplishment of even this modest goal.[11]

California's commission and its work haphazardly evolved from Congressional inattention, executive orders, and the press of local cir-

11. Prucha, *Great Father*, 1:360–61, 368, 397–99; and Trennert, *Alternative to Extinction*, 113, 179.

cumstances. Originally, Senator Frémont had introduced a bill providing for treaties of land cession, but because the senate was not convinced that California Indians had derived any land rights as a result of Spanish and Mexican sovereignty, the final law omitted treaty authorization and only permitted the appointment of three agents. The new agents' salaries were not provided for, but Congress had inadvertently passed a separate appropriation act based on Frémont's request for twenty-five thousand dollars "to enable the President to hold treaties with various Indian tribes in California," so the administration paid each agent three thousand dollars per year from this fund. To fill these positions President Millard Fillmore chose Oliver M. Wozencraft, a delegate to California's state constitutional convention, and outlanders Redick McKee and George W. Barbour. After consulting with the president, Interior Secretary A. H. H. Stuart directed them to act as a commission to "make such treaties and compacts with the Indians as may seem to be just and proper." The agents-cum-commissioners were supposed to ascertain the best "divisions of the Country having regard to the territory and the tribes ... for permanent Indian agencies." Then the appointees would assume their duties as agents and establish depots for Indian provisions and agents' residences. Congress had accidentally enabled the president to make treaties that it did not want, but eventually the senate would have the last word.[12]

Coincidentally, California Governor Peter Burnett prepared to launch a military offensive against Indians who were accused of stealing stock near the central mines. On October 25, 1850, he directed William Rogers, sheriff of El Dorado County, to call out "two hundred able bodied Militia" and permit them to choose a commander. The militia was to proceed as soon as possible "to punish the Indians engaged in the late attacks in the Vicinity of Ringgold and along the emigrant trail leading from Salt Lake to California." The governor ordered Rogers to assist the "emigrants and all others travelling the route." As soon as this force had carried out its mission, Burnett declared, the commander must disband the militia.[13]

Rogers promised the volunteer militia ample compensation, ranging from fifteen dollars per day for the commander to five dollars per day for privates, plus a one dollar per day allowance for each horse. Three hundred and nineteen men enlisted, including one surgeon with three assistants, guides, expressmen, and one gentleman whose official duty

12. *U.S. Statutes at Large*, 9:519, 558; Kelsey, "California Indian Treaty Myth," 227–29; and A. H. H. Stuart to the commissioner of Indian affairs, Oct. 9, 1850, M234:32.
13. Burnett to Rogers, Oct. 25, 1850, IWP.

was described as "musician." The volunteers elected Rogers their commander with the rank of colonel.[14]

On October 29 one of Rogers's scouting parties discovered the remains of some freshly butchered "Emigrant Cattle" near the North Fork of the Cosumnes River. The scout's commander reported that he was "necessarily on the lookout, [and] after travelling a few miles farther . . . discovered 150 or two hundred Indians who immediately fired upon me." The battle took place on the rim of a steep canyon, and both the Indians (probably Miwoks) and white fighters fell and tumbled down the steep walls. Three Indians were killed, but the Indian party forced the volunteers to retreat.[15]

On November 4, ten of Colonel Rogers's men fought with 150 Miwoks, some of whom were armed with shotguns and rifles. After five hours, fifteen Indians were killed, Rogers claimed, and "from the numerous Trails Marked with Blood there must have been a great many severely wounded." The Miwoks killed two volunteers, "Hugh Dixon (a Deleware Indian) Calvin Everts" and left one "Dangerously wounded, The Well Known Guide of Col Fremont Capt Francis De Allison." Rogers claimed that a general uprising was under way and assured his commander that he was determined to put it down.[16]

Brigadier General William M. Winn, commander of the state militia, was not impressed with Rogers's warning about an Indian war, but became alarmed at the number of men who had enlisted with Rogers and the excessive rates of pay he had promised. On November 11 Winn wrote to Governor Burnett, estimating the expense of the expedition at $22,500 per week. "Such a debt cannot be paid by the State," Winn warned, and besides the job should be done by federal troops. A state force should not exceed one hundred men, "considering the character of our people in the immediate vicinity of the Indian difficulties," added the general. "Col. Rogers says he knows nothing of military life for which he is not to blame," Winn concluded, "but the reports . . . show plainly that he does not, and that great difficulty must grow out of such irregularity." Governor Burnett took Winn's advice, ordering Colonel Rogers to reduce his force immediately to one hundred men and suggesting that the campaign be terminated soon, with "as little expense to the State as practicable." Subsequently General Winn wrote to Rogers. "I am inclined to the beleaf that you will soon be able to close the war with the Indians," the general observed, "and my advice to you is to do so as soon as possible." Winn informed Rogers that "the expense

14. Ibid.; and "Account Book," IWP, 35–36.
15. Rogers to Brig. Gen. Winn, Oct. 29, 1850, IWP.
16. Rogers to Winn, Nov. 4, 1850, IWP.

is immense without the means of immediate payment." Rogers took the advice of his commanders and disbanded his force on November 28, 1850.[17]

Winn's fears of exorbitant costs were well founded. The total cost of the one-month campaign in El Dorado County was $101,861.65. The state did not have the cash to cover this unforeseen expense, so the legislature issued $100,000 in bonds, appointed the spendthrift Rogers to be paymaster, and allowed him 7 percent of the money he disbursed in addition to his salary. Thus, Rogers collected nearly $5,500 for his militia service.[18]

The El Dorado County experience illustrated how lucrative a state-authorized Indian war could be for militia commanders, and how expensive it could be for taxpayers. By 1854 the Indian war debt amounted to more than nine hundred thousand dollars, which the United States eventually paid, partly because the state claimed that the federal government had failed to provide necessary military aid to suppress Indians, as indeed it had. In 1854 there were only twenty-five regular army companies with 1,229 enlisted men—873 recruits short of full strength—to serve in the entire Department of the Pacific, which included California and the Oregon and Washington territories. They could not respond to every local alarm, much less protect Indians from whites. Without enough federal troops to protect the frontier or to deter adventurous whites, the state sent more than twenty militia expeditions against the Indians through the Civil War period, mostly in the northern mining district.[19]

As was so often the case, the effects of white forays against Indians were not what state officials had intended. Instead of suppressing Indian livestock theft, they drove native people farther into the mountains and made them more dependent on raiding for subsistence. Whites retaliated with more military campaigns, thus creating a vicious cycle of violence (see fig. 8). In his 1851 message to the legislature, Governor Burnett explained that "the white man, to whom time is money, and who labors hard all day to create the comforts of life, cannot sit up all night to watch his property; . . . after being robbed a few times he becomes desperate, and resolves upon a war of extermination." There could be only

17. Winn to Burnett, Nov. 11, 1850, IWP; Burnett to Rogers, Nov. 15, 1850, IWP; Winn to Rogers, Nov. 25, 1850, IWP; and Rogers to Winn, Dec. 10, 1850, IWP.

18. "Account Book," IWP, 35; and *Statutes of California*, 1851, Chapter 125.

19. Joseph Ellison, *California and the Nation*, 97–102; Robert W. Frazer, ed., *Mansfield on the Condition of the Western Forts, 1853–54* (Norman, Okla., 1963), 182–83; and California State Archives, *Inventory of the Indian War Papers* (Sacramento, n.d.).

FIG. 8. Indian Ranchería on Dry Creek. A few days before whites attacked this Miwok ranchería and drove the inhabitants into the tules, in early 1853, an artist depicted the site on letter sheets. This community was at the mouth of Dry Creek where it flowed into the Mokelumne River, about twenty-five miles south of Sacramento. The most unusual feature of this ranchería is what appears to be a stockade. Did the Miwoks build this structure to defend against Mexican intruders or John Sutter? Or did they construct it for protection against immigrants in the 1850s?

one result, Burnett believed: "A war of extermination will continue to be waged between the races until the Indian race becomes extinct."[20]

In this atmosphere of impending genocide, the three federal treaty commissioners began their work in 1851. One week after the governor's message, the commissioners published their views in the *Daily Alta California*. Fearing a general Indian war, they counseled moderation in the mining districts. The commissioners pointed out the obvious implications of the Mexican cession for Indian policy. There was "*no farther west*" available for Indian removal, and the only policy alternatives were "*extermination* or *domestication*." The commissioners' juxtaposition of the stark alternatives of utter extinction and civilization was not unique to California. Discussions of Indian policy frequently used these terms to dramatize the problems of Indian-white relations. Of course, humanity dictated that the federal government should bend every effort to civilize the Indians in order to save them from extinction. In California, however, officials favored domestication not only for humanitarian reasons, but because it would secure "to the people of the State an element greatly needed in the development of its resources, viz: cheap

20. "Message to the California State Legislature," Jan. 7, 1851, *California State Senate Journal*, 1851, 15.

labor." In the Golden State, humanity and frontier economics seemed to go hand in hand.[21]

Governor Burnett soon stepped down and was replaced by John McDougal, but this change did not herald a new attitude towards California Indians. McDougal sent Colonel J. Neely Johnson to speak with the commissioners on behalf of the governor. The governor's message was simple and chilling: if the treaty negotiations were unsuccessful, Johnson warned, the state would "make war upon the [Indians] which must of necessity be one of extermination to many of the tribes."[22]

In March and April the commissioners negotiated the first two treaties on the Mariposa and San Joaquin rivers, while state volunteers fought the Mariposa Indian war, driving refugees into the arms of the commissioners. Models for subsequent negotiations, the first treaties set aside a large tract of land—as much as several hundred square miles— for the Indians and bound the federal government to provide teachers and farmers for native people (see map 5). For two years after ratification, the United States was also supposed to give the Indians thousands of beef and dairy cattle, and brood stock for horses, in addition to flour, cloth, thread, needles, various tools, and clothing. None of these items could be sold or exchanged without the consent of the Indian agent. In return, the Indian signatories relinquished their claim to any other lands and acknowledged the sovereignty of the United States.[23]

Since the agents were not specifically authorized to make treaties of land cession, Wozencraft explained their rationale to the commissioner of Indian affairs. The Indians had been driven into the mountains and were compelled to steal and fight. "They do not lack the *nerve* and *daring* of the best Atlantic Indians," he explained. Once accustomed to war, "their mountain fastnesses will be impregnable." "Our policy is . . . to get them down . . . in reservations, along in the foothills, bordering on the plains," with the miners "between them and the Mountains, forming a formidable Cordon, or barrier, through which it would be difficult to take their families unobserved" and where there would be "no place for Concealing Stolen Stock." In this way they could have "protection . . . learn the ways of civilization . . . and there become useful

21. "Address of the Indian Agents," *Daily Alta California*, Jan. 14, 1851, 2.

22. Barbour to Luke Lea, Feb. 17, 1851, M234:32; and McDougal to the Indian commissioners, Jan. 25, 1851, *California State Senate Journal*, 1851, 677.

23. The text of the unratified treaties is available in Charles J. Kappler, comp., *Indian Affairs: Laws and Treaties*, 5 vols. (Washington, D.C.: Government Printing Office, 1904–41), vol. 4; and on reel 8, T494. Robert F. Heizer compiled some of the treaties in *The Eighteen Unratified Treaties of 1851–1852 Between the California Indians and the United States Government* (Berkeley, 1972).

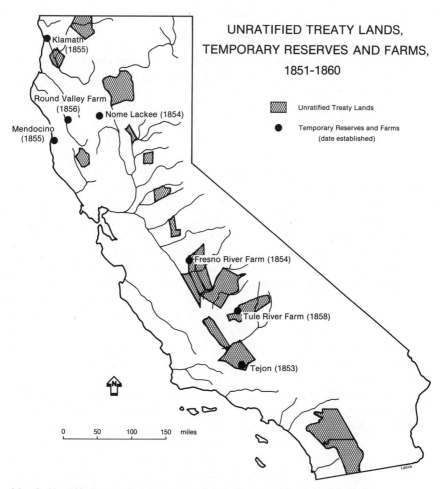

Klamath
(1855)

Round Valley Farm
(1856)
Nome Lackee (1854)

Mendocino
(1855)

Unratified Treaty Lands

Temporary Reserves and Farms
(date established)

Fresno River Farm (1854)

Tule River Farm (1858)

Tejon (1853)

N

0   50   100   150   miles

Lecce

MAP 5. Unratified Treaty Lands, Temporary Reserves, and Farms, 1851–1860

members of the community, instead of being a dead weight in the General Government," he concluded. In his mind, civilization would be a barrier to savage frontier warfare.[24]

After completing these first agreements the commissioners worked separately negotiating additional treaties and began their duties as agents. Redick McKee took charge of the coastal region north of San Francisco, including the northern mines; George Barbour got southern California; and Oliver Wozencraft assumed authority over the Sacramento and San Joaquin rivers and their tributaries. Altogether they

24. Wozencraft to Luke Lea, May 14, 1851, M234:32.

negotiated sixteen treaties that would establish reservations of more than 6.5 million acres from Tejon Pass to the Oregon border. Two other treaties concluded in southern California created reservations comprising slightly less than two million acres. In the mining regions the treaties removed Indians to places that the agents thought had no gold, although subsequent prospecting indicated otherwise. In the agricultural regions the treaties often created reservations next to large land-grant ranchos, thus making Indian workers available to the rancheros.[25]

For the most part, Indians who joined in the negotiations respected the provisions of the treaties. Seeing white encroachments and understanding that few choices remained to them, protection on substantial reservations must have seemed providential, especially to Indians whose traditional lands were set aside. The importance of the treaties to Indians is illustrated in the meeting of the Belgian argonaut Jean-Nicolas Perlot with an old chief named José (perhaps José Jesus?), probably a Miwok, somewhere near the Yosemite Valley. Mistaking Perlot for a government representative, José repeated treaty rights that he had memorized, explaining that the document gave his people the right to occupy their present site. No doubt José was not the only Indian who had memorized and asserted Indian rights under the treaties, placing his hopes in the good faith of the federal government.[26]

José and other Indians were bound to be disappointed in their confidence in the treaties, for California's white landholders did not find the agreements to their liking. At first the treaties received support in the agricultural community. Ranchers like Senator Bidwell used their influence with native people to encourage them to negotiate with the agents, but the nature of the treaties soon gave pause to landholders. By these treaties the federal government was required altogether to provide Indian people with hundreds of thousands of pounds of flour, thousands of dairy cattle, more than one thousand mules, mares, and stallions, and nearly twelve thousand beef cattle. Had the 1851 treaties been adopted, the reservations would have been federally subsidized livestock ranches with Indian proprietors. Native ranchers might have preferred to work their own herds and fields rather than those of white

25. Barbour and Wozencraft to Lea, March 5, 1851, and McKee to Wozencraft, June 4, 1851, M234:32; and "Schedule 4, Value of Lands, Articles and Chattels, and Services, Total Offsets, and Net Amount of Proposed Settlement," in Robert W. Kenny, *History and Proposed Settlement: Claims of California Indians* (Sacramento, 1944), facing p. 82. For examples of reservations near ranchos, see the treaties negotiated on May 14, June 4, July 12 and 18, Aug. 1, and Sept. 9 and 18, 1851, T494.

26. Jean-Nicolas Perlot, *Gold Seeker: Adventures of a Belgian Argonaut during the Gold Rush Years*, ed. Howard R. Lamar, trans. Helen Harding Bretnor (New Haven, 1985), 188–89.

ranches, an unappealing prospect for landholders in the gold rush economy.

In 1852 Bidwell reversed his position and earnestly opposed ratification of the treaties. Writing to U.S. Senator James McCorkle, Bidwell claimed that California was unique because so many Indians worked in the homes and fields of whites. Consequently, there was no way to differentiate between the "domesticated" Indians and the "frontier savages." Bidwell contended that the federal government should "*let them alone* [and] make laws *to protect* them against the brutal treatment that is often inflicted upon them." They would be "sure to cling around and shelter themselves," Bidwell wrote, "under the protection of him who treats them best."[27]

Even subagent Adam Johnston had misgivings about the treaties. The commissioners meant well, he told the commissioner of Indian affairs, but knowing little of the country, they laid out reservations "contiguous to and in some instances in conflict with the mining interests," so aggression would inevitably result. He suggested that all of the state's Indians—he estimated them at eighty thousand—be sent to the Tulare Lake area, which had excellent farm land that was "beyond the reach of the mining region." An alternative was to remove them east of the Sierras to the Carson Valley.[28]

Treaties that conflicted with agriculture and mining interests had little hope of finding support in California's state government. Before the commissioners had concluded a single treaty, Governor McDougal sent the ex-commander of the El Dorado expeditions, William Rogers, to Washington to inform President Fillmore about the condition of Indian affairs. McDougal's letter of introduction did not mention the commissioners, but obliquely informed the president that their work was ineffectual. Referring to the constant wars with native people, McDougal wrote, "I am ignorant of any adequate steps having been taken by the General Government to avert the evils so plainly imminent." With one hundred thousand "warriors" poised to strike the whites at any moment, McDougal claimed, there was "no alternative but to coerce submission." The governor asked for federal arms, ammunition, and money to pay volunteer troops. "It may seem to your Excellency that this is an extraordinary suggestion," declared the governor, "but you will remember that we occupy an extraordinary situation . . . with conditions peculiar to California and necessities that admit of neither question or delay."[29]

27. Bidwell to McCorkle, Dec. 20, 1851, enclosed in McCorkle to Luke Lea, Feb. 6, 1852, M234:32.
28. Johnston to Luke Lea, Jan. 30, 1852, M234:32.
29. McDougal to Fillmore, March 1, 1851, IWP.

After the treaties were negotiated, the California legislature did everything possible to thwart them. The state senate and assembly appointed committees to review the treaties, then voted to instruct California's congressional delegation to lobby against ratification. According to the state senate report forwarded to Congress, the proposed reservations included some of the state's most valuable agricultural and mineral land. The treaties would not "prevent mischief" or promote the Indians' happiness and were all the more unjust because there were not more than twenty thousand "Wild Indians" and "Mission Indians," an estimate that must have surprised the governor, who waited anxiously as one hundred thousand warriors prepared to decimate California settlements. The proposed reservations "would withdraw a large body of Indians who were now semi-civilized, from the locations, which they occupy under the paternal protection of the old residents of the country." The report proposed "a system of missions for the Indians," where they would be given annuity goods and taught to cultivate the land. Native people who were already "residing on private lands, with the consent of the owners, or engaged in cultivating their soil, should not be disturbed in their position." These Indians, the report argued, were "already in the best school of civilization."[30]

Opponents of ratification frequently cited the agents' corrupt beef contracts. The assembly committee report on the treaties called these contracts "high-handed and unprecedented frauds" and demanded a full investigation of the conduct of the agents. Charges of corruption were based on more than empty rumors. All the federal Indian agents were involved in questionable contracting practices. Redick McKee obligated the government to pay exorbitant prices for cattle owned by his son. George Barbour and Adam Johnston purchased cattle from Frémont at twice the market price, then gave receipts to James Savage for double the number of cattle that he actually delivered to the Indians. Agent Wozencraft made several deals for cattle that contractors never delivered. Often the contracts were verbal and Wozencraft accepted the mere word of a trader as proof of delivery, even when the cattle were not actually received. One ambitious cattle merchant later claimed that he offered Wozencraft a twenty-five-thousand-dollar bribe for such a con-

30. "Report of the Special Committee to Inquire into the Treaties Made by the United States Indian Commissioners in California," *California State Senate Journal*, 1852, 600–04; "Report of the Special Committee to Inquire into the Treaties Made by the United States Indian Commissioners in California," *California State Assembly Journal*, 1852, 202–05; and "Report of the Special Committee on the Disposal of Public Lands in California," *California State Senate Journal*, 1852, 575–88.

tract, but when the agent held out for sixty thousand the contractor balked and Wozencraft broke off the negotiations.[31]

Faced with wildly conflicting estimates of Indian numbers, their potential threat, true conditions, and raids on the public treasury, the United States Senate met in executive session and voted against ratification of the treaties on July 8, 1852. Nineteen Oregon treaties also met the same fate because local residents opposed them. These acts symbolized more than any others the failure of the federal government to take charge of Indian affairs, leaving them, for the time being, in the hands of state lawmakers and local interests. With Congress unwilling to concede that California Indians had land rights that needed to be respected, federal Indian policy would have to take a new direction.[32]

Shortly before the treaties were defeated Congress created the California Superintendency of Indian Affairs, and in March President Fillmore appointed the first superintendent, retired naval Lieutenant Edward F. Beale, who had served with Commodore Stockton in California and who was close to senators Frémont and Thomas Hart Benton. In fact, Beale had been a partner on Frémont's Indian beef contract. That fall the President also named three other men to posts in the California superintendency, all with long experience in California. Pierson B. Reading became a special agent to procure presents for the native people. Samuel Sheldon, who worked for Reading and formerly for Sutter, received an appointment as Indian subagent. Fillmore also appointed subagent Benjamin D. Wilson, an established southern California rancher since 1841.[33]

Superintendent Beale arrived in California and soon reported that Barbour, Wozencraft, and McKee were guilty of the "grossest mismanagement." Barbour had already resigned and the other two were soon dismissed. Beale set about creating a new design for federal Indian policy in California, proposing in October a system of "Military Posts" where Indian people would be "invited to assemble." Each post would be staffed with troops in proportion to the number of Indians there.

31. "Report of the Special Committee on the Disposal of Public Lands," 202–05; Beale to Lea, Sept. 30, 1852, M234:32; James M. Crane to Fillmore, Feb. 2, 1852, M234:32; Wozencraft to Lea, June 27, 1852, M234:32; and War Department to Interior Department, Sept. 15, 1852, M234:32.

32. See California's unratified treaties in T494. Each copy of the treaties is accompanied by a document indicating that the Senate did not ratify it. On Oregon, see Prucha, *Great Father*, 1:399; and Utley, *Indian Frontier of the American West*, 52–53.

33. Beale to Lea, Oct. 9, 1852, M234:32; Reading to Lea, Sept. 10 and Oct. 5, 1852, M234:32; Caughey, *The Indians of Southern California*; and Gerald Thompson, *Edward F. Beale*, 46–49.

The Indian agent in charge would adopt a "system of Discipline and instruction" for the Indians, who would pay for maintaining troops at each post by the sale of their "surplus produce." According to this proposal, Beale's reservations were intended to be temporary, so their locations could be changed when the surrounding white population demanded it. To activate his plan, Beale proposed to relocate every Indian between the Tuolumne River and Tejon Pass at a farm between the Fresno and San Joaquin rivers. He reported that the native people near the proposed reserve were well disposed towards his plan. Without waiting for approval, Beale purchased seed grain for planting in the winter of 1852–53.[34]

On March 31, 1853, Beale's proposal, endorsed by the commissioner of Indian affairs, resulted in an act of Congress authorizing five military reservations in California "for Indian purposes," not to exceed twenty-five thousands acres each, and appropriating $250,000 for removing and supporting the Indians. To avoid conflicts with miners and ranchers, reservations were supposed to be located on public lands with no white occupants. Beale established only the Sebastian reserve at Tejon Pass, and the original farm at the Fresno River, though not elevated to reservation status, remained in operation through 1860. The reservation land at Tejon, preempted by the government at Beale's urging, had been farmed for years by several hundred ex-mission Indians under the leadership of Tapatero (see fig. 9). They had raised wheat and corn, built adobe houses, and lived comparatively well. When he assumed control, Beale instituted a compulsory labor system to increase the crop yield, but he never succeeded in gathering more than eight hundred native people on the reserve. He drew upon his eighteen years of experience with naval discipline, applied with good results. "In my fields here, for instance," Beale informed the commissioner, "if I were to allow them to work when they pleased, but little would be done, for the industrious would be discouraged by the indolent; but as it is the indolent are punished and compelled to labor." Using this system the superintendent reported an 1854 crop surplus of 1.2 million pounds of wheat that could have been distributed to the state's starving Indians, but Beale argued against this. "We should not give any food to any Indians excepting those upon the reserve," he wrote, "as it would discourage those who have worked hard to raise it, to see it go into the hands of other Indians who have given no assistance."[35]

34. Beale to Lea, Sept. 16 and 30, 1852, M234:32; Beale to Lea, Oct. 29, 1852, M234:32; and Beale to Lea, Dec. 14, 1852, M234:32.

35. *U.S. Statutes at Large* 10:226; Edward H. Hill, *The Office of Indian Affairs, 1824–1880: Historical Sketches* (New York, 1974), 18–27; Henley to George Manypenny, Aug.

FIG. 9. Tejon Indians. Lieutenant L. R. Williamson found these former mission Indians living at Tejon in 1853. They became the core of the temporary reservation that California Indian Superintendent Edward F. Beale established. Conveniently for Beale, Williamson reported that the Indians already cultivated melons, pumpkins, and corn, thus giving Beale a head start in establishing a self-sufficient agricultural settlement. From R. S. Williamson, *Report of Exploration in California for Railroad Routes to Connect with Routes Near the 35th and 32nd Parallels of North Latitude* (Washington, D.C., 1856).

Beale purposely neglected native people in the rest of the state. Although Indians were in desperate straits in the mining districts, he reasoned, they constituted no substantial threat to miners who could take care of themselves. He chose Tejon Pass because the San Joaquin Valley Indians had a reputation as horse thieves and the reservation would protect Los Angeles ranchers. Indians who volunteered to go to Tejon would be welcome; otherwise they could shift for themselves. Even in the extreme conditions of the gold rush, few Indians accepted Beale's invitation. An exception was chief Weimah, a Nevada County Nisenan, who agreed to move to Sebastian, but other leaders were reluctant and stalled the move. To test Beale's sincerity the Nisenans sent fifty young men to report on reservation conditions the following year. But most Indians preferred to stay in their own country and take their chances without seriously investigating the new reservation. Life

29, 1854, M234:33; Beale to Manypenny, Feb. 8, 1854, M234:32; Beale to Manypenny, June 20, 1854, M234:33; and Office of the Second Auditor, Treasury Department, to Manypenny, Apr. 7, 1855, M234:34.

on a reservation carved out of Indian homelands was one thing, but to labor as permanent residents on what appeared to be a large white ranch was quite another. Subagent Reading, Beale's agent in northern California, used an emergency congressional appropriation to purchase eleven thousand dollars' worth of glass beads for Indian presents, and even Beale conceded that they were inappropriate for the needs of hungry Indians. Moreover, the Sebastian reserve's future was clouded because Beale had located it on a Mexican land grant, and the owners soon protested, although the reservation continued to operate while the grant's validity was being established. Still, Beale found many supporters. A policy that essentially left matters in the hands of local interests, giving no land to the Indians, was bound to be popular with Californians.[36]

Despite Beale's glowing reports of progress at Sebastian, in the summer of 1854 he was replaced by Thomas J. Henley, former postmaster of San Francisco. Henley was in complete accord with Beale's policy and enthusiastic about the Sebastian reserve, comparing it favorably with the success of the missions and New Helvetia. He thought that the Indians in the San Joaquin Valley easily could be removed to Sebastian, but it would take time to "colonize Indians in California according to the plans now in progress." Henley was not certain what sort of plan he would pursue with regard to native people in the mines. In every ranchería, he stated, could be seen "Disease, starvation and death in their most appalling forms." For the time being, the new superintendent was at a loss to improve their situation. "Time and circumstance," Henley wrote, "can alone determine the policy which should control our action towards them." In September Henley toured the central mines and found the Nisenan and Miwok Indians "in a most miserable and destitute condition." The failure of the acorn crop and the salmon runs made their predicament worse. Henley was convinced that "nothing but speedy removal [would] save them from entire annihilation." The Indians he spoke to were willing to go to a reservation, "and many expressed an anxiety to labor if it [could] be made a means of providing them with support."[37]

Superintendent Henley decided to build a reservation in northern California and sent H. L. Ford to explore the upper Sacramento Valley

36. Reading to Lea, Sept. 10, 1852, M234:32; and Thompson, *Edward F. Beale*, 55–56, 67.

37. Beale's activities at Tejon were investigated by the federal government, but he was later exonerated. See Henley and J. R. Browne to Manypenny, Dec. 8, 1854, M234:34; Henley to Manypenny, Aug. 28, 1854, M234:33; Henley to Manypenny, Sept. 13, 1854, M234:33; and Thompson, *Edward F. Beale*, 72–79.

near Tehama. There Ford met the Nomlaki people, greatly reduced in numbers, with only about three hundred still surviving. They agreed to work at the reserve "with good will" and were concerned because Mexicans had taken their women and children to sell in the valley. Ford gave presents to the Nomlakis and told them that Henley would be there in a few weeks. When Henley arrived, the Nomlakis agreed to help construct the reservation in return for protection from slave raiders who, Henley reported, "infested this portion of the country stealing Indian children to be sold as servants." The children were sold as orphans, but the truth was "that the parents had been murdered before the children could be captured." The Nomlakis immediately set up their ranchería on the proposed reserve and started gathering seed and acorns for the winter. They were quite content to gather their own food if only they were protected from slave raiders.[38]

Subsequently Henley went to Nevada County to talk to the Nisenans about going to the Nomlaki reserve. Apparently the Sebastian delegation's experience had not been positive, because the Nisenans refused to go. Much as they had before, the Nisenans merely agreed to send to the new reservation a "deputation of three from each tribe, about thirty in all," to help put up the agency buildings and plant crops. Henley reported that "Mr. S. P. Storms who speaks their language well and has resided among them since 1849 has been appointed Special Agent and will accompany the delegation above alluded to, to the reserve." Henley was surprised to find white opposition to removing Nevada County Indians, some of whom worked for whites, but added that "the force of public sentiment which is very strong on the other side will soon silence all opposition."[39]

Indeed, Henley's plan for removal of native people met with the approbation of many influential citizens of the state. After he talked with California's congressional delegation, senators John B. Weller (Frémont's successor) and William M. Gwin recommended Henley for personal loans amounting to fifteen thousand dollars in order to implement the removal policy immediately. Government agents had disappointed the Indians so often with false promises, California's congressmen declared, that if something were not done soon the native people would "have to be removed from the White Settlements by force."[40]

Early in December Henley reported that construction was well under way at Nomlaki. "Comfortable quarters for the season have been

38. Henley to Manypenny, Sept. 29, 1854, M234:33; and Henley to Manypenny, Oct. 15, 1854, M234:33.
39. Henley to Manypenny, Oct. 14, 1854, M234:33.
40. Henley to Manypenny, Oct. 16, 1854, M234:33.

erected," he wrote, "consisting of a frame building two stories high, thirty feet by twenty with a kitchen, a frame for a store house and commissary's quarters for the Indians who labor, and a comfortable stable with other small buildings for the chiefs." The Indians also had "erected their own huts" and were industriously "gathering acorns, grass seeds, and wild oats for their winter's provisions." Henley estimated that they had enough food to last two months. When their supply was exhausted, he would give each Indian three pounds of wheat or barley per day. According to Henley's figures, the cost of this ration would be only five to nine cents. "Although a very scant allowance," Henley admitted, it would be "quite enough and is more and better food than they have heretofore been accustomed to." He intended to give the Indians no meat, "so that for the article of beef which heretofore in the Indian Department in this state has cost more than everything else, the expense will be merely nominal." He had purchased two beef cattle, but "they were for the use of the white men."[41]

Thirty Nisenan "working hands" were with special agent Storms in a valley separate from the Nomlakis. The Nisenans had no provisions for the winter and so subsisted entirely on the meagre ration of grain that Henley allowed them. Despite the Indians' privation, Henley and Storms were satisfied with the work of the Nisenans, for "most of them were accustomed to labor before they came here."[42]

Early in 1855 Henley reported that twelve hundred Indians had been relocated at the Nomlaki reserve and had planted four hundred acres of grain. Soon the land under cultivation would be increased to one thousand acres. Henley concluded that the Indians were "highly pleased" with the "prospects of something substantial being done for them," and he anticipated no difficulty in bringing more native people to the reserve.[43]

Preparations for the arrival of the rest of the Nisenans continued through the summer of 1855, but no more Nevada County Indians appeared at Nomlaki. On July 16 several Nisenans ran away from the reserve, very likely returning to Nevada County to give an unfavorable account of life at Nomlaki. On August 22 the Nisenan Francisco arrived at Nomlaki to report the decision of the Indians in Nevada County on the proposed move to the reservation. Only Weimah would come to Nomlaki.[44]

Henley refused to accept the Nisenans' decision to remain in their

41. Henley to Manypenny, Dec. 8, 1854, M234:34.
42. Ibid.
43. Henley to Manypenny, Jan. 15, 1855, M234:34.
44. Henley to Manypenny, Sept. 19, 1855, M234:34.

homeland. Besides, the sentiments of Nevada County whites had changed in favor of removal, so in November he took reservation troops to Grass Valley to force the Indians to Nomlaki. Without enough wagons to take all the Nisenans, Henley took 150 of the "worst characters," leaving "none but those who would be industrious and peaceable." He contended that the Indians he selected were "in the habit of robbing and killing Chinese, and stealing from the cabins of miners." The remainder he left in the charge of Mr. L. Bouyer, a local rancher, with the understanding that they would be removed the following spring. Henley instructed Bouyer to protect the Indians from "abuse and ill-treatment" and to prevent them from "committing depredations upon the property of settlers." Bouyer was to see that Nisenan labor contracts were "properly enforced, so that they may not be defrauded out of the proceeds of their labor." Indians were permitted to reside at places for the purposes of fishing or gathering food; but if they became "troublesome or annoying" to whites, Bouyer was expected "to cause them immediately to be removed to his ranch." On November 1 Storms delivered 120 Nisenans to the agent in charge of Nomlaki reserve, thirty fewer than he started with, but he did not record whether they had died or escaped en route.[45]

The development of the temporary reservation system, culminating in the forced removal of Indians, marked a functional reconciliation of state and federal policies in California. Although the state and federal governments were never in perfect accord over Indian affairs, the state's needs were served by temporary federal reserves where Indians who were not amenable to local needs could be relocated. Over the next decade not only federal troops but state militia forced Indians onto nine temporary reserves in the northern part of the state. However, most Indians remained outside the reservation system, where they were subject to the indenture law. In 1860, while the northern wars were at their height, this law was amended to allow the indenture of prisoners of war and extended terms of service. Federal troops guarded Indian prisoners brought in by the militia and escorted them to reservations, an arrangement approved by the Indian superintendent. The northern Indian wars were carried on by Federal troops during the Civil War, when many of California's sixteen thousand volunteers were posted to the north for several years. By the end of the war Federal soldiers had subdued the region.[46]

45. Henley to Manypenny, Nov. 3, 1855, M234:34; and Henley to Manypenny, Nov. 15, 1855, M234:34.

46. See, for example, William C. Kibbe to John B. Weller, Nov. 29, 1859, IWP; and Kibbe to Weller, [Spring] 1859, IWP.

Indians on reservations received thin protection. Marauding whites killed and kidnapped Indians, stole stock, and harassed whites who tried to intervene. Henley, who abused his position by making Indians work on his land, was dismissed in 1859 for malfeasance and misapplication of funds. During the Civil War, President Lincoln appointed Edward Beale U.S. Surveyor General for California, a post that the former superintendent used to acquire title to Rancho El Tejon, the Mexican land grant that encompassed Sebastian reserve. He rented the reserve to the government for one thousand dollars per year until 1864, when the reservation finally moved to Tule River. Disastrously administered and shot through with corruption, the temporary reservations turned out to be a public burden. In 1860 Congress abolished the California superintendency and organized two districts, and the Indian Department systematically closed most of the reserves. The state superintendency was reestablished in 1864, but by 1869 only the Tule River, Round Valley, and Hoopa Valley reservations remained open. In 1860 the Indian commissioner directed a new agent in charge of the northern district to economize by making "suitable arrangements with the farmers and tradesmen" for Indian employment, and to keep only unemployable Indians on the reserves. There they were expected to "engage in daily labor" to "curtail the expenses of the service," or they would be left to "the control of the State, or subject to the mercy or charity of the white citizens."[47]

Most California Indians had long since been abandoned to the designs of local interests. At points of state and federal friction, Indian problems were resolved in favor of the state. Begun in 1846, the pattern of conciliating local interests continued through the 1860s, even as local conditions changed. The majority of Indians had to survive outside reservations and beyond the reach of any shadow of federal protection.

47. Carranco and Beard, *Genocide and Vendetta*, 60–61, 101–56; Thompson, *Edward F. Beale*, 137–55; A. B. Greenwood to John A. Driebelbis, July 30, 1860, in *Annual Report of the Commissioner of Indian Affairs, 1860*, Sen. Ex. Doc. 1, 36th Cong., 2d sess., ser. 1078, 455–56.

8

Indian Labor and
Population in the 1850s

When opponents of the 1851 treaties declared that Indians were already in "the best school of civilization," they assumed that employment in the white economy had intrinsic value beyond the pecuniary benefits that it provided. Indians who worked for whites were surely on their way up the ladder of civilization, or at least on the bottom rung, far above native people who remained in a "savage" condition. That whites benefited from Indian labor was well understood and nobody questioned the right of an employer to profit from the work of his employees, regardless of their race. The civilizing effects of an honest day's labor were highly regarded on the temporary reservations as well as on private farms. It was a happy coincidence that native labor would make the reservations self-sustaining. At first, the reserve system seemed to promise the best of all possible worlds: while permitting Indian workers to remain on white farms, it would remove troublesome natives to places where hard work would redeem them with little or no expense to the taxpayers.[1]

To bureaucrats, humanitarians, ranchers, and perhaps even the Indians themselves, labor on and off the reservation seemed to be the only certain way for native people to survive in the 1850s. Surely, Indians who adapted so readily to the changes of previous decades would prove flexible enough to meet the new requirements of California Indian life. In looking back on those turbulent years, it is tempting to view peaceful labor as preferable to the pervasive violence that was a growing cause of Indian population decline. Warfare killed untold numbers of Indians and drove thousands into marginally productive environments where malnutrition, starvation, and disease took a further toll. In view of this grim reality, reservations and ranchos seem to have been relatively benign institutions which, if properly managed, could have helped In-

1. In these respects the reservation was not a unique institution in nineteenth-century America. See David J. Rothman, *The Discovery of the Asylum: Social Order and Disorder in the New Republic* (Boston, 1971); and Takaki, *Iron Cages*, 181–88 and passim.

dians to survive in the 1850s. As it turned out, they were peculiarly ill suited for this purpose, regardless of what whites said at the time.

Reservation Promises and Reality

Contemporary observers seemed unable to understand why reservations failed to live up to the extravagant claims of Beale and his supporters. Failures were almost always portrayed as the result of corruption rather than any fundamental unsoundness of design. Typically, the 1858 reports of special agent J. Ross Browne showed corruption and mismanagement at all levels in the California superintendency, as indeed there were. He claimed, however, that the reservation system should not be pronounced a failure since it had not been given a fair trial. Properly managed by honest men, Browne believed, the temporary reserves could work.[2]

The Office of Indian Affairs was shocked at Browne's reports. To get a second opinion, its administrators sent special agent G. Bailey to California. Bailey confirmed Browne's charges, but decided that there was something wrong with the theory behind the institution. Referring to Nome Lackee, he wrote: "The Government provides a magnificent farm of 25,000 acres in one of the finest grain countries in the world, and stocks it at lavish expense: $17,160 are annually expended in salaries of overseers &c; $32,427 87/100 more are applied to the purchase of clothing, provisions and supplies of every description: an unlimited supply of Indian labor is furnished, and finally a net result is attaining of 11,950 bushels of grain." The system, wrote Bailey, did not "look beyond the mere feeding and clothing of Indians." Consequently, "there was no gain in the way of civilization to go to the credit side of the account," as Beale's plan had originally envisioned. Instead of self-supporting government farms operated by Indians who gained civilized habits, Bailey explained, the reservations were "simply Government Almshouses where an inconsiderable number of Indians are insufficiently fed and scantily clothed, at an expense wholly disproportionate to the benefits conferred." An average of only forty men were actually employed in farming, a tiny fraction of the total Nome Lackee population, which was estimated at twenty-five hundred. Since the produce of the farm could not feed all of them, almost two thousand were off "gathering berries, grass seed &c." About a half dozen Nevada County

2. J. Ross Browne, "Letter on the Condition of Indian Reservations in California," M234:35.

Nisenan girls were employed making straw hats, "but the great mass of the Indians appeared to have no occupation whatever."[3]

Bailey did not doubt that Indians could be employed successfully in farming. He had seen three hundred Indians living on the Lupillomi ranch near Clear Lake. Some of them were "capital vaqueros" for the rancher, while the rest of the men hired out to Napa and Sonoma county farmers at planting and harvest time. The rancher had given them several fields which they cultivated for their own benefit. In addition, they fished in the lake. With this combination of resources available to them, Bailey declared, these Clear Lake Indians were "the only really prosperous and happy ones I saw in California." Their relationship with the rancher was based on reciprocity: they worked for him; he protected and provided for them. "Can the Government vicariously establish such relations with the Indians?" Bailey wondered. He left the solution for "abler heads," but hinted that the government could not emulate the successful rancher. It simply was not "in the nature of things that one should work for another as he would for himself, and it was not to be expected that a salaried supervisor of a farm should manage it as profitably as the owner of it." The "radical defect of Mr. Beale's plan" was that Indian agents lacked the self-interest that economical ranchers possessed.[4]

Bailey described some of the elements of the Indian labor problem, but he did not quite grasp their full significance. He felt that Indians should never be permitted to leave the reserve, where they "should be kept constantly occupied." But what would two thousand Indians do? If forty men provided all the needed agricultural labor at Nome Lackee, even doubling or quadrupling the labor requirement would not have employed 10 percent of the males. When New Helvetia was at its height, several hundred Indians were employed during the harvest, but wage labor was not their sole source of support. They continued to rely on hunting and gathering while incorporating New Helvetia into their seasonal routine. To keep a large number of Indians "constantly occupied" with nontraditional tasks at a reserve, native people would have to abandon subsistence pursuits that whites defined as wasteful or retrograde, but which provided sustenance that reservation Indians continued to rely on. Perhaps without fully realizing it, bureaucrats expected Indians to exchange a meagre sufficiency for unemployment and less food.[5]

Reservation administrators soon learned that agricultural production alone would not support the Indians. In the summer of 1856 Superintendent Henley faced a small congressional appropriation and food

3. G. Bailey to C. E. Mix, Nov. 4, 1858, M234:36.
4. Ibid.
5. Ibid.

shortages caused by the drought of the previous year. Consequently he ordered the agents at Klamath, Tejon, Nome Lackee, and the Fresno River Farm to send out the Indians to gather wild food. Old men and women should be kept "constantly in the fields and woods, collecting such articles of food as can be procured," thus reducing "the issues from the products of the farm." The agents' reports commonly included estimates of the amount of natural food on hand. Grass seed, acorns, and salmon continued to be a substantial part of the Indian diet, and they were often procured off the reserves. Yokuts at the Fresno River Farm hunted wild horses to supplement their diet. At the same time, reservation Indians mined gold and worked for white ranchers.[6]

The Yuroks on the Klamath reserve preferred to feed themselves exclusively by hunting and gathering. Traditional subsistence patterns adequately fed the Yuroks, but frustrated the agent who regretted in 1856 that they had only cultivated thirty-six acres of potatoes. The Yuroks' "indisposition" to work he attributed to ignorance of the government policy and the Indians' natural pride and independence. They turned a deaf ear to the agent's arguments in favor of agriculture, saying that if the whites would leave them alone they could live as had their forefathers. During the 1850s Klamath agency labor reports showed that few Indians did any agricultural work. Perhaps the Yuroks made a wise decision. Farming the narrow benches along the Klamath River beneath the steep canyon walls seemed a precarious way to make a living. A single flood could wipe out a year's work. For these Indians, a conservative reliance on tried and true methods seemed best.[7]

Nonreservation Indians sometimes went to reserves to work. Tulare Lake Yokuts gleaned the Tejon fields; Yokuts and Tubatulabals from the San Joaquin, Kern, and Kings rivers helped with the harvests at the Fresno and Kings River farms. Indians from Tuolumne and Mariposa counties lived part of the year on reservations and spent the rest of their time in their homelands. In the winter of 1857, the Monache Indians came down from the mountains to ask the Fresno subagent for blankets and clothing. Although he sent them away disappointed, their arrival

6. Henley to James A. Patterson, June 14, 1857, M234:35; Henley to J. R. Vineyard, Aug. 7, 1857, M234:35; Henley to E. A. Stevenson, Aug. 7, 1857, M234:35; Henley to M. B. Lewis, Aug. 7, 1857, M234:35; Thomas P. Madden to Henley, June 22, 1857, M234:35; Lewis to Henley, Oct. 3, Oct 25 and Nov. 14, 1857, M234:35; Lewis to Henley, Nov. 15, 1858, M234:36; "Klamath Reserve Daily Report of Labor," Dec. 1, 1855, and Jan. 8, 1856, M234:35; and W. Wilby and S. Brooks to Lewis, Feb. 22, 1856, M234:35.

7. H. P. Heintzelman to T. J. Henley, July 13, 1857, in *Annual Report of the Commissioner of Indian Affairs*, 1857, Sen. Ex. Doc. 1, 35th Cong., 1st sess., ser. 919, 679; Klamath Indian "Reservation Labor Reports," Aug. 9–15, 1857, M234:35; Apr. 18–24, 1858, M234:36; and Oct. 2–8, 1859, M234:37.

shows that they were aware of the agency as a potential source of provisions.[8]

While many Indians were willing to work at reservations on a seasonal basis, most wanted to live in their traditional territory. Even if they had wanted to go to reservations, there would not have been enough food to support them. The predicament of the Kings River Indians shows how unexpected arrivals strained the Fresno River Farm, the least successful agricultural operation in the whole system. After several crop failures and short harvests, subagent M. B. Lewis dismissed it as an unlucky place. In 1858 drought ruined much of the Fresno farm's produce and sharply reduced forage and the hay crop in the southern San Joaquin area. The Wimilchi and Nutúnutnu Yokuts living near Tulare Lake were competing with the whites' cattle and pigs for scarce grass seed and acorns. Settlers, claiming that the Yokuts had killed some of their stock, forced about 250 Indians to move to the Fresno farm at gunpoint. Most of these refugees were women and children, for the men had retreated to the tules to hide out with the Tachis. From this haven the dispossessed tribesmen swore vengeance on the whites who had driven away their families. Lewis managed to persuade the Wimilchis and Nutúnutnus to go to the farm, but the Tachis refused to come out of the tules, saying that they preferred to die of hunger and cold with their friends and relatives. At the farm there was nothing to feed the new arrivals, so Lewis sent them off to the San Joaquin River to fish and dispatched teamsters to the Kings River to recover the Yokuts' acorn cache. Finally, the subagent had to purchase provisions to keep the Indians from starving to death.[9]

By the late 1850s the relationship of the Indians to the reservations had been turned on its head. To feed the Indian inmates, the agents had to rely on hunting and gathering. Independent natives used the reserves as part of their seasonal round, a situation hardly describable as the school of civilization that bureaucrats and politicians had envisioned. Instead of receiving security, food, and modern means of subsistence, the Indians subsidized the reservations with traditional food gathering.

8. M. B. Lewis to T. J. Henley, Jan. 4, 1858, M234:36; P. T. Herbert to Henley, Dec. 1, 1858, M234:37; T. P. Madden to Henley, June 22, 1857; and Lewis to Henley, Dec. 13, 1856, M234:35.

9. M. B. Lewis to T. J. Henley, May 8, 1858, M234:36; Lewis to Mr. Whitmore, Nov. 11, 1858, M234:36; Lewis to Henley, Nov. 14, 1858, M234:36; Justin Esney, W. G. McKinney, A. McNut, B. J. Hickel, and W. A. Tull to Lewis, Nov. 14, 1858, M234:36; Lewis to Henley, Nov. 15, 1858, M234:36; Lewis to Henley, Dec. 27, 1858, M234:37; Lewis to Henley, Jan. 8, 1859, M234:37; Lewis to J. Ross Browne, Feb. 28, 1859, M234:37; Lewis to Henley, Jan. 15, 1859, M234:37; Lewis to Henley, Dec. 31, 1858, M234:37.

Indians and the Market Economy

Most Indians lived off the reservations, preferring to survive in the midst of a white society. As we have seen, their experiences varied considerably: some entered the school of civilization by way of the indenture system; others were free laborers. The 1852 state census offers some insights into the world of working Indians during this troublesome time. Although incomplete and inconsistent, the census is the only comprehensive survey of the Indian population for its time. Since only "domesticated Indians" were enumerated, the manuscript census illuminated the lives of potential Indian workers. Unlike the federal census, the state document did not include individual household information. The census taker merely listed the name, age, sex, occupation, race, previous residence, and birthplace of people as he found them; but often much of this data was omitted for Indians. In most counties the census takers took down the name, age, and sex of each Indian, but seldom listed occupations. Nor did enumerators identify which—if any— Indians were indentured. Fortunately, entries for the Indians' white neighbors were usually complete, and by looking at the nearest white neighbors of the enumerated Indians and the size of the bracketed communities, we can reconstruct part of the Indian world.[10]

Table 8.1 identifies white neighbors on both sides of the Indians as miners, farmers, or "others." The statistics are broken down by the total number of Indians in each category, the number of places where Indians were found, the number of Indians in the smallest and largest communities, and the arithmetical mean size of Indian communities. Analysis of selected agricultural and mining counties shows that with few exceptions the largest Indian communities lived between miners or "others," while those who lived among farmers were in smaller groups. Evidently agricultural counties were less conducive to maintaining sizable Indian communities than were mining areas, which presumably provided fewer opportunities for Indian labor.

In Calaveras County all the enumerated Indians lived among miners, and a few Indians were identified as miners themselves (see map 4). Observers reported that gold mining was a substantial part of the the Miwok economy in Calaveras County until the placer deposits dwindled in 1854. Until then the Indians kept "tolerably comfortable" by traditional food gathering, using gold to purchase clothing, beef, bread, beans, and rice. Traders sometimes cheated the Miwoks out of their gold with liquor, and Indian drunkenness led to fights with whites and

10. Dennis Harris, "The California Census of 1852," 59–64.

TABLE 8.1. *Neighbors and Community Size of Domesticated Indians in 1852*

White neighbors (by occupation)	Total number of Indians	Number of Indian communities	Population range	Average size of Indian communities
Calaveras County				
Miner/Miner	1,623	23	1–1,160	70.6
Miner/Farmer	200	1	—	200.0
Miner/Other	24	7	2–6	3.4
Farmer/Farmer	0	—	—	—
Farmer/Other	0	—	—	—
Other/Other	0	—	—	—
Subtotal	1,847	31	1–1,160	59.6
San Joaquin County				
Miner/Miner	0	—	—	—
Miner/Farmer	0	—	—	—
Miner/Other	0	—	—	—
Farmer/Farmer	15	1	—	15.0
Farmer/Other	1	1	—	1.0
Other/Other	363	7	1–265	51.9
Subtotal	379	9	1–265	42.1
Sutter County				
Miner/Miner	0	—	—	—
Miner/Farmer	0	—	—.	—
Miner/Other	0	—	—	—
Farmer/Farmer	96	2	31–65	48.0
Farmer/Other	0	—	—	—
Other/Other	422	4	63–210	105.5
Subtotal	518	6	31–210	86.3
Yolo County				
Miner/Miner	0	—	—	—
Miner/Farmer	0	—	—	—
Miner/Other	0	—	—	—
Farmer/Farmer	30	8	1–9	3.8
Farmer/Other	104	5	6–62	20.8
Other/Other	15	2	1–14	7.5
Subtotal	149	15	1–62	9.9
Yuba County				
Miner/Miner	85	3	1–83	28.3
Miner/Farmer	0	—	—	—
Miner/Other	0	—	—	—
Farmer/Farmer	10	4	2–3	2.5
Farmer/Other	12	4	1–5	3.0
Other/Other	9	3	2–3	3.0
Subtotal	116	14	1–83	8.3

Continued on next page

TABLE 8.1.   (*continued*)

White neighbors (by occupation)	Total number of Indians	Number of Indian communities	Population range	Average size of Indian communities
Tulare County				
Miner/Miner	0	—	—	—
Miner/Farmer	0	—	—	—
Miner/Other	0	—	—	—
Farmer/Farmer	0	—	—	—
Farmer/Other	0	—	—	—
Other/Other	8,400	14	200–1,900	600.0
Subtotal	8,400	14	200–1,900	600.0
Shasta County				
Miner/Miner	41	3	1–25	13.7
Miner/Farmer	0	—	—	—
Miner/Other	5	3	1–3	1.7
Farmer/Farmer	0	—	—	—
Farmer/Other	38	4	1–30	9.5
Other/Other	3	3	1–1	1.0
Subtotal	87	13	1–30	6.7
Siskiyou County				
Miner/Miner	20	7	1–5	2.9
Miner/Farmer	0	—	—	—
Miner/Other	2	2	1–1	1.0
Farmer/Farmer	0	—	—	—
Farmer/Other	0	—	—	—
Other/Other	0	—	—	—
Subtotal	22	9	1–5	2.4

Source: 1852 California Special Census, California State Archives.

other Indians. In 1856 W. F. McDermott, a Calaveras County resident, reckoned that since 1850 the Miwok population had been reduced by about 60 percent. The causes, he believed, were cold winters, alcohol, and murder. By 1856 the fish were almost gone, game had become scarce, and even acorns were hard to come by. In 1858 a dozen or more bands remained, with forty to one hundred members each, but because they moved often, the special agent who described them found it difficult to ascertain their numbers. Frequently the rancherías split up because of dissatisfaction with their old chiefs, the malcontents uniting to form new communities or join other groups. The 1852 census probably illuminated this process, as it enumerated one very large community with over one thousand members and about twenty much smaller rancherías

in the county. The declining resource base on which the Miwoks depended no doubt exacerbated Indian social ferment.[11]

Statistics on age and sex ratios (table 8.2) provide one of the
most important indicators of Indian demographic health. Unfortunately, 1852 census takers were inconsistent in recording these vital
statistics. Some enumerators gave the age and sex of each Indian,
while others merely provided the estimated number who were older
or younger than twenty-one. The number of fertile women is of primary significance in understanding a population's reproductive potential. Where given, the female age cohort 15–39 approximates the
number of fertile women in the sample counties. The sex ratio indicates the number of men per one hundred women in each county.
Since the sex ratio is based on the whole population without regard
to age, it does not necessarily correspond with immediate reproductive potential. Like most other counties in 1852, Calaveras had a
shortage of Indian women, who were outnumbered by men by
nearly three to one. The few recorded females indicate that women
of childbearing age were rare, a demographic fact that did not bode
well for Miwok reproductive potential. The scarcity of children was
a result of declining birthrates that plagued Indian society.

The two counties in the northern mining district, Shasta and Siskiyou,
had very few enumerated Indians because of the frequent wars. The
recorded majority of Shasta County Indians had miners for neighbors,
and all except for one laborer were identified as servants. Apart from
two communities of twenty-five and thirty Indians each, the Indian servants lived in groups of one to three. The largest community lived with
Pierson B. Reading, who was identified as a farmer. His servants may
have mined for him in 1848 and probably worked on his Rancho Buenaventura, much as they had worked for Sutter and other Anglo rancheros
in the 1840s. In any case, Reading's Indians were an exceptional minority
in Shasta County, where most of the enumerated Indians lived near
miners or others.[12]

In neighboring Siskiyou County the manuscript census showed that
nearly all enumerated Indians were miners, but only nine were from
California. The rest of the Indian miners had come from Oregon, but
it is not known if they came voluntarily or under duress. It seems plausible, however, that the Oregonians emigrated of their own volition,

11. 1852 MS Census, Calaveras County; *Annual Report of the Commissioner of Indian
Affairs*, 1856, Sen. Ex. Doc. 1, 34th Cong., 2d sess., ser. 875, 792; Alex H. Putney to
T. J. Henley, Nov. 4, 1857, M234:35, Sept. 30, 1858, M234:37.

12. 1852 MS Census, Shasta County. By 1854, Oregon Indians spread the news of the
California Indian situation to Yakima and other tribes; see Miller, *Prophetic Worlds*, 111.

TABLE 8.2.   *Ages and Sex Ratios for Indians in Selected California Counties in 1852*

	Over 21	Under 21	60+	40–59	15–39	6–14	0–5	Total
Calaveras County: 297.2 males per 100 females								
Male	1,150	180	0	4	40	4	1	1,379
Female	321	124	0	1	18	0	0	464
TOTAL	1,471	304	0	5	58	4	1	1,843
San Joaquin County: not applicable								
Male	—	—	0	3	5	6	2	—
Female	—	—	0	1	2	1	0	—
TOTAL	118	190	0	4	7	7	2	328
Sutter County: 103.2 males per 100 females								
Male	—	—	—	—	—	—	—	258
Female	—	—	—	—	—	—	—	250
TOTAL	411	97	—	—	—	—	—	508
Yuba County: 2,180 males per 100 females								
Male	77	3	0	0	25	4	0	109
Female	0	0	0	0	4	0	1	5
TOTAL	77	3	0	0	29	4	1	114
Tulare County: 223.1 males per 100 females								
Male	—	—	—	—	—	—	—	5,800
Female	—	—	—	—	—	—	—	2,600
TOTAL	3,787	4,613	—	—	—	—	—	8,400
Shasta County: 204.2 males per 100 females								
Male	—	—	1	14	12	2	0	49[a]
Female	—	—	0	0	9	8	2	24[b]
TOTAL	—	—	1	14	21	10	2	73
Siskiyou county: 633.3 males per 100 females								
Male	—	—	0	1	11	7	0	19
Female	—	—	0	0	2	0	1	3
TOTAL	—	—	0	1	13	7	1	22

Source: 1852 California Special Census, California State Archives.

Note: This table is based on two kinds of figures. Some census takers noted the exact age and sex of each Indian; othes merely estimated those who were older or younger than 21.

[a]This number includes twenty males whose ages were not given.
[b]This number includes five females whose ages were not given.

following the route that Elijah and Pio-pio-mox-mox had pioneered a decade before. With California Indians hiding out to elude white soldiers, a few adventurous Oregon Indians may have thought Siskiyou County a good place to find employment in the mines.[13]

In both Shasta and Siskiyou counties, the census showed from two to six males for every female, and women of childbearing age were seldom seen. Violent conditions in the northern counties may have caused some Indian women to hide out with rebellious tribes, while others may have become victims of white kidnappers, as will be seen in the following chapter. Women had few good reasons to remain in contact with northern whites, and the limited opportunities to work in the northern mines favored Indian men. It was clear in 1852 that the prospects for Indian reproduction were not good among whites in the northern reaches of the state.

Before the gold rush most working Indians were employed in agriculture, yet the 1852 census enumerated comparatively few Indians in the interior agricultural counties. Sutter County, with more than five hundred, had the largest Indian population in the Sacramento Valley, but less than a fifth were definitely located adjacent to white farms. The rest were at the west end of Yuba City, at the mouth and along the banks of the Feather River, and across the Sacramento River opposite Colusa. Not surprisingly, sixty-five Indian people lived on John Sutter's Hock Farm and thirty-one resided on the ranch of Nicholaus Allgeier, a former Hudson's Bay man who had worked for Sutter in the 1840s. Regardless of their location, many of these Indians no doubt worked for white farmers part of the year, using Sutter and other ranchers as part of their seasonal round. The male and female populations were nearly equal, but since ages were not recorded it is impossible from these statistics to speculate on the Indians' reproductive potential.[14]

Continued agricultural work did not necessarily enhance Indian opportunities for survival. In 1856 John Sutter explained the deteriorating condition of Sutter County's Indians in a letter to Superintendent Henley. At Nicolaus there were only 15 Ollash Nisenans, down from 52 in 1846 (see table 3.2). In 1856 the Yukulme Nisenans, three miles down the Feather River from Sutter's Hock Farm, were "nearly extinct" and combined with the Hock Nisenans to form a community of 35, compared to 101 a decade earlier. About three miles up the Feather River from Hock Farm the diminishing Sisums had united with the Yubu Nisenans, rowdy Indians who Sutter thought were leading the other tribes astray

13. 1852 MS Census, Siskiyou County.
14. 1852 MS Census, Sutter County.

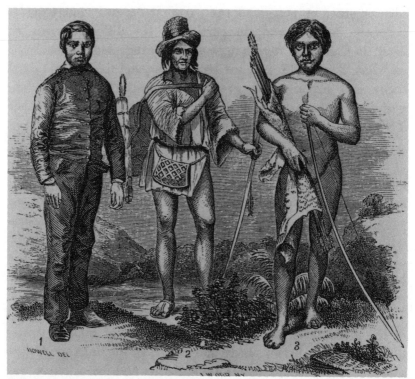

FIG. 10. Wahla, Chief of the Yuba Tribe. Nattily dressed Wahla is the only Indian identified in this composite picture, based on daguerreotypes. Wahla worked for Samuel Brannan, one of California's wealthiest men, and later became Governor Milton S. Latham's coachman. Latham educated Wahla and thought so highly of him that he commissioned Charles Nahl to paint a magnificent portrait of the Nisenan man that now hangs in the M. H. DeYoung Museum in San Francisco. Led by a man of apparent skill, it is no wonder that the Yuba Indians were independent and gave John Sutter trouble. From Frank Soulé, John H. Gihon, and James Nisbett, *The Annals of San Francisco* (New York, 1855).

(see fig. 10). They would drink and gamble all night, then go into the towns to amuse themselves during the day. Drinking in their rancherías led to frequent fights over women. Because "not all of them have Women," Sutter explained, competition for females was intense and sometimes ended in murder, as in the 1854 case of a Yukulme man who wanted to marry the widow of an Ollash chief. When she refused him, he shot and stabbed her to death, then eluded Sutter's attempt to capture him. Assaults on Nisenan women were common, according to Sutter, when the Indians were drinking.[15]

15. Sutter to Henley, Feb. 9, 1856, M234:35.

Another aggravating problem that concerned Sutter was that Indians refused to work for less than one dollar a day. Consequently, he preferred to hire white men who received slightly higher wages but ate less than Indians and were more reliable. Indians would work for a week, then rest for another, Sutter explained, taking their wages to Marysville to buy "bad Rhum and Whiskey and get Drunk and disorderly." Formerly Sutter had paid the Indians with "clothing and provisions," but in 1856 "nothing as the Dollars bring them to work."[16]

In towns, Sutter continued, the Indians did a little domestic work, fetching water and chopping wood. Nisenan men, some of whom had firearms, still hunted and fished when they could, but sold their game to whites for money and whiskey. Likewise, they sold their bows and arrows and other "curiosities" to buy bad liquor. Nisenans may have decided that bow hunting was archaic after they had acquired guns. Besides, not all traditional food gathering techniques were still permitted. Sutter complained that some settlers would not let Nisenan women gather acorns or grass seed, which were formerly staples of the Indian diet. With only men's work to supply the Indians, and with much of the men's earnings going for liquor, Sutter feared that the Nisenans would steal from his fields, orchards, and vineyards. Exasperated, Sutter asked Henley to remove the Indians, "or if you would give me the control *only of the* Hock & Yukulme Indians, I would make them work and pay them a reasonable Compensation, in food and Clothing."[17]

Henley acceded to Sutter's request, removed the troublemaking Yubu Nisenans, and appointed Sutter a special Indian agent; but first he went to Marysville and threatened to remove all of the Nisenans. Subsequently, the Hock, Yukulme, Sisum, and Ollash Indians went to Sutter and asked to remain in their native land, promising to work obediently and stay out of the towns. Sutter set aside a wheat field in front of their ranchería and agreed to plow and sow it for them. They would harvest the crop themselves, using Sutter's old reaping hooks. And they promised to work for Sutter "at reasonable prices . . . in clothing and provisions and not in money." Henley approved Sutter's request for some seed wheat to get them started, even though it did not conform to the policy of supporting Indians only on reservations. He justified the exception because of Sutter's standing as an old pioneer and his reputation for generosity and friendship to the Indians. He had no doubt that Sutter would be a faithful guardian of the Indians, many of whom,

16. Ibid.
17. Ibid.

Henley noted, had fought on the American side during the Mexican War.[18]

The Sutter County Nisenan rancherías were combining with one another to offset population losses in the 1850s, but the Indians also showed a remarkable independence, refusing to work for low wages and insisting on cash until forced to do otherwise. Even though Sutter had formerly bartered trade goods for Indian labor, the Nisenans' long association with him prepared them for the new cash economy that followed in the wake of the gold rush. Tragically, their fondness for liquor made alcohol the chief object of Indian cash purchases, at least according to Sutter. At the same time, alcohol and the scarcity of women strained the social conventions that governed sexuality and marriage. Sutter's complaints were no doubt a self-serving attempt to reclaim authority over the Indian labor force on terms that he had established in the 1840s. Yet, in order to keep the Nisenans on his property, he had to provide wheat fields for them. As we have seen, this special arrangement made it possible for whole communities of Indians to be supported. Once again, a variety of resources had to be available to Indian communities because they could not survive solely on agricultural employment.

Ironically, the evolution of Sutter's association with the Nisenans shows that in some ways the Indians had coped better with the turbulent 1850s than had Sutter. They readily accepted the cash economy, though they hardly thrived as a result. It was Sutter who resented the modern intrusion of free, waged labor in the agricultural economy. Caught up in a world that he had helped to create, he harked back to a simpler time when coercion and barter secured plenty of Indian workers. Desperately attempting to reclaim an aspect of the past that had served him well, Sutter appealed to federal authorities, who acquiesced to his requests much as they had to other local interests since 1846 (see fig. 11).

Nisenan competition for women probably indicated a deficit of fertile females, heralding future population decline, but demographic information is incomplete for Sutter County. Better data are available for Yolo County, an agricultural region west of the Sacramento River where most Indians had farmers for neighbors. The 1852 census listed a few as vaqueros, but occupations were not given for the greater number. Nevertheless, many of these people probably worked for their white neighbors in season. Among the Yolo Indians young males outnumbered women by more than two to one, emphasizing a historical pattern that

18. Henley to G. W. Manypenny, Dec. 4, 1856, M234:35; Henley to Sutter, Dec. 4, 1856, M234:35; and Sutter to Henley, Dec. 1, 1856, M234:35.

FIG. 11. View of an Indian Rachería, Yuba City, California. This Nisenan rancheria near John Sutter's Hock Farm, shown here in the 1850s, was probably similar to dozens of other Indian communities associated with Sutter in the 1840s. Traditional houses, granaries for storing acorns, and baskets were still in evidence, but shirts and dresses had replaced traditional garb. The men in this scene probably worked part of the time on Feather River ranches like Hock Farm.

had begun with Sutter: agricultural employment favored young, able-bodied males. In the 1850s there were few opportunities for Indian women on Anglo farms, and traditional women's work diminished as agriculture and mining encroached on former Indian territory. Agricultural counties were not hospitable places for traditional Indian communities and native women. Thus, farming regions discouraged family formation and were unfavorable for Indian biological reproduction.[19]

In the farming county of San Joaquin, incomplete data show age and sex ratios comparable to Yolo County's. Most of the Indians appeared to live in three rancherías on the Calaveras and Stanislaus rivers. The largest Indian community among the San Joaquin County farmers was that of Captain Truckee, a Northern Paiute who had come down from the Truckee River on the eastern slope of the Sierras. Truckee had always been friendly to white immigrants who traversed his country, and John C. Frémont had given him a letter that guaranteed Truckee safe passage among whites. He used his "rag friend" as a passport to California during the gold rush. In 1850 Truckee's six-year-old granddaughter, Sarah Winnemucca—who later had a stage career and promoted Indian welfare—accompanied the Paiutes to San Joaquin County.

19. 1852 MS Census, Yolo County.

On a previous trip Truckee had arranged to exchange Paiute labor for horses; Sarah, fearful of whites and badly frightened, was an unwilling companion. She thought of whites as cannibal owls who ate unruly children, an opinion that was not improved when some cowboys molested her older sister, Mary. However, after being nursed by a thoughtful white woman who had lost her own child, Sarah's view of whites changed for the better. Meanwhile, Paiute men applied themselves to various kinds of ranch work, tending livestock and running a ferry on the San Joaquin River. The women worked in the ranch kitchen. At the end of the season Truckee's band returned to Nevada with their new horses and guns that would help the Paiutes to hunt more efficiently, a necessity as increasing immigration scattered game and depleted the sparse grasses of the Humboldt River.[20]

In 1852 Truckee returned to the San Joaquin with fifteen companions. Apparently they comprised three families with eight children ranging from one to fourteen years of age. Sarah was not with them, but evidently her brothers Natchez and Tom were. The Northern Paiutes migrated to the valley by choice to tap a new source of food. Like the Oregon Indians, Truckee's band regarded California as a land of opportunity during the gold rush, despite the evident perils in the San Joaquin Valley. Likewise, Truckee's people were exceptional because they were able to find opportunities among whites in a far country. Local enumerated Miwoks lived in small rancherías that were associated with the ferries on the Calaveras, Mokelumne, and Stanislaus rivers and no doubt worked at agricultural jobs in season. Enumerators neglected to record sexual data for the Miwoks, but they doubtless displayed the same disparities that marked other interior Indians.[21]

Farther south in the same valley Yokuts Indians lived under far different conditions than the Paiutes and Miwoks near Stockton. Tulare County had a unique population structure among California's enumerated interior tribes in 1852: it was the only region where large communities remained the basis of Indian social life. Regrettably, the data are incomplete, for the census enumerator merely estimated the aggregates of men and women in fourteen rancherías, which were listed separately from the white population. Despite its shortcomings, the census shows that, as usual, men outnumbered women by more than two to one, although some rancherías had more women than others. Like so many other native people, the Tulare County Indians survived by com-

20. Gae Whitney Canfield, *Sarah Winnemucca of the Northern Paiutes* (Norman, Okla., 1983), 6–9.

21. 1852 MS Census, San Joaquin County; and Jack D. Forbes, *Native Americans of California and Nevada* (Healdsburg, Calif., 1969), 50.

bining hunting, gathering, mining, and working for whites; but with nearly fifty Indians for every white in the county, the Yokuts' main advantage was in numbers that gave them a measure of security from wanton white attacks. Living in large communities permitted the Yokuts to control their own social lives more than Indians who were forced into smaller and smaller native settlements as a result of demographic losses and white pressure on local resources. Moreover, in 1852 the sparseness of white settlement left large areas open to Indian exploitation.[22]

Racism, Mechanization, and Declining Indian Opportunity

During the 1850s the school of civilization in California had a limited enrollment and many truants. On federal reserves, agricultural labor did not sweep away traditional subsistence patterns, but rather complemented them. As self-sufficient enterprises, the reservations became dependent not merely on Indian labor, but on traditional native provender as well. Furthermore, no reservation provided enough work to absorb the total Indian labor pool; unemployment and underemployment were the lots of most reservation Indians.

Outside the reserves, Indians found comparatively few employment opportunities. Even as early as 1852, at the height of the gold rush demand for food, surprisingly few Indians worked in seasonal agricultural occupations. Why were Indians, who had been the principal source of agricultural labor until the gold rush, so quickly displaced in the interior farming counties?

Part of the answer is found in the nature of the new white population that employed Indians. Bound by racist ideas and unfamiliar with Indian labor, whites were reluctant to rely on native workers. And, as Sutter pointed out, Indian labor was no longer all that was available; white workers were more efficient, especially when Indians insisted on cash for their services. Sutter's statement of Indian wages may have been a little high, since others reported that Indians received seventy-five cents per day. Low Indian wages could have been offset by the increased efficiency of more-expensive white laborers who, according to Indian Office employees, did twice as much work. Furthermore, some farmers who relied on Indian labor set aside fields to help support rancherías year around, a practice provided for in the Indian indenture law. Most

22. 1852 MS Census, Tulare County; and P. T. Herbert to T. J. Henley, Dec. 1, 1858, M234:37.

farmers were unwilling to exchange productive land for Indian labor, which is one reason why the 1852 census shows comparatively few Indians living among farmers.[23]

There were few incentives to hire Indians in the 1850s, and the best-informed sources advised white farmers to reduce their reliance on manual labor. In 1854 the *California Farmer and Journal of Useful Sciences* urged farmers to substitute machines for people. The reason was simple: when a machine could "at a smaller cost . . . do the work which you are now doing with human hands, buy the machine if you can; and if you have not the means get them as soon as possible." Farmers heeded the suggestion. Two years later Eliza Farnham described the proliferation of farm machinery. Where in 1852 there had been undeveloped land, she saw "continuous grain fields, of six or eight miles in length, with, perhaps, a dozen reapers, of the best patent, marching up and down, leveling the tall thick harvest." Some of the reapers were manufactured locally, but by the mid-fifties Cyrus McCormack and other eastern manufacturers were exporting their wares to the West Coast. Reapers, seed drills, mowers, and threshers mechanized California agriculture (see fig. 12). On the large farms horse-powered treadmills ran threshers, and by 1860 portable steam engines had made their appearance. According to a twentieth-century estimate, the horse-drawn reaper alone cut the labor requirement to about half that of hand harvesting. If, as Indian Office employees claimed, native harvesters using sickles were only half as efficient as whites, then a mechanical reaper could reduce the need for Indian labor by three quarters. Moreover, farm laborers were plentiful in California. In 1860 the federal census showed California with the highest ratio of farm laborers to farmers in the United States. Two farmers in the Golden State shared one farm worker, while in Illinois the ratio was three to one, and in Indiana, four to one. While Indian population declined precipitously in the 1850s, native labor became a marginal rather than a critical resource. There were too many hands for too few jobs and Indian labor had become a surplus commodity on the California market. Just as the California economy could not absorb numerous Indian workers, the stopgap temporary reservations were incapable of supporting the native inmates who were already enrolled, much less care for the thousands of dispossessed native migrants who needed assistance.[24]

23. J. Ross Browne and E. F. Beale to Luke Lea, Apr. 2, 1857, M234:34; T. J. Henley to Charles E. Mix, Nov. 19, 1858, M234:36; and Henley to G. W. Manypenny, Sept. 4, 1856, in *Annual Report, Commissioner of Indian Affairs*, 1856, Sen. Ex. Doc 1, 34th Cong., 2d sess., ser. 875, 789.

24. Eliza Farnham, *California, In-Doors and Out; or, How We Farm, Mine, and Live*

Fig. 12. Bringing in the Harvest. In the 1880s these Miwok Indians brought in John McFarland's wheat harvest using the kind of machinery that had become available in the 1850s. Agricultural mechanization threw Indians out of work and made them less important in the California economy.

Thus, the public and private institutions that were supposed to save the Indians from extermination managed to provide salvation for only a small minority, at a cost of fragmenting Indian society and exacerbating population decline. For insofar as jobs were available for Indians, whites usually hired young men for heavy seasonal work. Consequently, women and children were ordinarily left behind to shift for themselves, a perilous situation in the 1850s. By no means were women irrelevant to the Indian economy, for wherever possible they continued to gather wild food against the lean winter months. The chronic shortage of women virtually everywhere in the interior in 1852 was a serious problem that threatened Indian survival, just as the shrinking Indian resource base did. Although there were not enough jobs for native men in the California economy, there were too many tasks for women as fewer of them became responsible for providing food to native communities. In ad-

Generally in the Golden State (New York, 1856), vi; *California Farmer and Journal of Useful Sciences* 1 (June 15, 1854):189; Paul W. Gates, ed., *California Ranchos and Farms, 1846–1862* (Madison, Wis., 1967), 42–44, 62; and Leo Rogin, *The Introduction of Farm Machinery in Its Relation to the Productivity of Labor in the United States during the Nineteenth Century* (Berkeley, 1931), 125–53.

dition, the lack of women presented a long-term demographic problem. Imbalanced sex ratios, coupled with shrinking populations in community after community, reduced chances for family formation. Moreover, the demography of the interior seems to suggest a world that was somehow more dangerous for Indian women than for men. That world we shall enter next.

9

"Between Two Grizzlies' Paws:"
Indian Women in the 1850s

California's rapidly changing demography helped to shape Indian women's lives. In 1850 there were only about seven thousand non-Indian and perhaps forty thousand Indian women in the state. Two years later Indians accounted for about one third of the enumerated female population, and in 1860 the federal census showed that only one of every fifteen women was an Indian. Once the gold rush began, there were always more than three men for every woman; and in 1852 there were nearly seven times more men than women, without adjusting for race. Ratios were often much higher in mining counties.[1]

Unbalanced sex ratios were typical of nineteenth-century mining frontiers; but in California, where Indians and whites commonly mingled, gender imbalances worked a special hardship on native women. While many white miners hoped to get rich quickly and return posthaste to their homes, wives, or sweethearts, those who planned to stay yearned for racially and culturally suitable mates. In the meantime, some argonauts looked to native women for sex and companionship.

The Sexual Frontier

In North America the Indian frontier was also a sexual frontier. The nature of interracial sexual encounters varied according to time, place, cultural norms, and circumstances. Not surprisingly, California proved to be both similar to and different from other sexual frontiers where Anglo, Hispanic, and Indian men and women united physically, if only briefly. The gold rush threw Anglos and Indians together in a violent melding that helped to further undermine declining native society. Sex-

1. The 1850 Indian population is based on a conservative aggregate estimate of 100,000, using a sex ratio of 125. For 1850 white and 1852 Indian and white population, see J. D. B. DeBow, *Statistical View of the United States* (Washington, D.C., 1854), 200–01, 394. For 1860, see Joseph C. G. Kennedy, *Population of the United States in 1860* (Washington, D.C., 1864), 28.

uality was somehow shorn of its regenerative power in native life. This tragic result is all the more poignant because it reflects on the most intensely personal of human experiences, and particularly, as we shall see, because Indian and white sexuality in California was suffused with violence.

In California interracial sexual encounters began with the arrival of the Spaniards, because the Hispanic sexual frontier had included Indian women as a matter of course since the sixteenth century. Sexual intercourse and frequent intermarriage were common, and these liaisons created the large mestizo population that underpinned Spanish and Mexican frontier settlements. In theory, mixed-blood Catholic Spaniards secured the far-flung Spanish Empire and produced tax revenues for the crown, while assuring that Catholicism would beat back paganism. In eighteenth-century California, priests often complained that soldiers seduced and raped neophyte women. At the same time, the friars hoped for mixed marriages and the large Catholic families that would result, but frontier California produced relatively few interracial marriages during Spanish and Mexican times. Nevertheless, California fit into the larger patterns of Hispanic-Indian sexual relations that had been established at the beginning of the colonial era.[2]

Anglos perceived a very different Indian frontier, which they construed to be sexually threatening. Unrealistically fearful of Indian virility, Anglos sought to protect their women from rapacious savages whose sexual appetites were unbridled by civilized conventions. In Anglo imaginations, the lustful Indian warrior who abducted the defenseless white virgin symbolized the sexual tension that was inherent in the westward movement. Interracial sex was clearly a part of the westering experience, but the Anglo pioneers' anxieties were a far cry from frontier realities. Indians who took women prisoners seldom violated them, reserving them instead for tribal adoption and marriage.[3]

On the other hand, Anglo men often had opportunities for sex with Indian women. As the men of the Lewis and Clark Expedition learned, many tribeswomen customarily offered sexual favors to outlanders. Lewis and Clark regarded the matter as simple prostitution, sex in exchange for payment, but for the Indians it could be more complicated.

2. Garr, "Rare and Desolate Land," 133–48; Céspedes, *Latin America: The Early Years*, 56–62; Cook and Borah, *Essays in Population History* 3:267–78, 304–10; Junípero Serra to Antonio Maria de Bucareli y Ursua, Aug. 24, 1775, in Serra, *Writings*, 2:149.

3. Richard Slotkin, *Regeneration Through Violence: The Mythology of the American Frontier, 1600–1860* (Middletown, Conn., 1973), 125, 357; Glenda Riley, *Women and the Indians on the Frontier, 1825–1915* (Albuquerque, 1984), 17–20, 209–10; Axtell, *Invasion Within*, 304–05.

Certain Plains tribes believed that coitus transferred power from one man to another by way of a female intermediary. Since the explorers and succeeding fur traders seemed to be endowed with great power, as evidenced by their technological wonders and trade goods, Indians often sought to use female sexuality to obtain some of the strong medicine that whites possessed. Besides, among Plains Indians sex was a means of establishing friendship and trade relations. The explorers did not ponder the deeper meanings of Indian sexual behavior, but instead saw Indian women as merely lubricious and amoral. So Indian women and white male explorers copulated, but each misunderstood the other's sense of these intimate meetings.[4]

Fur traders who stayed among Indians for prolonged periods developed a better understanding of the utility of sexual unions with tribeswomen. Not only did an Indian wife provide companionship and domestic service, she linked the trader with her tribe, opened trading possibilities, and gave him security under the tribe's sheltering wing. Although more lasting than the brief encounters that Lewis and Clark described, few fur trade marriages proved permanent. As the frontier was settled, mountain men often chose to abandon Indian mates and offspring who were not racially or culturally acceptable in Anglo society.[5]

In the latter part of the nineteenth century, when Indians were being pushed onto reservations, Indian prostitution grew as tribes were steadily dispossessed and impoverished. Troops who guarded the frontier from Indians also took their pleasure from Indian women, who were poor, desperate, and addicted to whiskey. As a result of the frontier experience, at least some Indian women eventually came to resemble the lascivious prostitutes that Lewis and Clark thought they had encountered in an earlier generation.[6]

Anglos who ventured to California brought stock ideas about Indian sexuality that had evolved over generations of frontier experience and ignorance about native people. In this imaginary scenario Indian men would assault white women, while Indian women offered their favors

4. James P. Ronda, *Lewis and Clark among the Indians* (Lincoln, 1984), 36–37, 62–64, 107–12, 131–32, 208–10, 232–33.

5. Swagerty, "Marriage and Settlement Patterns of Rocky Mountain Trappers and Traders," 159–80. Two detailed studies of Indian–fur trader relationships in Canada suggest parallels in the United States: Jennifer S. H. Brown, *Strangers in Blood: Fur Trade Companies in Indian Country* (Vancouver, B.C., 1980), 73–74, 111–30, 199–220; and Sylvia Van Kirk, *Many Tender Ties: Women in Fur Trade Society, 1670–1870* (Norman, Okla., 1980), 28–52, 231–42.

6. Anne M. Butler, *Daughters of Joy, Sisters of Misery: Prostitutes in the American West, 1865–1890* (Urbana, Ill., 1985), 9–10, 133–34.

to white men—a hellish vision of the gold rush sexual landscape that turned out to be partially correct, and even more chilling.

Whatever form it took, interracial sexuality was a matter of some importance to California Indians, for it affected marriage patterns, diplomacy, trade, and childbearing. Under ordinary conditions most California tribes welcomed marriage with outsiders, but the 1850s were not ordinary times. Indian population was declining and women were disappearing faster than men. Whatever their duration, sexual relations with whites were bound to have a negative impact on Indian society.

California Indians valued women and women's work highly because the acorns, pine nuts, and other plant foods they gathered were staples of the Indian economy. As elsewhere in North America, California Indians regarded marriage as a diplomatic arrangement that strengthened trading and security needs. Marriage, therefore, was in part an explicitly economic relationship that underscored the importance of women in Indian society. Discontinuity in this time-honored pattern of work in marriage meant disruption of Indian communities.[7]

Like other societies, California Indians regulated sexual behavior in and out of marriage. All tribes expected sexual fidelity in marriage as an ideal and viewed adultery as a legitimate cause for divorce, although transgressions were not always seriously regarded. Pre- and extramarital sex occurred, but true prostitution appears to have been rare. The northern tribes placed many barriers in the way of sexual expression, even limiting the time of year when married couples could copulate. The Karoks avoided sex because, it was said, they preferred to devote their energy to the pursuit of wealth. On the other hand, at the Achumawi girls' puberty ceremony the celebrants sang ribald songs and had intercourse "back in the bushes"; the Pomos thought of courtship as a time of sexual enjoyment. Among California natives sexual mores seem to have varied considerably, but northern Indians tended to be more proscriptive than the central tribes.[8]

Indian and white ideas about women, sex, and marraige did not fit well together. Whites denigrated Indian women as racially inferior and regarded food gathering as evidence of cultural backwardness. As elsewhere in North America, the "squaw drudge" stereotype indicated a state of savagery. Indeed, the slur "digger" derived from women's work—getting roots and tubers with a sharpened digging stick. Empha-

7. Willoughby, "Division of Labor among the Indians of California," 2:68; Bean, "Social Organization in Native California," 106–9; Bushnell and Bushnell, "Wealth, Work, and World View in Native Northwest California," 133.

8. On sex and marriage, see Heizer, *Handbook*, 148, 173, 181, 186, 232, 295, 296, 327, and 502.

sizing these negative views, whites often described native women as slaves because they appeared to work harder than men. Disparagement of mens' work—hunting and fishing—stemmed from the misapprehension that such activities were trivial pastimes rather than important economic contributions. In short, whites did not accept the native sexual division of labor. When whites hired Indians, they ordinarily employed men in the "male" occupations, such as field hands and cowboys, that white society dictated (see fig. 13).[9]

Before the gold rush, as we have seen, some Anglo settlers had taken Indian wives, accepting for the time being the more liberal Hispanic attitudes about miscegenation or perhaps emulating the temporary alliances that the fur trade usually spawned. In any event, most Anglos subsequently gave up their Indian partners when prospective white mates began to arrive. During the gold rush some white newcomers took native partners, much as had their pre–gold rush counterparts, no doubt regarding their conjugal arrangements as temporary alliances of convenience that would make their brief California residence more comfortable. Few newcomers succeeded in making fortunes, and many postponed—sometimes forever—their homeward journeys. In the meantime, forbidding racial and cultural stereotypes notwithstanding, white men and Indian women became sexual and sometimes marriage partners.[10]

In one sense, it is surprising that sexual activity occurred at all, because many white miners' letters, diaries, and reminiscences indicate that they found Indians singularly unappealing. Charles D. Ferguson hoped that his soul would animate the "body of a bird or beast rather than that of a Digger Indian, more especially," he added, "one of the female branch." Edmund Booth wrote home to his wife giving descriptions of Indian women, whom he considered repugnant in all ways—a

9. See Robert C. Buchanan to E. D. Townsend, Aug. 1, 1853, "Reports Relating to Indian Customs," RG 393; David Smits, "The 'Squaw Drudge': A Prime Index of Savagism," *Ethnohistory* 29 (1982):281–306; and Rawls, *Indians of California*, 49.

10. Antonia I. Castañeda, "The Political Economy of Nineteenth-Century Stereotypes of Californianas," paper presented at the Pacific Coast Branch meeting of the American Historical Association, San Francisco, Aug. 12–14, 1982; Sherburne F. Cook, "The American Invasion," 75–92; Cook, "Trends in Marriage and Divorce since 1850," 1–29; Andrew J. Rotter, " 'Matilda for Gods Sake Write': Women and Families on the Argonaut Mind," *California History* 58 (Summer 1979):128–41. For intermarriage patterns elsewhere, see Lecompte, "Independent Women of Hispanic New Mexico," 17–35; Swagerty, "Marriage and Settlement Patterns of Rocky Mountain Trappers and Traders," 159–80; special issue on *metis* in *American Indian Culture and Research Journal* 6, no. 2 (1982); the special issue on Navajo women, *American Indian Quarterly* 6 (Spring/Summer 1982); and Van Kirk, *Many Tender Ties*.

Fig. 13. Washerwoman, Yosemite Valley, 1870. Some Indian women found employment doing domestic chores for white men. Although the cult of true womanhood emphasized the spiritual side of women, feminine work roles were physically demanding. This woman made a living doing laundry for tourists who came to the famous valley.

reaction that might be considered *de rigueur* under the circumstances. William Perkins described Indian women who lived near Sonora as naked, dwarfish creatures about four feet tall, with pendant breasts, long thin arms, and heavy thighs. The women that Perkins described seemed to him more like mythical creatures than flesh-and-blood human beings. So little did Indian women resemble his ideal of feminine anatomy that Perkins found it "difficult to tell the sexes apart." Even Dame

Shirley, the foremost female observer of mining camp life, could find only one "moderately pretty" Indian woman. The rest she compared with "Macbethian witches" for their "haggardness of expression, and ugliness of feature."[11]

To be sure, native women aged quickly from hard work, malnutrition, and the dislocations of the gold rush. In the early years they dressed in traditional garb, wearing simple skirts made of bark, grass, or skins, and adorned the upper halves of their bodies only with necklaces. Later they adopted white clothing, sometimes wearing cast-off garments or making new ones with cloth purchased from traders. Unaccustomed to public seminudity and unsympathetic to the dire poverty that the gold rush brought to the Indians, white miners were disposed to disparage native women because they did not measure up to Victorian ideals. Nevertheless, nineteenth-century photographs, paintings, lithographs, and drawings show that there were many young California Indian women whom some men undoubtedly found attractive.[12]

Alliances of Convenience

Victorian ideals, moral scruples, and aesthetic preferences did not keep white men from cohabiting with Indian women in the 1840s, and during the gold rush some whites established similar relationships. Since few whites bothered to solemnize their unions with Indian women, it is impossible to determine the number of mixed marriages. Sherburne F. Cook estimated that several thousand such unions may have occurred during the 1850s, but this estimate may have been too liberal. Census evidence rarely indicated mixed couples, and most of them were in the northern region.[13]

Even in the rough-and-ready 1850s miscegenation was frowned on in

11. Ferguson, *Experiences of a Forty-Niner*, 197; *Edmund Booth (1810–1905) Forty-Niner: The Life Story of a Deaf Pioneer Including Portions of His Autobiographical Notes and Gold Rush Diary, and Selections from Family Letters and Reminiscences* (Stockton, Calif., 1953), 42; *Three Years in California: William Perkins' Journal of Life at Sonora, 1849–1852*, ed. Dale L. Morgan and James R. Scobie (Berkeley, 1964), 145; and Louise Amelia Knapp Smith Clappe, *The Shirley Letters from the California Mines, 1851–1852*, ed. Carl I. Wheat (New York, 1949), 12–13.

12. See the fine book of photographs with commentary by Theodora Kroeber and Robert F. Heizer, *Almost Ancestors: The First Californians* (San Francisco, 1968); and Theodora Kroeber, Albert B. Elsasser, and Robert F. Heizer, *Drawn from Life: California Indians in Pen and Brush* (Socorro, N.M., 1977).

13. Cook, "American Invasion," 77; and Census, Trinity County, 1860 MS.

mining communities. Not only was it incongruent with Anglo-American racial and sexual ideals, many whites thought it downright dangerous. White accounts of the Pomo killings of Stone and Kelsey indicate that the two whites had taken chief Augustin's wife and kept her in their cabin. Whites reasoned that Augustin's jealousy caused the Indian attack and that the Indian woman assured its success by pouring water down the barrels of her captors' rifles.[14]

Cohabiting with an Indian woman could be particularly perilous in the strife-ridden north country. In Mattole Valley the white man Buckskin Jack made the mistake of killing the brother of the woman he lived with while he was out with a company of volunteers. To avenge her brother, the woman cut Jack's throat while he slept. He survived the wound, however, and killed her with a knife. As a consequence, Jack's neighbors "resolved to drive off all 'squaw men' " if they did not get rid of their women. The local "squaw men" complied, perhaps fearing the wrath of their white neighbors more than their Indian consorts.[15]

White men did not always give up their Indian women so easily. In 1859 state militia Captain John P. Jones (later a United States senator from Nevada) forced whites to give up their native women as part of his campaign against the Pit River Indians. All of the men asked to marry the Indian women, but Jones forbade it and sent the women to reservations by way of the Sacramento River settlement Red Bluff. One of the disappointed men, Joseph Roff, a government contractor who furnished hay to Fort Crook in northeastern California, followed the women and their military escort to Red Bluff, where he tried to hire some men to kidnap his woman. After they failed, he followed the prisoners to the Mendocino Reservation on the Pacific coast and married the Indian. They settled near Round Valley and had two little girls who died in childhood. When their mother died soon after, Roff sold out and left the valley.[16]

It is clear that some white men and Indian women tried to transcend frontier conditions and form stable families, but they had to suffer the disapprobation of the Anglo-American community. William Brewer, who would soon receive a professorship at Yale, declaimed with rancor against the "squaw men" he met in the foothills of the Sierra Nevada in 1864. He asserted that they were all "rank Secessionists" and " 'poor white trash' from the frontier slave states, Missouri, Arkansas, and Texas." Brewer never met a good Union

14. Palmer, *Napa and Lake Counties*, 56.
15. Marysville *Weekly Express*, Aug. 21, 1858, quoted in Heizer, *They Were Only Diggers*, 34.
16. Elijah Potter, "Reminiscences," MS, Bancroft Library.

man living in "that way," but he probably did not look very hard for exceptions to his rule for miscegenation. In1864 secessionist was one of the worst epithets a Union man could use. In applying this term to whites who lived with native women, Brewer revealed his low opinion of interracial marriage by linking it to the supposed disloyalty of men who took Indian wives.[17]

Considering the social disapproval of miscegenation that prevailed among Anglo-Americans, what drove white men to choose Indian sexual partners? Were they, as Brewer suggested, from a particular class, the dregs of the frontier, men who were not bound by the restraints that conventional society placed on sexual behavior? Or were they somehow transformed by their frontier experiences? One of the few documents that gives insights regarding these questions is Isaac Roop's leather-bound Roop House Register, in which he kept an account of emigrants who came through Honey Lake Valley and made random comments on life in the 1850s. Roop was a cut above the average frontiersman. A widower and former postmaster of Shasta County, he eventually became territorial governor of Nevada.[18]

According to Roop's register, when there was "Nothing to Drink" in the valley, life was "Dam Dull." He and his companions relieved the monotony by hunting. On one excursion Roop bagged "all told, two grizzlys, one Antelope and a digger squaw este noche [tonight]," a cryptic comment that could have meant that he either killed her or slept with her. It is certain, however, that Roop and his male friends were anxious to encourage white women to stay in the valley, either for brief encounters or as wives. The valley men used whiskey to seduce the haggard pioneer women who came over Beckwourth Pass, but none of them stayed. After two years of watching thousands of men and hundreds of women pass his cabin door, Roop and his male companions were desperate. In August 1856 one of the men wrote, "They [wagon] Benches was crowded with Girls" and "Roop was fixing some plan to stop them in this Valley." But Roop's plotting was to no avail. Later in August three of his cohorts "struck after a Negro Wench," but the results of the expedition were not recorded. It was a bad month for single men in the valley. One of them "followed one train some twelve miles for a *Woman* (found she was married) Came back in disgust." When Mr. Long from Kansas left Honey Lake with his wife and two

17. *Up and Down California in 1860–1864: The Journal of William H. Brewer, Professor of Agriculture in the Sheffield Scientific School from 1864 to 1903*, 3d ed., ed. Francis P. Farquhar, (Berkeley, 1966), 546.

18. Roop House Register, 1854–1857, MS, California Room, State Library, Sacramento.

daughters, an anonymous writer in the register asked, "Why in 'Gods Name' can't some of the Women stop here?" When a man named Kingsbury "caught one of the girls rubbing her leg," one of Roop's friends "took a stiff milk punch on the strength" of merely hearing of the incident.[19]

Roop's feelings of sexual frustration were not unique. Henry B. Sheldon, a young unmarried Christian missionary from New England, wrote home saying that he wanted "nothing physically more than '*the other half*'." Sheldon could have satisfied his physical needs quite easily in San Francisco, where he found nearly one thousand courtesans who were the "*aristocracy*" of the city. He hoped that the arrival of upstanding single women and families would help to improve the social conditions of the state. Brother Sheldon eventually fulfilled his desire for companionship by marrying his New England sweetheart.[20]

Not all Californians could send for a wife as Sheldon did. They had to satisfy their needs for female companionship, sex, marriage, and family life with the few females who were available in the state. White men who sought relationships that conformed to nineteenth-century norms had to marry in a very small pool of white, socially acceptable women or remain celibate bachelors. The alternatives were to consort with prostitutes, associate with racially unacceptable women, or engage in deviant sexual outlets. White men engaged in all of these forms of sexual behavior in California; most probably thought of their liaisons with Indians as an expedient that would not be needed once there were enough white women in the state. Even though Anglo-American society did not accept them, the few men who established long-term relationships with Indians honored the monogamous, nuclear family model. In that sense, they conformed to accepted standards of sexual behavior.

Prostitution

If marriages helped some Indian women to survive, prostitution offered others and their families a way to cope with the destitution that the gold rush had caused. The argonaut Herman Francis Reinhart frankly explained how an illicit liaison occurred in southern Oregon in 1851. Two Indian women and a girl came to his camp begging for flour, sugar, and

19. Ibid.
20. Sheldon to "Dear Friends," July 26, 1852; Sheldon to "Dear Friends," June 25, 1852; Sheldon to "Dear Father," Mar. 9, 1854, H. B. Sheldon Papers, California Room, State Library, Sacramento.

bread, leading Reinhart's companion, a blacksmith named Ashcraft, to ask if they would have intercourse with him in return for "some bread and a handkerchief or some sugar." Ashcraft struck a bargain with the youngest woman, who was about twenty and had lost one eye. The Indians ate; then Ashcraft "went off with the one-eyed one." After they returned, the young woman's husband arrived and accused his wife of mischief with Ashcraft. The couple scuffled briefly, but the older woman and the girl convinced the husband that his wife had not misbehaved. Reinhart later learned that the woman had lost her eye as punishment for adultery, as was customary in her tribe.[21]

As in Oregon, hunger and privation drove California Indians to prostitution. In 1853 E. A. Stevenson, an Indian Office employee, reporting on the conditions in El Dorado County, found that "poverty and misery" forced native women to "open and disgusting acts of prostitution" from which they contracted syphilis. In one camp Stevenson saw nine women who were "so far advanced with this disease that they were unable to walk." Even a change in the weather could cause a noticeable increase of Indian prostitutes in towns, living as they did on the raw edge of starvation. After heavy rain in 1858, women came to Shasta City to "procure their bread and clothing in a manner the most infamous." They gathered "in small groups squatted . . . along side walks from sundown to a late hour of night." Shasta City residents believed that the federal government should be responsible for feeding destitute Indians to eliminate native streetwalkers. In any case, white Shastans believed Indian prostitutes to be a "vile nuisance, calling loudly for abatement."[22]

Even where the federal government supposedly had the power to discourage Indian prostitution, it was unable to do so. In 1857 Lieutenant LaRhett Livingston reported that all the Indians near Fort Miller in Fresno County were diseased as a result of intercourse "with the worse class of whites to be found in any country." The lieutenant stated that debased whites gave Indians liquor and that on any day an observer could "see a dozen Indians reeling drunk." The existence of debauched Indians near the post had "the worst possible effect upon the Troops." So many of his men had contracted venereal diseases, Livingston claimed, that it was "likely to prove extremely prejudicial" to Fort Miller's strength and efficiency.[23]

21. *The Golden Frontier: The Recollections of Herman Francis Reinhart, 1851–1865*, ed. Doyce B. Nunis, Jr., (Austin, 1962), 45.

22. Stevenson to Thomas J. Henley, Dec. 31, 1853, and Nevada *Journal*, Nov. 12, 1858, quoted in Heizer, *Destruction of the California Indians*, 13–16, 280.

23. Livingston to Major W. W. Mackall, Mar. 9, 1857; and William J. L'Engle to

Because syphilis had a negative impact on Indian birth rates, its presence in the native population had a special significance. With the population sharply declining, syphilis made it difficult to recover losses through reproduction. In 1858 special Indian agent Jonathan Markle of Cloverdale provided a horrifying description of the result of the disease on Lo-co, a young Indian girl among the Indians whom he looked after. His physician explained that it was the worst case he had ever seen, "the *clitoris* being entirely eat away." The doctor said it would cost at least twenty dollars to treat her, and the prognosis was so uncertain that "if she was a white girl he would not touch the case at all." Markle promised to do "anything to save her," but hoped that the Indian Office would defray the expense of treatment. Women who were not cared for by someone like Markle could hardly afford to pay for treatment themselves. The going rate for Indian labor in Sonoma County was seventy-five cents per day, so an Indian would have had to work a month to pay for Lo-co's medical attention.[24]

Rape and Forced Concubinage

Prostitution offered short-term economic benefits to some women, but at very high long-term costs to their personal health and tribal reproductive potential. But at least Indian prostitutes could exert some control over their lives by choosing the circumstances of their sexual transactions and bargaining over prices. Not all women were able to retain even that meagre scrap of self-respect, for sexual assaults on Indians were frequent. The state's newspapers commonly reported cases of rape and forced concubinage in the mining districts during the 1850s. The *Daily Alta California*'s 1858 report of assaults on Trinity County Indians was typical. In the northern mines, the newspaper declared, there was a class of men who, when they could not "obtain a squaw by fair means, [would] not hesitate to use foul." They would "drag off the squaw" and "knock down her friends" if they interfered. Indian women frequently fled to the mountains "to avoid the violence of men who, under the influence of liquor, [would] not hesitate to do any deed." The *Alta* asserted that Indian families had been driven from their homes "in the dead of winter by crowds of drunken men" who could not be prose-

Livingston, Mar. 9, 1857, quoted in Heizer, *Destruction of the California Indians*, 272–74.

24. Sherburne F. Cook, "The Indian Versus the California Mission," *Ibero-Americana* 21 (1943):28–29; and J. Markle to T. J. Henley, Dec. 17, 1858, M234:37.

cuted because, except in cases involving violations of the law banning liquor sales to Indians, Indian testimony was inadmissible in California courts.[25]

Indian women were not safe even when they were on Indian reservations. In 1856 the San Francisco *Bulletin* carried a story of a reserve where "some of the agents, and nearly all of the employees" were "daily and nightly . . . kidnapping the younger portion of the females, for the vilest purposes." The article averred that the "wives and daughters of the defenseless Diggers" were "prostituted before the very eyes of their husbands and fathers, by these civilized monsters, and they dare not resent the insult, or even complain of the hideous outrage." The next year four state militiamen were guarding some Indian prisoners on Butte Creek. John Breckenridge, a guard, complained in the Red Bluff *Beacon* that "one Cain, a miner came . . . and claimed a squaw" and tried to take her away. When the guards stopped him, he returned "with a mob of forty-five men" and a deputy sheriff, released the Indians, and took the Indian woman he claimed to Dogtown, where he married her even though her Indian husband was still alive. Breckenridge believed "that the only motive of the mob was to secure the squaws and keep them on the creek."[26]

Sexual molestation of Indians was not unusual. When three Indian women ventured into Mariposa, white men there "so bedeviled and tormented" them that "they were almost frightened out of their wits." The incident moved the editor of the Mariposa *Gazette* to compose a poem declaring that he

> Had rather be an innocent lamb
> between two grizzlies' paws
> Than take the desperate chances
> of three unprotected squaws.[27]

The Indian women's fears of white men were sometimes evident in their outward behavior. When Chilean Vicente Pérez Rosales arrived on Weber Creek in 1849, he met with a group of Indian men and women, probably Miwok, "naked and carrying bows and arrows." When the Indians saw Rosales and his companions the native women "squatted

25. "Cruelty to Squaws," *Daily Alta California*, Jan. 17, 1858, 1; San Francisco *Bulletin*, Sept. 13, 1856, quoted in Heizer, *Destruction of the California Indians*, 278.

26. Breckenridge's statement to the *Beacon* is printed in the San Francisco *Bulletin*, Nov. 9, 1857, and quoted in Heizer, *Destruction of the California Indians*, 279.

27. Howard C. Gardiner, *In Pursuit of the Golden Dream: Reminiscences of San Francisco and the Northern and Southern Mines, 1849–1857*, ed. Dale L. Morgan (Stoughton, Mass., 1970), 143.

down to make themselves as inconspicuous as possible." A few Chilean men approached the Indian women, who "took off, running like deer back up the hill."[28]

Indian women were not always overawed by rapacious whites. During an attack on a Clear Lake Pomo community, one white assailant "happened to run across a comely squaw hidden in the brush," took "a fancy to her," and tried to capture her. She fought him off with all the "might of her insulted and outraged sympathy for her people," and the man reported that he was as glad to get away from her as "to escape with his life from the clutch of a she bear." A few years later the Nisenan demanded that a white named "Big Tom" return one of their kidnapped women, but he refused. Consequently they attacked Tom's camp, rescued the woman, killed all the whites, and cut Big Tom into a thousand pieces. Retaliation for assaults on Indian women was a common cause of violence in gold rush California (see fig. 14).[29]

Sexual Violence and the Gold Rush

Interracial rape, one of the great fears of white men and women on the frontier, materialized as an important factor in gold rush Indian-white relations. But white, not Indian, men were the perpetrators, and Indian women were the victims. Why was California's sexual frontier so different from white expectations and experience in this respect? Partly, of course, because opportunities for white rapists abounded in California. Indian men were often away at work, leaving their women unprotected. Furthermore, other conditions in gold rush California seemed to encourage the rape of Indian women. According to modern theories of rape and criminality, these crimes were not only possible but predictable. Even though more than a century separates modern sexual deviants from gold rush assailants, explication of current ideas about sexual assault helps to explain the historical causes of interracial rape and suggests some of its consequences.

Again, demographic circumstances come to the fore. The white gold rush population was composed mostly of young males who left home

28. Beilharz and López, *We Were 49ers!* 51–52.

29. Palmer, *History of Napa and Lake Counties, California*, 58; Sacramento *Daily Democratic State Journal*, Sept. 1, 1855, and Marysville *Weekly Express*, Aug. 21, 1858; Sacramento *Union*, Oct. 1, 1858, quoted in Robert F. Heizer, ed., *They Were Only Diggers: A Collection of Articles from California Newspapers, 1851–1866, on Indian and White Relations* (Ramona, Calif., 1974), 29, 34–35.

Fɪɢ. 14. Mono Women. Four Mono women posed in front of a traditional bark house in the Sierra Nevada foothills in the late nineteenth century. Indian women were especially vulnerable to assaults when men were out harvesting crops or doing other seasonal labor that took them away from home. These women had long since adopted white clothing, but they evidently continued to use baskets. Courtesy of the California State Library.

to seek their fortunes. Studies of modern juvenile offenders have shown that young rapists lacked a strong attachment to families and were estranged from home environments. Moreover, when compared with delinquents who did not commit sex crimes, rapists had a significantly higher exposure to delinquent peers who supported deviant acts. Likewise, many young men were isolated from the ameliorating influences of home, church, and moral society in California. Not all of them could emulate Brother Sheldon, who dutifully wrote his parents to express his personal and moral anxieties. And for those young men who looked for bad company, there was plenty to be had in California. Reporters of California rapes often mentioned that the perpetrators were part of the "worst" set in the mines, young men who were especially prone to criminal actions. The reported group assaults on Indian communities could well have been supported by the type of violent subculture that modern researchers describe.[30]

Bad moral conditions and isolation were not the only forces that propelled sexual assaults in California. Although rape is a sex crime, modern research has shown that sex is not the sole driving force behind the act. The psychologist A. Nicholas Groth describes rape as a complex act that serves several retaliatory and compensatory needs for the rapist. "It is an effort to discharge his anger, contempt, and hostility toward women," to "counteract feelings of vulnerability and inadequacy in himself and assert his strength and power to control and exploit." Furthermore, the rape act is an attempt to "deny sexual anxieties," to reaffirm "identity, competency and manhood," to "retain status (in gang rape) among male peers," and finally "to achieve sexual gratification." Although rape defends against anxiety, expresses conflict, and gratifies the sexual impulse, Groth reasons that the act is associated "more with conflict and stress than with pleasure and satisfaction." Sexuality, therefore, is not the sole or the primary motive for rape, but is the means by which conflicts arising out of anger and frustration are discharged. The assailant is often moved by a "progressive and increasing sense of failure" and extraordinary stress that temporarily overwhelms him. According to Groth, rape represents a crisis for the assailant who is unable to cope with other conditions in his life.[31]

In the early 1850s many young California men certainly faced changing conditions that could have produced extraordinary stress. Having immigrated to the mines to gain quick wealth, they soon learned that it was becoming increasingly difficult to obtain easy riches from freely available placers because the best claims were already taken and the surface wealth had been skimmed off. In the first years employment of Indian miners made a few whites wealthy and no doubt added to less-successful white miners' general animosity toward native people. The historian Rodman Paul has shown that throughout the 1850s miners' daily wages declined as the placers played out. Moreover, capitalists progressively took over the mines as expensive hard rock and hydraulic mining became necessary to exploit deeper auriferous deposits. Arriving as independent entrepreneurs, individual miners found themselves absorbed into a growing pool of wage laborers, a fate that many had hoped to escape by going to California.[32]

Yet persistent stories about independent miners who struck it rich

30. Suzanne S. Ageton, *Sexual Assault Among Adolescents* (Lexington, Mass., 1983), 111–12.

31. *Men Who Rape: The Psychology of the Offender* (New York, 1979), 60–61.

32. Paul, *California Gold*, 171–72.

continually teased avaricious appetites. The constant possibility of fabulous wealth, combined with the manifest difficulty of obtaining it, must have been a constant irritation to some men who were unable to profit in the rush for gold. Frustration alone may have led some to commit violent acts, including rape. However, it has been shown that sustained levels of nonaggressive stimulus—even a constant irritating noise—can trigger aggressive behavior, especially if the perpetrator has been previously exposed to aggressive models. Occasional violence on the overland trail, military experience in the Mexican War, and exposure to mob violence and lynchings provided plenty of aggressive models for gold seekers. It may be that the continuing nonaggressive stimulus of gold strikes along with exposure to frontier violence caused some men to rape.[33]

While the frontier may not have been as violent as popular literature has suggested, most white immigrants believed that the potential for Indian and white violence was very real. Even though actual aggression by Indians was comparatively rare, white frontier folk vented their anxieties by alternately fomenting "Indian scares" where none really existed, by circling the wagons, posting guards, "forting up," and acting hysterically. While Indian rapists were uncommon, the fear of Indian sexual assaults inflamed white mens' and womens' imaginations, although in quite different ways. Women yearned for male protection from assaults, while men sought to live up to the protective—and aggressive—behavior that society and their womenfolk expected of them. Men did not always have to fight Indians to protect females from the fate worse than death, but real and imagined Indian threats and white responses provided aggressive models that made California Indian women targets for the sexual violence of frontiersmen.[34]

Many white men believed that Indians were their enemies and that the country had to be wrested from them by every available means. According to Julia and Herman Schwendinger's recent research on rape, rapists' disdain for women "may be fused with racial, class, religious, or national chauvinism" and applied "to women who are held in even greater contempt because they represent and epitomize a particular social group." The Schwendingers assert that this analysis is no less valid where rape is explicitly illegal—as it was in gold rush California—for in a social context where inequality exists, poor white men can demonstrate their worth by raping women who are supposed to be from an inferior

33. Julia R. Schwendinger and Herman Schwendinger, *Rape and Inequality* (Beverly Hills, 1983), 201; Dolf Zillmann, "Excitation Transfer in Communication-Mediated Aggressive Behavior," *Journal of Experimental Social Psychology* 7 (July 1971):419–34.

34. Riley, *Women and Indians*, 83–119, 168.

class. Thus, "sexual aggression can support colonialism, slavery," and, by logical extension, the conquest of California Indians.[35]

Rapists frequently justify their crimes by defining their victims as inferior or especially blameworthy, or by denying that any wrong was done. In the nineteenth century assailants imbued with the common racial prejudices of their day and culture could twist the facts of frontier life to define Indian women as legitimate victims of sexual abuse. Thus, native women were both enemies and objects. According to French researchers, gang rapes offer a particularly apt example of this phenomenon. The rapist believes that it is possible to attack the victim because "she is wrong, and more exactly, she has to suffer for being wrong. . . . " "Not only is she an enemy, she is wrong and has to pay; furthermore she is an object, an experimental object at the mercy of the group." Applied to the social context of the gold rush, this analysis has the grim ring of truth. Inexorably, Indian women became objects through which violent men could express deep anxieties inherent in the frontier experience, sexual fears, and fantasies that were part of the normative value system of Victorian American culture as well as the unique circumstances of California life.[36]

All forms of interracial violence reinforced the idea that men without the civilizing influence of white women would act in an uncivilized way. As one observer put it, white rapists did not "behave themselves as white men should." In an unregulated masculine world men could become white savages by brutally abusing Indian women or by marrying them and tacitly rejecting the principle of racial purity. In either case, according to conventional Anglo values, white women were needed to correct the situation by providing suitable mates and an improved moral atmosphere. Furthermore, the gold rush experience revealed the weakness of Victorian sexual ideology by showing how frail a thread held men to the straight path of accepted sexual behavior. Throughout the mining districts there was palpable evidence that males easily fell away from the right way of living. In the Golden State, there was precious little to make up for what Brother Sheldon called the "loss of home influence" and a society of friends who provided the necessary peer pressure that kept men from deviant behavior. He could only hope for a better day when emigration would bring virtuous women and families

35. Schwendinger and Schwendinger, *Rape and Inequality*, 202–04.

36. P. Robert et al. quoted in E. A. Fattah, "The Use of the Victim as an Agent of Self-Legitimization: Toward a Dynamic Explanation of Criminal Behavior," in *Victims and Society*, ed. E. C. Viano (Washington, D.C., 1976), 105–29.

to California, a hope which in his case was happily consummated. For others, such hopes were vain.[37]

The Impact of Interracial Sex

Whatever the motives of whites may have been, their sexual forays had important results in native communities. Indian victims of rape likely displayed some of the somatic and emotional symptoms of rape trauma syndrome that modern psychologists have described. Rape-induced somatic reactions include physical wounds, tension, sleeplessness, gastrointestinal irritations, and genitourinary disturbances. On an emotional level, victims are often stricken by fear, guilt, anger, and humiliation. They must often undergo long-term reorganization of their lives as a result of rape trauma. Nightmares, increased motor activity, and fearfulness shape the existence of assaulted women. Depending on the circumstances of the attack, they fear being alone, or going in crowds, the indoors, outdoors, or people behind them. And, significantly, some raped women develop a fear of normal sexual activity. There is no reason to believe that Indian women were not similarly affected. Indeed, if raped women exhibited an aversion to sex, rape trauma syndrome may have contributed to low birthrates. Moreover, given the small size of Indian communities, fear of rape may have affected many women who were not themselves victims as they tried to help their friends and relatives cope with the consequences of rape.[38]

Another somatic result of rape and other interracial sex was venereal disease, which tended to reduce birthrates and lower resistance to other illnesses that infected the postcontact Indian population. In addition, some sexual liaisons resulted in the birth of an undetermined number of mestizo children who were raised by Indian women. Most half-caste Indian children who survived the 1850s were raised in Indian society and contributed to the persistence of native cultures. Because of rapid population losses all children, regardless of their ancestry, should have been welcomed into Indian communities.[39]

Sherburne F. Cook claimed that Indians increased abortion and infanticide to do away with unwanted children fathered by whites. Scant

37. Sacramento *Union*, Oct. 1, 1858, quoted in Heizer, *Destruction of the California Indians*, 279–80.

38. Ann Wolbert Burgess and Lynda Lytle Holstrom, "Rape Trauma Syndrome," *American Journal of Psychiatry* 131 (Sept. 1974):981–86.

39. Cook, "American Invasion," 82.

evidence supports his contention, but infanticide was reported in the missions and ethnographers have recorded it in some tribes. The Cahtos killed deformed children and the Sinkyone disposed of bastards. Because twins were thought to be unlucky, the Konkow Maidus killed them and their mothers. The Pomos used infanticide to limit population growth, but other tribes apparently never took up the practice. Indians driven by fear and hatred of whites may have killed half-white babies, but the gold rush would have been an especially inappropriate time to begin the destruction of children.[40]

The extent of abortion and infanticide will never be known, and the 1860 census data for Indian birth ratios and infant sex ratios offer little help (see map 6 and table 9.1). The anomalies in infant sex ratios that are evident in the San Joaquin and northern districts indicate a surplus of girls and boys, respectively, skewed statistics that could suggest that sex-selective infanticide was at work. But similar infant sex ratios appear in the published censuses for white populations in several counties. Thus, it is not plausible to attribute Indian statistical peculiarities to infanticide.

Among most California Indians, however, the 1860 census shows a clear trend. In virtually every age cohort in every county there were substantially fewer women than men. Indian women left tribal society and joined white households as servants and wives, but not in large numbers, as the next chapter demonstrates. Besides, Indians in white society were enumerated in 1860, so the census accounts for errant Indian women. If census data for Indian women were inaccurate then census officers in thirty-six of forty-two counties underenumerated Indian women, a degree of consistency that seems to militate against inadvertent error. On the other hand, the fact that some counties that reported a surplus of Indian women or had an abundance of women in particular age cohorts argues against the idea that racist notions or consipiracy caused undercounts. Some native women may have hidden from census officers because they feared assaults, but it is difficult to accept this as the cause of a statewide phenomenon affecting nearly all tribes, ages, and conditions. There are errors in the census, no doubt, but the general trend showing a deficit of women is hard to deny and ought not to be slighted. All Indians were at risk during the tumultuous 1850s, but women's chances for survival were measurably worse than men's. Brutal assaults, deadly diseases, and general privation killed women and left their communities' reproductive potential in doubt.

Region and county Indian reproduction rates varied substantially.

40. Ibid., 90–92; and Heizer, *Handbook*, 104, 142, 196, 245, 259, 267, 295, 327, 357, 381, 421, 440, 511, 652.

MAP 6. California Counties, 1860. Shaded areas indicate counties with Indian populations analyzed in chapter 10.

The Sacramento Valley had a very low crude birth ratio of about one child for every two potential mothers, and this was typical of counties with large Indian populations in that region. The San Joaquin Valley Indians had about the same birth ratio as white women (1.7); however, Tulare and Fresno counties' comparatively high reproduction and population overshadow three other counties with only fourteen Indians and three children altogether. Mother Lode Indians appeared to have a strong reproductive rate, even though their numbers had been reduced by nearly nine thousand since 1852. But only Plumas and Yuba counties

TABLE 9.1.   *Indian Sex Ratios and Crude Birth Ratios by Region and County in 1860*

	Population in 1852	Population in 1860	0-to-1-year-old sex ratio	1-to-14-year-old sex ratio	Crude birth ratio
Sacramento Valley					
Butte	30	121	0	250.0	0.3
Colusi	66	75	1:0	142.8	1.4
Sacramento	80	251	1:0	166.7	0.6
Sutter	514	10	0	0:3	1.5
Yolo	152	0	—	—	—
Tehama	—	656	0	136.4	0.5
Subtotal	842	1,113	2:0	138.5	0.5
San Joaquin Valley					
Fresno	—	3,294	67.8	93.0	1.7
Merced	—	4	0	0	—
San Joaquin	379	4	0	1:0	0:1
Stanislaus	—	6	0	2:0	2.0
Tulare	8,207	1,340	0	158.5	1.4
Subtotal	8,586	4,648	67.8	98.6	1.7
Mother Lode					
Calaveras	1,982	1	0	0	0:1
El Dorado	—	8	0	1:0	0.3
Mariposa	4,533	7	0:1	0:2	1.5
Nevada	3,226	5	0	300.0	4.0
Placer	730	7	0	150.0	5:0
Plumas	—	108	0	460.0	1.6
Tuolumne	590	6	0	0	0:2
Yuba	120	72	200.0	110.0	1.4
Subtotal	11,181	214	100.0	205.0	1.5

Continued on next page

had populations large enough to yield statistically significant results, and in Plumas there was a marked lack of young girls. In the northern district several counties showed very strong reproductive potential alongside counties with very low birth ratios. High birthrates and healthy sex ratios may have been evident because so many northern Indians hid out during the 1850s, thus avoiding some of the consequences of contact.

Reproduction rates varied considerably depending on Indian values, the number of fertile women, potential marriage partners, the extent of intermarriage, and white assaults. Since reproduction was offset by high death rates, even groups that appeared to have healthy birthrates would be lucky to hold their own in coming years.

Indian women could resist or acquiesce and somehow make the best of a very bad situation, but in sexual matters they had little freedom of

TABLE 9.1.   (*continued*)

	Population in 1852	Population in 1860	0-to-1-year-old sex ratio	1-to-14-year-old sex ratio	Crude birth ratio
Northern District					
Del Norte	—	266	100.0	100.0	0.6
Humboldt	—	153	0	107.0	5.9
Klamath	—	46	1:0	250.0	2.4
Mendocino	187	1,054	100.0	164.4	1.8
Shasta	73	8	0	1:0	0.3
Siskiyou	26	51	0	233.3	1.0
Trinity	4	100	200.0	118.2	1.4
Subtotal	290	1,678	140.0	144.5	1.6
Statistics for Other California Women in 1860					
Whites	171,841	323.177	103.2	105.3	1.7
Free colored	2,206	4,086	105.6	99.5	1.2
Asians	—	34,933	100.0	462.3	0.3

Sources: Adapted from Joseph G. Kennedy, *Population of the United States in 1860* (Washington, D.C., 1864), 26–27; and J. D. B. DeBow, *Statistical Review of the United States* (Washington, 1854), 394.

Note: Sex ratios are determined by the formula: males/females × 100. Crude birth ratios are determined by dividing the total number of children by the total number of women between the ages of fifteen and thirty-nine. When one of the numerical values is zero, relationships—of men to women and of children to potentially fertile women—are expressed with a colon. Statistics are based on the total Indian population within each region. Certain counties did not exist in 1852. For example, Fresno County was part of Tulare County, and Humboldt was part of Klamath.

choice. It is difficult to imagine that they were not fearful, angry, and resentful because of rape and the necessity of prostitution and concubinage. We can only guess about the effects of Indian-white sexual relations on Indian family life. Did Indian husbands give sympathy and support to their raped spouses, or did sexual assaults create strains on Indian marriage and family life that could not be eased? The answer to this question no doubt varies from case to case and culture to culture, but rape and other forms of sexual exploitation almost certainly inflicted damage on individual Indians and their society that transcended the immediate harm inherent in the acts themselves.

While much of the intimate history of Indian-white sexual life will remain hidden, what is known reveals a social landscape pockmarked with sexual violence. To survive the gold rush era, Indian women had to run a sexual gauntlet, while their kinfolk and friends helplessly watched their sense of community, chastity, and morality being assaulted by white men who dreamed of a new community of racial purity, sexual continence, and Christian ethics—a community that they would found with white women.

10

Uncertain Refuge:
The Household and
Indian Survival in 1860

In 1851 John Bidwell, Sutter's old friend and one-time employee, explained his conception of California Indian affairs to U.S. Senator J. W. McCorkle. The prominent Butte County farmer said that California conditions were altogether different from those in eastern states. California's settlers did not have to contend with Indians only on the frontier; they were "all *among* us, *around* us, *with* us—hardly a farm house—a kitchen without them." A farmer who needed laborers told Indians to "go into his fields" and fed and clothed them in return. Bidwell thought Indian workers looked up to a farmer with "a kind of filial obedience to his commands" and expected from him "a kind of parental protection." The earnest farmer contrasted his description of agrarian paternalism with the activities of "malicious and brutal vagabonds" who roamed the country murdering Indians. Such depredations caused native people to retaliate in kind, "thereby exposing the industrious miner to dangers and death." In these desperate times, Bidwell believed, Indians were "sure to cling around and shelter themselves under the protection of him who treats them best."[1]

Bidwell described a future for California Indians that was based on the past. Writing when demands for labor were at their peak, he assumed that Indians would find safety in a free market that demanded native services. Indeed, he asserted that native workers would be able to choose the employers who best protected and cared for them. But this was not to be. During the 1850s demand for Indian labor rapidly declined as California's mining and agricultural technology developed. Indians continued to work for whites; but try as they might, it was increasingly difficult for them to get work, let alone find employers who would treat them well.

1. Bidwell to McCorkle, Dec. 20, 1851, enclosed in McCorkle to Luke Lea, Feb. 6, 1852, M234:32. On Bidwell's life, see Rockwell D. Hunt, *John Bidwell: Prince of California Pioneers* (Caldwell, Idaho, 1942).

The Indian future turned out to be far different than Bidwell had imagined. By 1860 only thirty-two thousand California natives had survived the vicissitudes of the preceding decade. Murder, starvation, and disease claimed thousands of lives and the survivors had to reckon with entirely new conditions of life. The future of Indian society would be based not only on the sheer number of natives, but on social circumstances that encouraged or retarded procreation. According to the demographer Sherburne F. Cook, native numbers continued to fall until about 1900, when they reached a nadir of between twenty and twenty-two thousand. Cook postulated that Indian demographic decline was due partly to a "palpable fall in the birthrate concerning which we have little factual knowledge." This lack of knowledge is not surprising. Like other poor working people, the California Indians left no well-documented record of their daily lives. By using techniques derived from social history and demography, however, it is possible to gain a fuller understanding of the gold rush's effect upon native reproduction and survival. At the same time, this analysis provides insights into the ways that Anglo and Hispanic traditions merged on the Spanish borderland frontier during a time of rapid modernization.[2]

The 1860 federal census offers a wealth of information on Indian people at the household level. Census takers, who received two cents for each person counted, enumerated 17,798 Indians in California, by far the highest Indian population enumerated in any state. Excluded were reservation Indians, those in flight or rebellion, and native people "retaining their tribal character," who were estimated to number 13,540. The manuscript census includes such demographic data as name, age, sex, and usually occupation. Often marital status is indicated or can be inferred from circumstantial evidence. In addition, all data were organized on the basis of each dwelling visited by the census officer, thus making possible an analysis of the household. Since the enumerated Indians frequently lived in close association with whites, the manuscript census provides a close-up view of their relations with one another.[3]

2. Cook, *Population of the California Indians*, 44–73; and Cook, "Destruction of the California Indian," 14–19.

3. *U.S. Statutes at Large*, 9:428–36; table VI, "Chinese, Japanese, and Civilized Indian Population at Each Census," in Francis A. Walker, comp., *A Compendium of the Ninth Census (June 1 1870)* (Washington, D.C., 1872), 18; table I, "Population by Age and Sex," in Joseph C. G. Kennedy, comp., *Population of the United States in 1860* (Washington, D.C., 1864), 22–27, 605. Sherburne F. Cook found the published 1860 census a "very poor enumeration" that could be "discarded completely" for his purpose of establishing the total number of Indians in the state (*Population of the California Indians*, 53). Apparently he did not examine the census carefully. Cook erroneously criticized C. Hart Merriam's "Indian Population of California" (*American Anthropologist*, n.s., 7., no. 4

The census indicated several general demographic characteristics of the California population that must be taken into account for the study of Indian people in 1860. The state contained 379,994 persons, 70 percent of whom were males and 60 percent of whom were white males. Overall, the population was young—nearly 60 percent were under thirty. Of the four racial categories identified in the census—white, colored, Indian, and Asian—all showed exceedingly high sex ratios that usually portend reproduction problems unless immigration or intermarriage with other groups provides new females of childbearing age.[4]

Like the white population, the enumerated Indians were mostly young males (see table 10.1). Theoretically, this Indian population was the soundest reproductive group because it had the highest female-to-male ratio. Statistically, however, Indian women bore fewer live children and raised fewer of them to maturity than their white counterparts. The published census reveals that the Indian population had been redistributed since 1852. Predictably, the highest reported county Indian population was 3,294 in Fresno County (formerly part of Tulare County) in the San Joaquin Valley (see map 6). Yet numbers for the San Joaquin had declined by more than 6,000 during the eight years since the state

---

[1905], 594–606) because Merriam correctly stated that the 1860 census indicated there were 31,338 Indians in the state. Cook overlooked the fact that the census takers estimated there were 13,540 Indians not enumerated in Kennedy's *Population in 1860*, 605. Cook did not examine the manuscript census returns. Another critic of the 1860 census, Francis A. Walker, superintendent of the 1870 census, incorrectly stated that most of the 17,798 California Indians enumerated in 1860 were on reservations and should not have been included in the computation of the representative population (*Compendium of the Ninth Census*, 19). Actually, there were no reservations in many counties that reported substantial Indian populations. In 1860 the Indian Office did not provide complete population estimates for California reservations, but in 1858 and 1859 Indian agents estimated there were 10,500 Indians on reserves, a figure that far exceeded the 1860 census totals for the counties in which the reservations were located. In 1861 the Indian Office reported that there were perhaps 8,000 Indians on the reservations, but even this figure was criticized as inflated. See *Annual Report, Commissioner of Indian Affairs*, 1858, Sen. Ex. Doc. 1, 35th Cong., 2d sess., ser. 974, 643; 1859, Sen. Ex. Doc. 1, 36th Cong., 1st sess., ser. 1023, 805–11; and 1861, Sen. Ex. Doc. 1, 37th Cong., 2d sess., ser. 1117, 760. Much of the information about Indians in households is inferred from the order in which the census takers listed the inhabitants. The household head was named first, followed by his spouse and children, if any. Other residents were listed after the family unit. For an example of how such inferences can be used, see Barbara Laslett, "Household Structure on an American Frontier: Los Angeles, California, in 1850," *American Journal of Sociology*, 81 (July 1975):109–28.

4. Sex ratios (males per 100 females) were 238.1 for whites, 227.3 for coloreds, 2,000 for Asians, and 147.1 for Indians (Kennedy, *Population in 1860*, 28). See also Teitelbaum, "Factors Associated with the Sex Ratio," 90–109; and Eblen, "Analysis of Nineteenth Century Frontier Populations," 399–413.

TABLE 10.1.   *Regional Indian Population by Age and Sex in 1860*

Age and sex	Southern region	Central Coast region	Sacramento Valley region	San Joaquin Valley region	Northern region
0–14					
M (%)	16.9	19.8	13.0	14.0	24.4
F (%)	14.3	13.9	7.4	14.3	19.4
Sex ratio	118.2	142.4	175.7	97.9	125.8
15–39					
M (%)	26.6	31.1	47.7	39.6	22.3
F (%)	23.4	17.0	25.1	17.1	28.4
Sex ratio	113.7	182.9	190.0	231.6	78.5
40–59					
M (%)	7.7	7.4	4.7	8.6	3.4
F (%)	5.2	3.4	1.2	2.4	1.9
Sex ratio	148.1	217.6	391.7	358.3	178.9
60+					
M (%)	3.4	4.7	0.8	3.1	0.3
F (%)	2.3	2.6	0	1.0	0
Sex ratio	147.8	180.8	N/A	310.0	N/A
Total population					
Male	4,640	1,690	884	3,059	314
Female	3,834	992	450	1,625	310
TOTALS	8,474	2,682	1,334	4,684	624

Source: 1860 Federal Manuscript Census, California State Archives.

census. Mother Lode mining counties reported nearly 9,000 fewer Indians. While some Sacramento Valley counties reported increases of several dozen, it is difficult to find positive meaning in this statistic because the state had created some new counties and had redrawn old county boundaries after 1852. More important are the substantial drops in counties which had had significant Indian populations eight years previously. Sutter County Indians decreased from over 500 to 10, and Yolo from 152 to zero. The few reported increases probably resulted from Indians migrating from other counties. Sex ratios and age statistics varied from county to county, too.[5]

The differing regional population patterns displayed in table 10.1 assume a larger significance when viewed through the microscope of household analysis. To analyze these trends it is helpful to divide California into five areas with distinct settlement histories: the southern, central coast, Sacramento Valley, San Joaquin Valley, and northern

5. Kennedy, *Population in 1860*, 22–28.

regions. Hispanic people settled the first two regions, so their impact on Indian populations can be compared to that of Anglos elsewhere. Within selected precincts in each region, the Indian population is analyzed according to family structure and the ethnicity of heads of households. The correlation of ethnicity and family structure shows significant variations in patterns of Indian household life throughout California.[6]

The southern region was originally the home of numerous tribes with large populations. These people, like other California Indians, divided their labor between the sexes, with men hunting and fishing and women gathering plant foods. Parents often arranged the marriage of their children, a practice that reflected the economic and social utility of the unions. Most couples lived in single-family households near the husband's parents. Generally speaking, only chiefs, shamans, or other powerful men had more than one wife.[7]

The Indians in the southern region were the first California native people to experience Hispanic colonization. Beginning in 1769, Spanish soldiers and missionaries founded a system of missions, presidios, and pueblos. Indian neophytes formed a labor pool for the missions, which were the primary economic institutions in the colony; but they died at a rapid rate, thus requiring the Franciscans to recruit new converts from the interior valley. Still the demographic decline continued, undercutting

6. The southern region includes Los Angeles, Santa Barbara, San Bernardino, and San Diego counties. The central coast region includes Alameda, Contra Costa, Marin, Mendocino, Monterey, Napa, Santa Clara, Santa Cruz, San Francisco, San Mateo, and Sonoma counties. The Sacramento Valley region includes Butte, Colusa, El Dorado, Nevada, Placer, Plumas, Sacramento, Sierra, Solano, Sutter, Tehama, Yolo, and Yuba counties. The Northern region includes Del Norte, Humboldt, Klamath, Shasta, Siskiyou and Trinity counties. Note that these were the counties as the boundaries were drawn in 1860. A no-family household did not contain an identifiable conjugal couple, while a simple-family household included a couple and their offspring, if any. The simple-family-plus-others households contained a family unit as well as unrelated residents. An extended-family household included blood-related kin in addition to the nuclear group. A multiple-family household had two or more conjugal couples and their offspring. Peter Laslett's definition of family structure is relied on here, except that the term *simple family* rather than *nuclear family* is used, and single parents with children are included in the no-family category so that a clear idea of Indian families capable of reproduction can be obtained. See Peter Laslett, ed., *Household and Family in Past Time* (Cambridge, England, 1972), 34.

7. Heizer and Elsasser, *Natural World of the California Indians*, 45–52. The tribes in the southern California culture area are Chumash, Alliklik, Kitanemuk, Fernandeño, Gabrieleño, Juaneño, Luiseño, Cupeño, Diegueño, Serraño, Cahuilla, and Kamia. The Great Basin groups in the southern region are Kawaiisu, Vanyume, and Chemehuevi. The Colorado River tribes—Mohave, Halchidoma, and Yum—were not considered in this study because they occupied areas peripheral to southern California settlement (ibid., 29, and Heizer, *Handbook*, 511, 523, 544–45, 556, 572, 581–82, 589, 602).

the missions' source of labor and causing their decay as the economic mainstay for Spanish California. After 1821 Mexican independence led to the secularization of the missions, the distribution of their vast property holdings, and the dispersal of the neophytes. Some of the Franciscan-trained natives returned to their homes in the interior, while others found work in the Mexican settlements or on large land-grant ranchos that replaced the missions as the dominant institutions in the province. Under Mexican sovereignty, Indians remained California's basic labor force. Eighty years of relations with Hispanic people led to a statewide decline in Indian population from an estimated 300,000 to about 150,000. Due principally to disease, the decline took sharpest effect in the mission and rancho districts.[8]

During the gold rush Los Angeles grew rapidly and became an important regional trading center. Anglo immigrants displaced many of the old Mexican landholders, but Indians remained as house servants and field hands. Their subservient position was institutionalized to a certain extent by Chapter 133, which provided for the arrest and indenture of loitering and intoxicated Indians. Local authorities, added another feature: every week in Los Angeles Indian prisoners were "auctioned off to the highest bidder for private service." At the week's end the rancheros paid these coerced Indians partly with liquor, helping to assure enough intoxicated Indians for the next auction and a steady supply of labor. Under the threat of arrest and auction, Indians competed fiercely for a limited number of steady jobs as house servants at wages reportedly ranging from fifty cents to one dollar per day.[9]

The sample household analysis of Los Angeles Indians illustrates the results of these local social and economic conditions (see table 10.2). More than half of the Indians lived in non-Indian households, and most of them lived in no-family quarters on nearby ranchos with other male

8. Cook, "The Indian Versus the California Mission," 1–194; Cook, "The Physical and Demographic Reaction of Nonmission Indians," 1–55; Robert Archibald, *The Economic Aspects of the California Missions* (Washington, D.C., 1978), 142–58; Francis F. Guest, "An Examination of the Thesis of S. F. Cook on the Forced Conversion of Indians in the California Missions," *Southern California Quarterly*, 61 (Spring 1979):1–77; Hurtado, "Controlling Californian's Indian Labor Force: Federal Administration of California Indian Affairs during the Mexican War, 1846–1849," *Southern California Quarterly* 61 (Fall 1979):217–38; and George Harwood Phillips, "Indians in Los Angeles, 1781–1875: Economic Integration, Social Disintegration," *Pacific Historical Review* 69 (August 1980):427–51; Phillips, *Chiefs and Challengers*; and Cook, *Population of the California Indians*, 43.

9. Leonard Pitt, *Decline of the Californios: A Social History of the Spanish-Speaking Californians, 1846–1890* (Berkeley 1966), 121; and Phillips, "Indians in Los Angeles," 440–41, 443, 451; and Los Angeles Common Council minutes, August 16, 1850, quoted ibid., 444.

TABLE 10.2.   *Los Angeles County Sample Households, 1860*

Household type	Ethnicity											
	Non-Indian			Indian			Mixed			Total		
	C	N	%	C	N	%	C	N	%	C	N	%
No-family	52	125	261.8	16	75	16.1	0	0	0	68	200	42.8
Simple-family	0	0	0	4	15	3.2	6	15	3.2	10	30	6.4
Simple-family + others	51	93	19.9	2	8	1.7	13	42	9.0	66	143	30.6
Extended-family	1	7	1.5	0	0	0	0	0	0	1	7	1.5
Multiple-family	6	35	7.5	2	45	9.6	3	7	1.5	11	87	18.6
TOTAL	110	260	55.7	24	143	30.6	22	64	13.7	156	467	99.9*

Source: 1860 Federal Manuscript Census, California State Archives.

C = the number of households with Indian members; N = the number of Indians in each category; % = the percentage of the sample Indian population in each category.

*Total percentage varies from 100.0 because of rounding.

workers. Nearly 20 percent of the Indians were household servants in non-Indian homes. About 30 percent of the sample Indian population lived in Indian-headed households, but less than half lived in dwellings with identifiable conjugal couples. Almost as many Indians lived in mixed households as in Indian-headed families.

Examples from the manuscript census provide additional insights into the nature of Los Angeles Indians' town and country life. Typically, Indian household servants lived in the homes of people who were at least moderately well-to-do. A twenty-five-year-old Indian servant named María, for example, lived in the house of the Polish merchant David Solomon, his wife, and three children. Solomon owned $1,000 in real estate and $4,000 in personal property. María, no doubt, assisted Mrs. Solomon with domestic chores and the many tasks associated with raising three children who were all less than five years old. Indian men as well as women worked as domestics and occasionally an Indian couple served in a household, but this was rare.[10]

Some of the major landholders on the town's outskirts kept large houses filled with family, friends, and employees. Abel Stearns, a Massachusetts man who became one of the wealthiest southern Californians, lived with his wife and nineteen unrelated people, including Juan and Antonio, Indian laborers. One of Stearns's neighbors, Mexican Cali-

10. 1860 MS Census, Los Angeles County, 30, 32, 35.

fornian Julian Chaves, was a person of more modest means, but he kept eight Indian servants, including six males in their twenties. The former American fur trapper William Wolfskill, according to the manuscript census, kept more Indians on his rancho than any of his Los Angeles counterparts. Altogether there were thirty-seven Indians living on Wolfskill's property, including eleven male farm workers, eight washerwomen, a servant, and their children. Wolfskill's rancho was an exception; most ranchos kept only a few workers except during peak seasons of the year.[11]

Compared with those in other regions, Los Angeles Indians married non-Indians fairly often (see tables 10.2–10.6). There were twenty-two households with mixed couples—about 14 percent of the households sampled. Los Angeles Indian women had spouses from Mexico, Kentucky, and elsewhere. The estates of their non-Indian spouses varied greatly, from moderate wealth to apparent pauperism.[12]

George Harwood Phillips has recently described the history of Los Angeles as a dual process of "economic integration" and "social disintegration." Phillips writes that Indian society disintegrated as a result of its limited and essentially exploited economic role, and that the disintegrative process was indicated by Indian drunkenness, vice, and violence, "which in turn led to drastic population reduction." A main contributor to the decrease in Indian numbers was disease. Moreover, household analysis shows that comparatively few Indians lived in situations in which reproduction and child rearing were feasible. In short, the Los Angeles social order that integrated most Indians into non-Indian and no-family households substantially contributed to their overall demographic decline. Social disorder, at least as contemporary whites defined it, may have been an ancillary symptom of Los Angeles' social and economic conditions.[13]

The 1860 household patterns of Los Angeles Indians were substantially different from those in other parts of Hispanic California. The divergency of living conditions is illustrated in the central coast region. Like interior Indians, those on the coast belonged to the central California culture area and were basically monogamous and patrilocal, although occasional polygyny existed. With Spanish settlement in the

11. Ibid., 57, 113–14; Doris Marion Wright, *A Yankee in Mexican California: Abel Stearns, 1798–1848* (Santa Barbara, Calif., 1977); and Iris Higbie Wilson, "William Wolfskill," in LeRoy Hafen, ed., *The Mountain Men and the Fur Trade in the Far West* (10 vols., Glendale, Calif., 1965), 2:351–62. For Julian Chaves, see "Pioneer Register," in Bancroft, *History of California*, 3:758.

12. 1860 MS Census, Los Angeles County, 6, 13.

13. Phillips, "Indians in Los Angeles," 427–28, 451.

eighteenth century, Central Coast Indians entered the Franciscan missions, where they suffered the usual consequences of disease and demographic reduction. During the 1820s and 1830s, mission secularization dispersed the Indians to the surrounding ranchos and urban settlements, where they worked as herdsmen and servants. By the time of the gold rush, the central coast Indians were gaining social acceptance in the Mexican community. Increasingly, people of undiluted Indian ancestry were recorded in local records as *vecinos* and *vecinas* (citizens) rather than *indigenas* (Indians).[14]

In 1860 the Indian population of the central coast region was only about one third as large as that of the southern region (see table 10.1). The central coast Indians were mostly young males, although the age distribution and sex ratios were not so radically imbalanced as those in other parts of California. The ratio of females of childbearing age to males shows there was an important deficit of potentially fertile women in the Indian population.

In the town of Monterey and its surrounding ranchos, the correlation of household types and ethnicity shows that a majority of Indians lived in Indian households, while most of the remainder lived in non-Indian households (see Table 10.3). By household type, Indians were distributed about equally among households categorized as no-family, simple-family, and simple-family-plus-others. The largest correlative Indian group was living in simple-family households, while the next largest number of Indians lived in non-Indian simple-family-plus-others households. About 32 percent of the population sample lived in Indian and non-Indian no-family household settings.[15]

The Monterey census indicates that Indians played economic roles similar to those in southern California. Most men were unskilled laborers working on ranchos, while women labored as domestics in the homes of affluent Anglos and Hispanos. Household servants were usually between fifteen and forty years old, although servants as young as eight were recorded. The Indian domestic staff in the David Spence home offers an example. Spence, a wealthy merchant and landowner, lived with his wife, their son and daughter-in-law, and two grandchildren. The Spences kept three female Indians to serve them, aged twenty-five, twelve, and eight. Spence's home was like those of his landed Mexican

14. Tribes of the central coast region were Pomo, Wappo, Coast Miwok, Costanoan, Esselen, and Salinan. See Heizer and Elsasser, *Natural World of the California Indians*, 29; Heizer, *Handbook*, 259, 296, 488, 490, 502; Malcolm Margolin, *The Ohlohne Way: Indian Life in the San Francisco-Monterey Bay Area* (Berkeley, 1978), 83–84; and Cook and Borah, *Essays in Population History*, 83–84.

15. Kennedy, *Population in 1860*, 26–27; and 1860 MS Census, Monterey County.

TABLE 10.3. *Monterey County Sample Households, 1860*

Household type	Non-Indian			Indian			Mixed			Total		
	C	N	%	C	N	%	C	N	%	C	N	%
No-family	14	16	11.9	8	27	20.2	0	0	0	22	43	32.1
Simple-family	0	0	0	8	37	27.6	3	6	4.5	11	43	32.1
Simple-family + others	18	36	26.9	1	5	3.8	1	4	3.0	20	45	33.6
Extended-family	1	3	2.2	0	0	0	0	0	0	1	3	2.2
Multiple-family	0	0	0	0	0	0	0	0	0	0	0	0
TOTAL	33	55	41.0	17	69	51.5	4	10	7.5	54	134	100.0

Above the ethnicity columns: **Ethnicity**

Source: 1860 Federal Manuscript Census, California State Archives.

C = the number of households with Indian members; N = the number of Indians in each category; % = the percentage of the sample Indian population in each category.

contemporaries—the Garcías, Sepulvedas, and de la Torres. In Monterey's genteel Anglo and Mexican society, for those households classified as simple-family-plus-others, Indian servants were the "others."[16]

Monterey Indian simple-family and no-family households differed in their social composition, but they were similar in other respects. Both types of households were composed of working people variously identified as laborers and servants. In some cases the census even identified children as servants. For example, in the Indian simple-family household apparently associated with the rancho of County Treasurer Thomas Day, the Indian parents as well as their children (ages eleven, four, and one) were identified as farm servants. In the mind of the census taker, as this classification implies, Indian occupational status was to some extent hereditary.[17]

Indian and white household arrangements in Monterey were the result of several generations of Hispanic colonization and tradition. Like those in Los Angeles, Monterey's Indians were integrated into the social and economic structure, but they had an additional measure of control over their lives because they headed most of their own households. Still, the deficit of potential Indian mothers and the relative lack of identifiable conjugal couples meant that the Monterey population could not easily

16. "Pioneer Register," Bancroft, *History of California* 5:730–31 (on David Spence's career); 1860 MS Census, Monterey County, 9, 10, 12, 15.
17. 1860 MS Census, Monterey County, 33.

TABLE 10.4.   *Butte County Sample Households, 1860*

Household type	Non-Indian C	Non-Indian N	Non-Indian %	Indian C	Indian N	Indian %	Mixed C	Mixed N	Mixed %	Total C	Total N	Total %
No-family	11	15	12.6	6	85	71.4	0	0	0	17	100	84.0
Simple-family	0	0	0	0	0	0	2	3	2.5	2	3	2.5
Simple-family + others	10	16	13.5	0	0	0	0	0	0	10	16	13.5
Extended-family	0	0	0	0	0	0	0	0	0	0	0	0
Multiple-family	0	0	0	0	0	0	0	0	0	0	0	0
TOTAL	21	31	26.1	6	85	71.4	2	3	2.5	29	119	100.0

Source: 1860 Federal Manuscript Census, California State Archives.

C = the number of households with Indian members; N = the number of Indians in each category; % = the percentage of the sample Indian population in each category.

sustain itself. Moreover, while Monterey Indians lived in relative peace, they also lived in poverty. As in Los Angeles, Indians in Monterey comprised a part of the working class whose reproductive future was in doubt.

Indian household structures in Hispanic California were rooted in the past. Reliance on Indian labor, large domestic staffs, and the presence of mestizo families were hallmarks of Spanish settlement. Anglo-Americans adopted Hispanic frontier practices, but modified them to suit their needs and predilections, a process that is displayed more dramatically in interior household patterns. The 1860 census enumerated only a handful of Indians in the mining counties of the Sierra foothills, but recorded modest populations in the bordering Sacramento Valley agricultural counties. More than 60 percent of the male Indians were under forty, about twice the number of their female cohorts. Proportionately, there were more Indian women of childbearing age in the Sacramento Valley than in any other region except the northern, but they produced fewer children. Indians over forty were downright rare, accounting for less than 7 percent of the population (see table 10.1).

Reasons for these disparities are found in the household structure of Indians in Butte County (see table 10.4). More than 70 percent of the Butte Indians lived in Indian no-family households, and most of them were male workers. The remaining Indians were about equally divided between non-Indian no-family and simple-family-plus-others households as workers and servants, and three Indians lived in mixed households.

Most remarkably, in the 1860 Butte census there were no identifiable Indian conjugal couples.

The Indian living arrangements on John Bidwell's Rancho Chico illustrate the kind of household that dominated Indian life in Butte County. Bidwell kept fifty-two Indians on his rancho, and fifty-one of them lived in Indian no-family households in four dwellings that were segregated by sex. Thirty-nine male herders, gardeners, and farm laborers lived in three households. Eleven women day laborers lived in a separate dwelling headed by a male named Yummarine, whom the census taker identified as chief. Ten of the women were in their prime childbearing years, between the ages of sixteen and thirty-one, yet there were no children listed in the census. Given the segregated living conditions, the absence of children was not surprising. In 1860 the Indians at Rancho Chico were there to work, not to raise families or sustain tribal populations.[18]

The Butte County ranchos with Indian households like those on Rancho Chico were all large operations. Bidwell owned $52,000 in real estate and $55,640 in personal property. Former Pennsylvanian J. A. Keefer employed twelve young Indian men and four young women on his property. He owned $3,800 worth of land and personal property valued at $10,000. Similarly, R. W. Durham claimed $8,000 in real estate and personal property worth $2,000 and employed twenty-one male Indians, all except one in their twenties.[19]

As in Monterey, most of the Butte County Indians who lived in non-Indian simple-family-plus-others households were servants; but unlike their coastal counterparts, most were young males. On the whole, Butte servants lived in modest homes of white couples with some money, although there were occasional servants in impoverished households.[20]

On the whole, Butte County contrasted sharply with Monterey and Los Angeles in its demographic composition. The Sacramento Valley Indian population seemed precariously based on one generation, with a sharp deficit of women of childbearing age, although the whole Butte

18. 1860 MS Census, Butte County, 37–39. Dorothy Hill reviewed the Butte census and claimed that Indian children were "unlisted," but she does not cite evidence to support her assertion that Indians were permitted to retain their "customary dwelling structures, food, and religious customs," even though Bidwell "forced" them to accept "new occupations" (*The Indians of Chico Rancheria* [Sacramento, 1978], 27–29). Paul Wallace Gates also reviewed the manuscript census and found in it the importance of Indian labor to Bidwell's grain farming (Gates, ed., *California Ranchos and Farms*, 45–46, n. 7). See also Anne H. Currie, "Bidwell Rancheria," *California Historical Society Quarterly* 36 (Dec. 1957):313–25.

19. 1860 MS Census, Butte County, 46, 54.

20. For example, ibid., 21, 27, 35, 59.

native population may have been more broadly based than the census shows. In the margin of the manuscript census an officer wrote "16 Indians in Rancheria unemployed," implying that Indians who did not work were not enumerated. The census showed no other unenumerated Indian communities in the county, but it is evident that to have stable family lives, Indian people would have to establish them outside the social and economic realm of 1860 Butte County ranchos, where the sexes were segregated and marriage and child rearing were discouraged.[21]

In 1860 living conditions for Indians in California's interior were by no means uniform. At the southern end of the valley, in the San Joaquin region, Indian household structures were very different from those in the Butte County sample. The gold rush had an uneven impact on the San Joaquin region's Indian population. San Joaquin, Mariposa, Merced, and Stanislaus counties were virtually depopulated, but Fresno County (formerly a part of Tulare County) had 3,294 Indian people, the largest Indian population in the state, and adjacent Tulare County had 1,340 Indians. Fresno County Indians remained a substantial majority, since there were 999 whites and 312 other non-Indians in the county.[22]

The concentration of Indians in Fresno County was due in some measure to the presence of the Fresno River Farm subagency, which operated until 1861. To augment the farm's produce, some of the agency Indians worked on local ranchos. Even Indians who lived in the mountains relied to some extent on the Fresno River Farm. For example, the Mono Indians worked for white settlers during planting and harvest times, mined gold in the winter and the spring, and gathered "the natural products of the mountains," a subagent reported. In addition, the Mono Indians received some food and clothing at the government farm. With all these sources of supply the Monos had "been able to provide themselves with a comfortable living for Indians." Until it closed, the Fresno River Farm was a temporary refuge for Indians whom whites had dispossessed.[23]

The Fresno County household sample reveals another distinctive pattern. Almost 90 percent of the Fresno Indians lived in Indian households; more than 50 percent of the sample population lived in dwellings containing identifiable conjugal couples. Fewer Indians lived in all kinds of

21. Ibid., 46.

22. *1860 Census*, 28.

23. Hill, *The Office of Indian Affairs*, 19–27; Edward F. Beale to Lea, Dec. 14, 1852, M234:33; and *Annual Report of the Commissioner of Indian Affairs*, 1859, Sen. Ex. Doc. 1, 36th Cong., 1st sess., ser. 1023, 809–10.

TABLE 10.5.   *Fresno County Sample Households, 1860*

	Ethnicity											
Household type	Non-Indian			Indian			Mixed			Total		
	C	N	%	C	N	%	C	N	%	C	N	%
No-family	15	43	8.9	29	169	34.9	0	0	0	92	484	100.1*
Simple-family	0	0	0	11	58	12.0	2	2	0.4	13	60	12.4
Simple-family + others	9	10	2.1	20	147	30.4	1	2	0.4	30	159	32.9
Extended-family	0	0	0	0	0	0	0	0	0	0	0	0
Multiple-family	0	0	0	5	53	11.0	0	0	0	5	53	11.0
TOTAL	24	53	11.0	65	427	88.3	3	4	0.8	92	484	100.1*

Source: 1860 Federal Manuscript Census, California State Archives.

C = the number of households with Indian members; N = the number of Indians in each category; % = the percentage of the sample Indian population in each category.
*Total percentage varies from 100.0 because of rounding.

non-Indian homes than in any other region, and less than 1 percent lived in mixed households (see table 10.5).

Not only did Fresno's native people live in Indian households, they lived in their own communities. One of these communities contained 286 Indians in thirty-seven households. The census officer recorded a forty-year-old man named Wuemekana as chief of the community. Wuemekana lived with his wife and three children, a sixty-year-old servant, the servant's wife, and their three children, plus a forty-year-old woman. No other household listed a servant in this large community. Except for Wuemekana's servant, the census taker indicated no non-Indian occupations but occasionally noted that a man was a "brave," which apparently indicated a different status, at least in the mind of the white officer. In other communities the census taker found a "Great War Chief," a woman "fortune-teller," and several male Indian "doctors."[24]

Native people defined their own household and social relationships within Fresno County's Indian communities, even though they worked periodically for white ranchers. Outside the Indian communities the patterns in non-Indian no-family households were similar to those found in Butte. Young Indian men lived with whites as servants. Most of the non-Indian household heads appeared to be men of moderate means or better, with sufficient capital to afford a servant.[25]

24. 1860 MS Census, Fresno County, 41–48.
25. Ibid., 1.

TABLE 10.6. *Trinity County Sample Households, 1860*

Household type	Non-Indian			Indian			Mixed			Total		
	C	N	%	C	N	%	C	N	%	C	N	%
No-family	9	12	15.2	1	1	1.3	0	0	0	10	13	16.5
Simple-family	0	0	0	0	0	0	18	35	44.3	18	35	44.3
Simple-family + others	8	9	11.4	0	0	0	8	16	20.3	16	25	31.7
Extended-family	0	0	0	0	0	0	0	0	0	0	0	0
Multiple-family	0	0	0	0	0	0	2	6	7.6	2	6	7.6
TOTAL	17	21	26.6	1	1	1.3	28	57	72.2	46	79	100.1*

Source: 1860 Federal Manuscript Census, California State Archives.

C = the number of households with Indian members; N = the number of Indians in each category; % = the percentage of the sample Indian population in each category.

*Total percentage varies from 100.0 because of rounding.

Although Fresno County Indians remained the local majority population and many of them retained substantial control over their community and household lives, they were somewhat reliant on the white economy and federal assistance for survival. Far from being autonomous native societies in Indian country, the Fresno Indians were a dependent and declining refugee population with a deficiency of women of childbearing age.

The last example of Indian household life comes from the northern region, where Hispanic colonization had no direct effect. During the gold rush, however, the north became a battleground and Indians withdrew to isolated mountains hideouts. As might be anticipated, federal census takers enumerated fewer Indians in the northern region than in any other area in the state, and the small Indian population in the 1860 census presented a unique demographic picture (see table 10.1). There were nearly as many Indian women as men in the total population and more women of childbearing age than their male cohorts. Children under fourteen formed more than 40 percent of the Indian population; nearly 95 percent of the enumerated native people were under forty.

The Trinity County household sample is likewise unique (see table 10.6). Nearly three quarters of the sample population lived in mixed simple-family and multiple-family households. All of the conjugal couples consisted of white males and Indian females. The census takers counted racially mixed offspring as Indians, sometimes recording such children as half-breeds. Typically, the husbands of these unions were landless farmers and miners with little or no personal property. Most of the males were between twenty and forty years of age, but their spouses were very young, usually between the ages of thirteen and twenty.[26]

The emotional depth of these unions is difficult to judge and it is not unreasonable to suspect that many were temporary alliances of convenience for the white men. Still, the manuscript census indicates that about half of the white partners conferred their last names on their spouses and children. Two families from the manuscript census offer illustrations of this point. David Peters, a landless Pennsylvania blacksmith with $190 worth of personal property, headed a mixed household in Trinity County. Peters was thirty and his Indian wife, Ellen Peters, was eighteen. They had a two-month-old infant son named Samuel Peters. On the other hand, J. Stewart, a propertyless miner in his thirties from Maine, lived with the teenaged Indian Mary Jane and her two-year-old daughter, Mary Ann. Peters seemed to have married and legitimized— at least for the census taker—his young son. Stewart apparently did not seek to formalize his relationship with Mary Jane or her daughter.[27]

Conjugal coupling did not necessarily indicate conjugal bliss or a humane attitude on the part of the white men who lived with Indian women. A white army officer remarked on the casual brutality that erupted in one mixed household in 1862. A frontiersman who had lived in the northern region with an Indian woman for years without warning beat "his own child's brains out against a tree and kill[ed] the squaw, its mother" because he had no other way of getting rid of them, and "to keep them from falling into another persons hands." These intimate murders convey the terrible possibilities of a mixed household in the war-torn and remote northern region.[28]

The Trinity County Indian and white social arrangements were distinct from those in other regions in the state. There was no place for Indian households within white society. Indian labor was important specifically in the context of the family, where women performed the wifely duties of housework and child rearing. Trinity Indians who lived in non-Indian households had a place in arrangements that resembled those in Butte and Fresno counties. Young Indian men lived in white

26. 1860 MS Census, Trinity County, 31 and 33–35, gives examples of such households.

27. Ibid., 31, 40.

28. U.S. Department of War, *War of the Rebellion Records: A Compilation of the Official Records of the Union and Confederate Armies* (70 vols., Washington, D.C., 1880–1901), vol. 50, part 1, 73–75.

households as servants, acting, in a sense, as surrogate wives—cooking, cleaning, and serving for white men.[29]

The regional patterns of Indian and white household life found in the 1860 census illustrate the variety of the native experience in the decade following the gold rush. In regions with Hispanic traditions, individual Indians and families were integrated into the larger society as rancho workers and servants in middle- and upper-class homes. Out of the direct path of the gold rush and in areas with substantial Hispanic populations, Anglos in Los Angeles and Monterey counties seemed to conform to the social patterns of their Hispanic neighbors. In contrast, Butte County ranchers used Indians as workers but rigidly segregated Indian households by sex. In this Anglo-dominated region, white settlers valued Indian labor, but the Indian family had no role in Butte society. To the south in Fresno County, Indians were the majority and maintained their own communities with households that they defined. Nevertheless, Indians in Fresno County relied on whites for seasonal work on farms and livestock ranchos. In Trinity County Indians filled the usual servant's role in non-Indian households, but more of them lived in mixed homes as the spouses and children of white men. These different patterns marked the range of household life for Indians who were permitted to live in white society.

Despite the regional variations in households, two trends can be seen throughout California. Except in the northern region, there were fewer women of childbearing age than their male cohorts. Even in the north, a significant number of potentially fertile Indian women lived with white men, thus creating a shortage of women available to Indian men. The scarcity of potential mothers was a severe problem for California's Indian population, already under stress and in rapid, prolonged decline. The second trend apparent in the manuscript census is the movement of a large proportion of Indians into living situations that were not conducive to reproduction, which explains in part the fall in the birthrate that Cook noted some years ago. To our understanding of Indian death and survival we may now add the limiting effects of household arrangements that discouraged Indian marriage and child rearing. Ironically, economic and social integration created conditions that permitted individual Indians to survive, but also contributed to an overall decrease in native numbers.

A better knowledge of Indian and white household arrangements raises an old and troubling problem that extends beyond California's borders: Given the economic and social possibilities of nineteenth-cen-

29. 1860 MS Census, Trinity County, 27, 31, 71, and 91.

tury America, was integration into white society better for Indians than segregation or even armed resistance? In Anglo and Hispanic California, the transformation of native Californians from a racial and cultural majority into a working-class minority contributed to their drastic, tragic population decline. When two streams of European civilization rushed together in California, native people were soon nearly obliterated on the northwestern flank of the Spanish borderlands frontier. Yet California Indians somehow quietly persisted, living in a land that was radically transformed during the course of a single lifetime. For them, the 1860 census charts the landscape of survival and demographic decline.

Conclusion

To an extent extraordinary for Indians in the nineteenth-century United States, native Californians were subject to the vagaries of the market economy. Elsewhere the fur trade usually introduced Indians to the capitalist economy, but permanent white settlement generally left few places for Indian workers. In California, however, the advent of market agriculture did not push Indians aside, but drew them in as farm workers. In the 1840s Indians were practically the sole source of agricultural labor and whites used every possible means to obtain their services. Slavery, debt peonage, and wage labor all had a place in Mexican and Anglo California. The California experience is not suprising when compared with other frontiers and other times. The historian Howard Lamar has argued perceptively that frontier conditions often encouraged the use of coerced as well as free labor. Ethnically distinct people of color were prime candidates for labor exploitation, and in this sense California Indians shared much with black slaves, Aleut contract workers, and Mexican peons.[1]

Labor, coerced or free, did not prove to be the salvation of California Indians, for white racial attitudes as well as changing economic circumstances in the 1850s limited Indian chances for survival. The gold rush created new demands for labor, but both mining and farming rapidly became less dependent on Indian workers. Consequently, by 1860 there were fewer jobs for Indians than there had been a decade earlier. At the same time, state militia and slavers brutally attacked Indians who were unemployed or who were not confined to the reservations. Neither employment nor reservation life promised complete protection from marauding whites or starvation, and thousands of Indians—particularly those in the north—preferred to retreat from white society and take their chances on the run.

The state and federal governments alike implemented Indian policies that were rooted in the Indians' longstanding role in the agricultural economy. In 1850 the state passed Chapter 133 providing for the indenture of loitering and minor Indians, a law that was designed to assist

1. Lamar, "From Bondage to Contract," 293–96, 317.

211

whites in gaining access to Indian labor. Subsequently the federal government established an ill-conceived reservation system that failed because policy makers misunderstood the Indian role in the agricultural economy. Believing that reservations could be self-sustaining and that all able-bodied Indians could be employed in missionlike institutions, federal officials failed to achieve either goal. Exasperated administrators had to rely on Indian hunting and gathering to supplement reservation production. Indians came to regard the reservations as part of their seasonal round and few remained there permanently. Finally, the commissioner of Indian affairs understood the reservations to be supplemental to the market economy and directed his agents to find jobs for Indians on local farms. The reservation could not function as it was supposed to and the market could only absorb a fraction of the available Indian labor. Thus, Indian workers—on and off the reservations—were consigned to underemployment and poverty.

Caught between the reservation and the rancho, Indians saw their numbers decline quickly in the 1850s. The nadir did not occur until 1900, but by 1860 most of the reduction had already taken place. In succeeding decades the decline proceeded more slowly, a fact that did not indicate demographic stability so much as the inability of Indians to recover from the devastation of the 1850s. Only in the twentieth century have native Californians been able to increase their numbers.[2]

Some reasons for population decline are obvious. Disease, starvation, and violence, probably in that order, accounted for thousands of deaths. At the same time, the survivors seemed unable to produce enough offspring to recover population losses. The low natality was related to the Indians' place in the market economy and to the ubiquitous shortage of fertile women. As early as 1846 the New Helvetia census showed that the more closely Indians associated with whites, the smaller was the proportion of native women in the total Indian population. This imbalance was partly due to the selective nature of the seasonal agricultural economy that required male field workers. Moreover, women apparently faced perils that were gender-specific. Abduction, rape, prostitution, and forced concubinage threatened women's lives while removing them from the Indian reproductive cycle. At the same time, venereal diseases debilitated women and men alike, reducing their ability to reproduce. The inclusion of Indians in the work force further limited reproductive opportunities by separating families and segregating the sexes. The frontier experience was especially hard on Indian women, whose travails were reflected in statistics that showed fewer

2. Cook, *Population of the California Indians*, 44–77.

women than men—the hallmark of native California demographics during the frontier era.

Whether forced or free, Indian labor provided only for individual survival. Far from becoming a basis for the persistence of native communities, the market economy tended to break down the native family and ranchería society. The native family, with its complex network of blood and fictive kin that once provided stability in native society, became a casualty on the California borderland frontier.

From a historiographical perspective, the frontiers of Turner and Bolton collided in California, where the combination of Hispanic and Anglo traditions did deadly work among the Indians. The demographic impacts of the two frontiers were determined by two distinct impulses. Hispanics aimed to integrate Indians and Anglos sought to segregate them. In Hispanic America comparatively liberal ideas about intermarriage and the customary inclusion of Indian workers in the larger society did not stop native demographic decline, but built a foundation for a mixed-blood population that would replace Indians. In the mid-nineteenth century Anglo-Americans segregated Indians on reservations and destroyed recalcitrants, rather than integrating them into white society. Although there was little in Anglo-American tradition to encourage Indian integration at any level, Anglos in labor-scarce California readily followed the Hispanic model and accepted Indian workers. But when the Anglo-American people took full control of California, Indians had to compete in an economy that had a surplus of labor and in a racist society that discouraged intermarriage. Thus, the living space for Indians on the margins of white society steadily eroded.

Hispanic and Anglo traditions coexisted uneasily in the 1850s, when California's Indians were expected to survive in the workplace and on segregated reservations. The 1852 and 1860 censuses show the approximate number of Indians within white society, while reservation counts give the number of Indians who were officially segregated. Together, these figures define the number of Indians who were tolerated within the new state. In 1852, before any reservations existed, the state census enumerated approximately thirty-one thousand domesticated Indians. In 1860 nearly eighteen thousand Indians were enumerated in the federal census, and in 1859 Indian agents estimated that there were about ten thousand reservation inmates, although this may have been an overstatement. The total, approximately twenty-eight thousand, was about the number of Indians that white Californians would allow in the state. This figure was 15 to 30 percent higher than the Indian population nadir of twenty to twenty-four thousand at the end of the century. Bearing in mind the aphorism that there are lies, damned lies, and statistics, it should be understood that this is by no means a scientific demographic formula. Rather, it serves to underscore a basic point: in California, both Anglo and Hispanic traditions *limited* Indian survival in the 1850s and defined the upper limits of California Indian population for the second half of the nineteenth century.[3]

To return to the question posed at the end of the last chapter: Were Indians better off when segregated from white society or when integrated into it? We are fortunate that this question is merely academic for us; California Indians faced this dilemma daily in the 1850s. To nineteenth-century Anglo policy makers, segregation seemed the only way to protect Indian populations; yet California contained so many Indians that the newcomers found it inconceivable to set aside sufficient land for their needs. The few Indians who resided on reservations lived in poverty. The only white-approved alternative—working for white landowners—was potentially destructive because working in the white community fragmented Indian society even though it sustained individuals. Indian flight and rebellion brought military reprisals that wiped out whole communities. Some Indians, like the Monos, moved constantly from the reservation to private ranches to hunting and gathering grounds, making use of all available opportunities to create a new seasonal round. Other native people chose one survival strategy or another and lived or died with it.

Insofar as Indians lived in a distinctly dangerous world, they deserve full credit for surviving in it. Far from being passive, they fought and accommodated according to their needs and local conditions. The Miwoks and Yokuts best exemplify the flexible spirit with which native Californians faced the abrupt changes of an unpredictable age. Beginning as hunters and gatherers, some became Christian neophytes who lived out their lives in the Franciscan missions. Others chose to be horse-thief Indians who fought Mexicans, allied with fur traders, resisted Sutter, marched with the California Battalion, opened the southern mines, and peacefully accommodated to the reservation. Of all the interior Indians enumerated in 1860, the Yokuts retained the largest measure of control over their communities. Yet even they could not ward off the effects of disease and a resource base that diminished year by year. Most Indians in California were overwhelmed in the 1850s, but that does not mean they became mere observers of their fates. Indeed, the regional patterns that can be identified so clearly in the censuses

3. Ibid.; Kennedy, *Population in 1860*, 26–27, 605; *Annual Report of the Commissioner of Indian Affairs*, 1859, Sen. Ex. Doc. 1, 36th Cong., 1st sess., ser. 1023, 805–8; and *Annual Report of the Commissioner of Indian Affairs*, 1861, Sen. Ex. Doc. 1, 37th Cong, 2d sess., ser. 1117, 757, 828–29.

were due in part to choices that these people made to control their own lives.

But statistics do not tell the story of survival as eloquently as the lives of Indians like José Jesus, Sarah Winnemucca, Estanislao, Tomquit, and many others (see fig. 15). Even after Anglos had established control and Indians were no longer significant in the work force, some Indians were not quickly forgotten by the whites who supplanted them. Anashe, a Gualacomne Miwok headman who consistently sided with Sutter, deeply impressed whites who knew him in the 1840s. In 1862 Sutter remembered Anashe fondly when Samuel Hensley suggested naming a steam tugboat for the Miwok man. Among the first Indians to meet Sutter in the Sacramento Valley in 1839, Anashe remained friendly to him throughout the 1840s. While other Indians fought him, "Anashe always proved a great friend," Sutter recalled, "not only to me but to all whites." Sutter demonstrated his regard for the Miwok headman during the measles epidemic of 1847. Anashe's daughter was one of the victims and Sutter spent a considerable amount of time and energy trying to cure her. Although she died, Anashe remained loyal to Sutter. It is not known what became of Anashe during the gold rush, but evidently he was dead in 1862. In the old pioneer's opinion, "the Indian chief was well worthy of being" the namesake of the new steam vessel. It was ironic that whites applied an Indian's name to a device that represented the age of steam, industrialization, and modernization—the very forces that displaced California Indians.[4]

Indians like Anashe were easy to remember pleasantly through the hazy glow of pioneer memory. Other Indians—especially those who were not always helpful to whites—found no acclaim in California. Anashe's contemporary, the Muquelemne Miwok headman Maximo, had also supplied Indian workers for New Helvetia, but he broke with Sutter when the Swiss colonizer killed Maximo's son Raphero. After Maximo withdrew his support, Sutter retaliated by seeing to it that the Miwok leader was driven off his land. Nevertheless, Maximo continued to live in the Mokelumne River country, surviving the gold rush and subsequent decades as well.[5]

Sutter, who had profoundly influenced Indians in California, in some ways shared their fate. Though he was lionized as a founding pioneer, the old adventurer lost all of his California land. Eventually he retired to Pennsylvania and petitioned Congress for money he claimed the

4. "The Launch of a Tug Boat," Sacramento *Union*, Sept. 29, 1862, 1; Sutter et al., *New Helvetia Diary*, 58–101.

5. "An Aged Indian Chief," Sacramento *Daily Record Union*, May 25, 1885, 4.

Fig. 15. Mike Clenso in Old Age. Mike Clenso, one of the Nisenan laborers who built New Helvetia, survived the tumult of the gold rush and lived to an old age. He posed in clothing that was typical of Indian workers in the late 19th century.

FIG. 16. Miwok Indians. In the early 1880s these unidentified Indians lived and worked on the McFarland Ranch on the Cosumnes River near Galt. Could the elderly man in the background be Maximo? Certainly he was one of the Miwok leader's contemporaries.

government owed him for his services during the Mexican War. As it turned out, the federal government served Sutter no better than the Indians, for Congress never gave him a cent. Living his final years in penury, he was reduced to accepting charity from a stranger interested old pioneers. Sutter died in the summer of 1880, bitterly disappointed because Congress had not paid his claim.[6]

As would be expected, Sutter's relatives marked his passing with deep personal mourning. Not all Californians mourned for him, however. Five years after Sutter was in the grave, an old Indian man wearing a dilapidated felt hat visited the town of Galt. It was Maximo, perhaps one hundred years old and bent with age. A sparse gray beard covered the tattoos on Maximo's chin, and his pierced nose was destitute of the ornaments he wore as a young man. He spoke in English to a newspaper editor about the 1840s, of helping Sutter and other whites, of the killing of his son and his anger with the lord of New Helvetia. Despite his troubles with Sutter, Maximo maintained friendly relations with other

6. Sutter to Rudd, Oct. 30, Nov. 7, and Dec. 26, 1879, RM; and Emil Victor Sutter to Rudd, Aug. 10, 1880, RM.

whites, supplying them with workers when Indian labor was in demand. Maximo may have taken secret pleasure in knowing that he had outlived his old nemesis, Sutter. In the end, survival was Maximo's revenge. After Sutter killed Maximo's son and the Indian's first wife died, Maximo remarried and fathered more children. The Sutters were all gone, but there were still Muquelemnes in California (see fig. 16).[7]

Simple survival required flexibility, tenacity, and even heroism of Indians like Maximo. Nevertheless, Indians finally watched California slip from their grasp as newcomers stripped them of their lands and technology robbed them of a livelihood. Indians could affect their destinies, but they were not the masters of the new California. The few survivors would remain impoverished and dispossessed casualties of a new age. If mastery of new conditions eluded California's Indians, they were little different in that respect from other people who have been forced to adapt to novel situations. While native Californians coped with change, industrialism and the mechanization of agriculture in Western Europe and the United States were forcing other rural people into new ways of life. Their struggles, successes, and failures were often masked by the very processes that adversely affected them. California Indians had fewer options than whites who faced radical change, so shifting conditions took a deadly toll. The result for Indians was demographic disaster, but the importance of the California Indian experience extends far beyond high morbidity and depressed natality rates. Their story shows clearly the human costs of bringing California into the ambit of the modern world economic system. That so few Indians survived is stark evidence of the prodigious upheavals of a remarkable time. That any Indians survived is testimony that abhorrent conditions can produce courage and strength in people, a tribute to the persistence of humankind.

7. "An Aged Indian Chief," Sacramento *Daily Record Union*, May 25, 1885, 4.

Sources

I. Manuscripts

A. National Archives, Washington, D.C.
1. Records of the United States Army Continental Commands, 1821–1920 (Record Group 393).

   Letters Sent by the Governors and Secretary of State of California, 1847–1848. National Archives Microfilm Publication M182.
   Records of the Tenth Military Department, 1846–1851. National Archives Microfilm Publication M210.
   Records of the Pacific Division. Letters Received.
   Records of the Department of the Pacific. Reports Relating to Indian Customs.
2. Records of the United States General Accounting Office (Record Group 217).

   Selected Records of the General Accounting Office Relating to the Frémont Expeditions and the California Battalion, 1842–1890. National Archives Microfilm Publication T135.
3. Records of the Bureau of Indian Affairs (Record Group 75).

   Documents Relating to the Negotiations of Ratified and Unratified Treaties With Various Indian Tribes, 1801–1869. National Archives Microfilm Publication T494.
   Letters Received by the Office of Indian Affairs, 1824–1881. California Superintendency. Letters Received, 1849–1880. National Archives Microfilm Publication M234.

B. California State Archives, Sacramento
1. Records of the Military Department. Adjutant General.

   Indian War Papers.
2. Records of the California Department of State.

   1860 Federal Manuscript Census. Schedule A.
   1852 California Special Census. Schedule I.
3. Records of the State Legislature.

   State Senate. Old Bill File.

C. The Bancroft Library, Berkeley

1. Manuscript Collections

Archives of California, 1767–1850. Departmental State Papers. Benecia.
Bigler, John. Correspondence and Papers.
Booth, Joseph W. Diary, 1852–1853.
Dixon, H. S. G. Letter to H. H. Bancroft, May 1, 1875.
Fitch, Henry Delano. Papers.
Henley, Thomas Jefferson. Letter to George W. Manypenny, April 14, 1855.
Knight, Thomas. Papers and Account Book.
McKinstry, George A. Papers
Reading, Pierson Barton. Correspondence and Papers.
Sadler, Warren. Journal, Reminiscences, and Miscellaneous Papers.
Sutter, John Augustus. Correspondence and Papers.

2. Pioneer Reminiscences

Ayres, Irwin. "Biographical Sketches." MS.
Bernal, Juan. "Memoria de Juan Bernal nativo californio, de 67 años de edad, hijo lejitimo de Joaquin Bernal, soldado qe. de cuera de la compania de Sn. Francisco." MS.
Chamberlain, John. "Memoirs of California Since 1840." MS.
Cotton, A. R. "Across the Plains in 1849." MS.
Gonzalez, Don Mauricio. "Recollections of California History."
Potter, Elijah. "Reminiscences." MS.
Sutter, John A. "Reminiscences of General John Augustus Sutter." MS.
Wiggins, William L. "Reminiscences." MS.
Wozencraft, Oliver. "Indian Affairs." MS.
Yates, John. "Sketch of a Journey in the Year 1842 from Sacramento California through the Valley by John Yates of Yatestown." MS.

D. The Huntington Library, San Marino

Fort Sutter Papers
Leidesdorff, William Alexander. Collection.

E. California Room, State Library, Sacramento

Burrows, Rufus C. "Anecdotes Concerning Early Experiences in California 1848–1858." Typescript.
Journal of a Passenger on the Palmetto Mining Company Voyage from Charleston, South Carolina. MS.
Marsh, John. Collection.
McKinstry, George. Collection.
Reading, Pierson B. Collection.
Roop, Isaac. Roop House Register, 1854–1857. MS.
Sheldon, H. B. Papers.
Sutter, John A. Collection.

F. Lilly Library, Bloomington, Indiana.

Rudd, Smith. Collection.

II. Printed Government Documents

A. United States

President of the United States.

Message of the President of the United States Containing the Proceedings of the Court Martial of Lieutenant John C. Frémont. Senate Executive Document 18, 30th Cong., 1st sess. (serial 507).

Message from the President... to the Two Houses of Congress.... House Executive Document 8, 30th Cong., 1st sess. (serial 515).

Message from the President... to the Two Houses of Congress... at the Commencement of the Second Session. Senate Executive Document 1, 30th Cong., 2nd sess. (serial 537).

Message from the President... Communicating Information Called for by... the Senate... Relating to California and New Mexico. Senate Executive Document 18, 31st Cong., 1st sess. (serial 557).

Department of the Interior. Secretary of the Interior.

Report of the Secretary of the Interior... of the Correspondence between the Department of the Interior and the Indian Agents and Commissioners in California. Senate Executive Document 4, 33d Cong., spec. sess. (serial 688).

Annual Report of the Secretary of the Interior, 1849. Senate Executive Document 5, 31st Cong., 1st sess. (serial 570).

Department of the Interior. Office of Indian Affairs. *Annual Report of the Commissioner of Indian Affairs.*

1849. Senate Executive Document 5, 31st Cong., 1st sess. (serial 569).

1850. Senate Executive Document 1, 31st Cong., 2d sess. (serial 587).

1851. Senate Executive Document 1, 32d Cong., 1st sess. (serial 613).

1852. Senate Executive Document 1, 32d Cong., 2d sess. (serial 658).

1853. Senate Executive Document 1, 33d Cong., 1st sess. (serial 690).

1854. Senate Executive Document 1, 33d Cong., 2d sess. (serial 746).

1855. Senate Executive Document 1, 34th Cong., 1st sess. (serial 810).

1856. Senate Executive Document 1, 34th Cong., 2d sess. (serial 875).

1857. Senate Executive Document 1, 35th Cong., 1st sess. (serial 919).

1858. Senate Executive Document 1, 35th Cong., 2d sess. (serial 974).

1859. Senate Executive Document 1, 36th Cong., 1st sess. (serial 1023).

1860. Senate Executive Document 1, 36th Cong., 2d sess. (serial 1078).

1861. Senate Executive Document 1, 37th Cong., 2d sess. (serial 1117).

Department of War. Secretary of War. Office of Indian Affairs. *Annual Report of the Commissioner of Indian Affairs.*

1837. Senate Document 1, 25th Cong., 2d sess. (serial 314).

1848. House Executive Document 1, 30th Cong., 2d sess. (serial 537).

Department of War. *War of the Rebellion Records: A Compilation of the Official Records of the Union and Confederate Armies.* 70 vols. Washington, D.C.: Government Printing Office, 1880–1901.

United States Statutes at Large. Vols. 4, 5, 9, 10.

B. State of California
  California State Senate Journal.
  California State Assembly Journal.
  Statutes of California

III. Published Primary Sources

A Faithful Translation of the Papers Respecting the Grant Made by Governor
  Alvarado to John A. Sutter. Sacramento: Sacramento Book Collectors' Club,
  1942.
Booth, Edmund. Edmund Booth (1810–1905) Forty-Niner: The Life Story of a
  Deaf Pioneer Including Portions of His Autobiographical Notes and Gold Rush
  Diary, and Selections from Family Letters and Reminiscences. Stockton, Calif.:
  San Joaquin Pioneer and Historical Society, 1953.
Brewer, William H. Up and Down California in 1860–1864: The Journal of
  William H. Brewer, Professor of Agriculture in the Sheffield Scientific School
  from 1864 to 1903. 3d ed. Edited by Francis P. Farquhar. Berkeley: University
  of California Press, 1966.
Brooks, George R., ed. The Southwest Expedition of Jedediah S. Smith: His
  Personal Account of the Journey to California, 1826–1827. Glendale, Calif.:
  Arthur H. Clark, 1977.
Bryant, Edwin. What I Saw in California. 1848. Reprint. Berkeley: University
  of California Press, 1985.
Bunnell, Lafayette Haughton. Discovery of Yosemite and the Indian War of
  1851 which Led to that Event. 4th ed. Los Angeles: G. W. Gerlicher, 1911.
Carr, John. Pioneer Days in California. Eureka, Calif.: n.p., 1891.
Carter, Harvey Lewis, ed. "Dear Old Kit:" The Historical Christopher Carson,
  with a New Edition of the Carson Memoirs. Norman: University of Oklahoma
  Press, 1968.
Caughey, John Walton, ed. The Indians of Southern California in 1852: The
  B. D. Wilson Report and a Selection of Contemporary Comment. San Marino,
  Calif.: The Huntington Library, 1952.
Clappe, Louise Amelia Knapp Smith. The Shirley Letters from the California
  Mines, 1851–1852. Edited and introduced by Carl I. Wheat. New York: Alfred
  A. Knopf, 1949.
Cook, Sherburne F., ed. "Colonial Expeditions to the Interior of California:
  Central Valley, 1800–1820." University of California Anthropological Records
  16, no. 6 (1960):239–292.
——— "Expeditions to the Interior of California: Central Valley, 1820–1840."
  University of California Anthropological Records 20, no. 5 (1962):151–214.
Dale, Harrison C., ed. The Ashley-Smith Explorations and the Discovery of a
  Central Route to the Pacific, 1822–1829. Rev. ed. Glendale, Calif.: Arthur H.
  Clark, 1941.
Davis, William Heath. Sixty Years in California. San Francisco: A. J. Leary,
  1889.

Delano, Alonzo. *Life on the Plains and Among the Diggings*. Auburn and Buffalo, N.Y.: Miller, Orton, and Mulligan, 1854.

Farnham, Eliza. *California, In-Doors and Out; or, How We Farm, Mine, and Live Generally in the Golden State*. New York: Dix, Edwards, 1856.

Ferguson, Charles. *The Experiences of a Forty-niner during Thirty-four Years Residence in California and Australia*. Cleveland: Williams Publishing Co., 1888.

Frazer, Robert W., ed. *Mansfield on the Condition of the Western Forts, 1853–54*. Norman: University of Oklahoma Press, 1963.

Gardiner, Howard C. *In Pursuit of the Golden Dream: Reminiscences of San Francisco and the Northern and Southern Mines, 1849–1857*. Edited by Dale L. Morgan. Stoughton, Mass.: Western Hemisphere, 1970.

Garner, William Robert. *Letters from California, 1846–1847*. Edited by Donald Munro Craig. Berkeley: University of California Press, 1970.

Gates, Paul W., ed. *California Ranchos and Farms, 1846–1862*. Madison: The State Historical Society of Wisconsin, 1967.

Gayton, Anna H., ed. "Estudillo Among the Yokuts." *Essays in Anthropology Presented to A. L. Kroeber in Celebration of His Sixtieth Birthday*. Edited by Robert H. Lowie. 1936. Reprint. Freeport, N.Y.: Books for Libraries Press, 1968.

Hammond, George P., ed. *The Larkin Papers*. 11 vols. Berkeley: University of California Press, 1951–68.

Hastings, Lansford W. *The Emigrant's Guide to Oregon and California*. Cincinnati: George Conklin, 1845.

Hawgood, John A., ed. *First and Last Consul: Thomas Oliver Larkin and the Americanization of California, A Selection of Letters*. 2d ed. Palo Alto, Calif.: Pacific Books, 1970.

Heizer, Robert F., comp. "Names and Locations of Some Ethnographic Patwin and Maidu Villages." Berkeley: University of California Research Facility Contributions, no. 9 (1970):96.

——— *The Eighteen Unratified Treaties of 1851–1852 Between the California Indians and the United States Government*. Berkeley: University of California Archaeological Research Facility, 1972.

Heizer, Robert F., ed. *George Gibbs' Journal of Redick McKee's Expedition through Northwestern California in 1851*. Berkeley: University of California Archaeological Research Facility, 1972.

Heizer, Robert F., ed. and comp. *They Were Only Diggers: A Collection of Articles from California Newspapers, 1851–1866, On Indian and White Relations*. Ramona, Calif.: Ballena Press, 1974.

——— *The Destruction of the California Indians: A Collection of Documents from the Period 1847 to 1865*. Santa Barbara, Calif.: Peregrine, Smith, 1974).

Jackson, Donald, ed. *The Journals of Zebulon Montgomery Pike, with Letters and Related Documents*. 2 vols. Norman: University of Oklahoma Press, 1966.

Jackson, Donald, and Mary Lee Spence, eds. *The Expeditions of John Charles Frémont*. 3 vols. Urbana: University of Illinois Press, 1970–73.

Maloney, Alice Bay, ed. *Fur Brigade to the Bonaventure: John Work's California Expedition, 1832–1833*. San Francisco: California Historical Society, 1945.

Marsh, John. "Letter of Dr. John Marsh to Hon. Lewis Cass." *California Historical Society Quarterly* 22 (1943):315–22.

Perkins, William. *Three Years in California: William Perkins' Journal of Life at Sonora, 1849–1852*. Edited by Dale L. Morgan and James R. Scobie. Berkeley: University of California Press, 1964.

Perlot, Jean-Nicolas. *Gold Seeker: Adventures of a Belgian Argonaut during the Gold Rush Years*. Edited by Howard R. Lamar. Translated by Helen Harding Bretnor. New Haven: Yale University Press, 1985.

Phelps, William D. [Webfoot]. *Fore and Aft: Or, Leaves from the Life of an Old Soldier*. Boston: Nichols and Hall, 1871.

Quaife, Milo Milton, ed. *Echoes from the Past, by General John Bidwell; In Camp and Cabin by Rev. John Steele*. Chicago: The Lakeside Press, 1928.

Reinhart, Herman Francis. *The Golden Frontier: The Recollections of Herman Francis Reinhart, 1851–1865*. Edited by Doyce B. Nunis, Jr. Austin: University of Texas Press, 1962.

Rich, E. E., ed. *The Fort Vancouver Letters of John McLoughlin*. 3 vols. London: Champlain Society for the Hudson's Bay Record Society, 1941–44.

Serra, Junípero. *Writings of Junípero Serra*. Edited by Antonine Tibesar. 4 vols. Washington, D.C.: Academy of American Franciscan History, 1955–66.

Sullivan, Maurice S., ed. *The Travels of Jedediah Smith: A Documentary Outline Including the Journal of the Great Pathfinder*. Santa Ana, Calif.: Fine Arts Press, 1934.

────── *Jedediah Smith: Trader and Trail Breaker*. New York: Press of the Pioneers, 1936.

Sutter, Johann August (John Augustus). *The Diary of Johann August Sutter*. San Francisco: Grabhorn Press, 1932.

Sutter, John A., et al. *New Helvetia Diary: A Record Kept by John A. Sutter and His Clerks at New Helvetia, California, from September 9, 1845, to May 25, 1848*. San Francisco: Grabhorn Press, 1939.

Taylor, Bayard. *Eldorado: Or, Adventures in the Path of Empire*. 1850. Reprint (2 vols in 1). Glorietta, N. M.: Rio Grande Press, 1967.

Uldall, Hans Jørgen, and William Shipley, comps. *Nisenan Texts and Dictionary*. University of California Publications in Linguistics, vol. 46. Berkeley: University of California Press, 1966.

Wilbur, Marguerite Eyer, trans. and ed. *A Pioneer at Sutter's Fort, 1846–1850: The Adventures of Heinrich Lienhard*. Calafía Series, no. 3. Los Angeles: The Calafía Society, 1941.

IV. Newspapers

California Farmer and Journal of Useful Sciences.
California Star.

Californian.
Daily Alta California.
Marysville *Weekly Express.*
Sacramento *Daily Democratic State Journal.*
Sacramento *Daily Record Union.*
Sacramento *Union.*

V. Books, Articles, and Secondary Sources

Ageton, Suzanne S. *Sexual Assault Among Adolescents.* Lexington, Mass.: Lexington Books, 1983.

American Indian Culture and Research Journal 6, no. 2 (1982). Special issue on *Metis.*

American Indian Quarterly 6 (Spring/Summer 1982). Special issue on Navajo women.

Anderson, Gary Clayton. *Kinsmen of Another Kind: Dakota-White Relations in the Upper Mississippi Valley, 1650–1862.* Lincoln: University of Nebraska Press, 1984.

Andrews, Thomas F. "The Controversial Hastings Overland Guide: A Reassessment." *Pacific Historical Review* 37 (1968):21–34.

Archibald, Robert. *The Economic Aspects of the California Missions.* Washington, D.C.: Academy of American Franciscan History, 1978.

Axtell, James, ed. *The Indian Peoples of Eastern America: A Documentary History of the Sexes.* New York: Oxford University Press, 1981.

———. *The European and the Indian: Essays in the Ethnohistory of Colonial North America.* New York: Oxford University Press, 1981.

———. *The Invasion Within: The Contest of Cultures in Colonial North America.* New York: Oxford University Press, 1985.

Bailyn, Bernard. *The Peopling of British North America: An Introduction.* New York: Alfred A. Knopf, 1986.

Bakker, Elna. *An Island Called California: An Ecological Introduction to Its Natural Communities.* Berkeley: University of California Press, 1971.

Bancroft, Hubert Howe. *History of California.* 7 vols. San Francisco: The History Company, 1886–90.

Bartlett, Richard A. *The New Country: A Social History of the American Frontier, 1776–1890.* New York: Oxford University Press, 1974.

Bean, Lowell John. "Social Organization in Native California." In *Native Californians: A Theoretical Retrospective.* Edited by Lowell John Bean and Thomas C. Blackburn. Socorro, N.M.: Ballena Press, 1976.

Beattie, George William. "Spanish Plans for an Inland Chain of Missions in California." *Historical Society of Southern California Annual Publication* 14 (1929):243–64.

———. *California's Unbuilt Missions: Spanish Plans for an Inland Chain.* Los Angeles, 1930.

Beilharz, Edwin A., trans., and Carlos U. López, ed. *We Were 49ers! Chilean Accounts of the California Gold Rush*. Pasadena, Calif.: Ward Ritchie Press, 1976.

Bennyhoff, James A. *Ethnogeography of the Plains Miwok*. Center for Archeological Research at Davis, no. 5. Davis: University of California, 1977.

Berkhofer, Robert J., Jr. *The White Man's Indian: Images of the American Indian from Columbus to the Present*. New York: Alfred A. Knopf, 1978.

Billington, Ray A. "Books that Won the West." *American West* 4 (1967):25–32, 72–74.

Bledsoe, A. J. *History [of] Del Norte County, California, with a Business Directory and Traveler's Guide*. Eureka, Calif.: Humboldt Times Press-Wyman & Co., 1881.

Bolton, Herbert E. "The Mission as a Frontier Institution in Spanish American Colonies" and "Defensive Spanish Expansion and the Significance of the Borderlands." In *Bolton and the Spanish Borderlands*. Edited by John Francis Bannon. Norman: University of Oklahoma Press, 1964.

Borah, Woodrow W. "Sherburne Friend Cook (1896–1974)." *Hispanic American Historical Review* 55 (1975):749–59.

Broadbent, Sylvia M. "Conflict at Monterey: Indian Horse Raiding, 1820–1850." *Journal of California Anthropology* 1 (1974):86–101.

Brown, Jennifer S. H. *Strangers in Blood: Fur Trade Company Families in Indian Country*. Vancouver: University of British Columbia Press, 1980.

Brown, Richard D. *Modernization: The Transformation of American Life, 1600–1865*. New York: Oxford University Press, 1976.

Burgess, Ann Wolbert, and Lynda Lytle Holstrom. "Rape Trauma Syndrome." *American Journal of Psychiatry* 131 (1974):981–86.

Bushnell, John, and Donna Bushnell. "Wealth, Work and World View in Natve Northwest California: Sacred Significance and Psychoanalytic Symbolism." In *Flowers of the Wind: Papers on Ritual, Myth and Symbolism in California and the Southwest*. Edited by Thomas C. Blackburn. Socorro, N.M.: Ballena Press, 1977.

Butler, Anne M. *Daughters of Joy, Sisters of Misery: Prostitutes in the American West, 1865–90*. Urbana: University of Illinois Press, 1985.

California State Archives. "Inventory of the Indian War Papers." Sacramento, n.d.

Canfield, Gae Whitney. *Sarah Winnemucca of the Northern Paiutes*. Norman: University of Oklahoma Press, 1983.

Carranco, Lynwood and Estle Beard. *Genocide and Vendetta: The Round Valley Wars of Northern California*. Norman: University of Oklahoma Press, 1981.

Castañeda, Antonia I. "The Political Economy of Nineteenth-Century Stereotypes of Californians." Paper presented at the Pacific Coast Branch meeting of the American Historical Association, San Francisco, Aug. 12–14, 1982.

Céspedes, Guillermo. *Latin America in the Early Years*. New York: Alfred A. Knopf, 1974.

Cohen, Felix S. *Handbook of Federal Indian Law*. 1942. Reprint. Albuquerque: University of New Mexico Press, n.d.

Compendium of the Ninth Census. Washington, D.C.: Government Printing Office, 1870.

Compendium of the Tenth Census. Rev. ed. Washington, D.C.: Government Printing Office, 1885.

Connelly, Mark Thomas. *The Progressive Response to Prostitution in the Progressive Era.* Chapel Hill: University of North Carolina Press, 1980.

Cook, Sherburne F. "Population Trends Among the California Mission Indians." *Ibero-Americana* 17 (1940):1–48.

———. "The Mechanism and Extent of Dietary Adaptation Among Certain Groups of California and Nevada Indians." *Ibero-Americana* 18 (1941):1–59.

———. "The Indian Versus the Spanish Mission." *Ibero-Americana* 21 (1943):1–294.

———. "The Physical and Demographic Reaction of the Nonmission Indians in Colonial and Provincial California." *Ibero-Americana* 22 (1943):1–55.

———. "The American Invasion, 1848–1870." *Ibero-Americana* 23 (1943):1–111.

———. "The Epidemic of 1830–1833 in California and Oregon." *University of California Publications in American Archaeology and Ethnology* 43 (1955):303–25.

———. "The Destruction of the California Indians." *California Monthly* 79 (December 1968):14–19.

———. *The Conflict Between the California Indians and White Civilization.* Foreword by Robert F. Heizer and Woodrow Borah. Berkeley: University of California Press, 1976.

———. *The Population of the California Indians, 1769–1970.* Berkeley: University of California Press, 1976.

Cook, Sherburne F. and Borah, Woodrow. "Mission Registers as Sources of Vital Statistics: Eight Missions of Northern California." In *Essays in Population History.* 3 vols. Berkeley: University of California Press, 1971–79.

Coy, Owen. "Evidences of Slavery in California." *Grizzly Bear*, no. 6 (1916): 1–2.

Cronon, William. *Changes in the Land: Indians, Colonists, and the Ecology of New England.* New York: Hill and Wang, 1983.

Currie, Anne H. "Bidwell Rancheria." *California Historical Society Quarterly* 36 (1957):313–25.

Dasmann, Raymond F. *The Destruction of California.* New York: Collier, 1966.

DeBow, J. D. B. *Statistical Review of the United States.* Washington, D.C.: Government Printing Office, 1854.

Degler, Carl N. *At Odds: Women and the Family in America from the Revolution to the Present.* New York: Oxford University Press, 1980.

Dillon, Richard. *Fool's Gold: The Decline and Fall of Captain John Sutter of California.* New York: Coward McCann, 1967.

Dutschke, Dwight. Interview with author. July 14, 1987.

Easterlin, Richard A. "Factors in the Decline of Farm Family Fertility in the United States: Some Preliminary Research Results." *Journal of American History* 63 (1976):600–14.

————. "Population and Farm Settlement in the Northern United States." *Journal of Economic History* 36 (March 1976):45–75.

Eblen, Jack. "An Analysis of Nineteenth-Century Frontier Populations." *Demography* 2 (1965): 399–413.

Edmunds, R. David. *The Shawnee Prophet*. Lincoln: University of Nebraska Press, 1983.

Ellison, Joseph. *California and the Nation, 1850–1869: A Study of the Relations of a Frontier Community with the Federal Government*. University of California Publications in History, 16. Berkeley: University of California Press, 1927.

Ellison, William Henry. "The Federal Indian Policy in California, 1846–1860." *Mississippi Valley Historical Review* 9 (June 1922):37–67.

Evers, Hans-Dieter, Wolfgang Clauss, and Diana Wong. "Subsistence Reproduction: A Framework for Analysis." In *Households and the World-Economy*. Edited by Joan Smith, Immanuel Wallerstein, and Hans-Dieter Evers. Beverly Hills: Sage Publications, 1984.

Faragher, John Mack. *Women and Men on the Overland Trail*. New Haven: Yale University Press, 1979.

Fattah, E. A. "The Use of the Victim as an Agent of Self-Legitimization: Toward a Dynamic Explanation of Criminal Behavior." In *Victims and Society*. Edited by E. C. Viano. Washington, D.C.: Visage Press, 1976.

Fernandez, Ferdinand F. "Except a California Indian." *Southern California Quarterly* 50 (1968):169.

Forbes, Jack. *Native Americans of California and Nevada*. Healdsburg, Calif.: Naturegraph, 1969.

————. "The San Francisco Bay Region: An Analysis of Racial Origins." *Aztlan* 14, no. 1 (1983):175–89.

Galbraith, John S. "A Note on the British Fur Trade in California." *Pacific Historical Review* 24 (1955):253–60.

Garr, Daniel. "Planning Politics and Plunder: The Missions and Indian Pueblos of Hispanic California." *Southern California Quarterly* 54 (1972):291–312.

————. "A Rare and Desolate Land: Population and Race in Hispanic California." *Western Historical Quarterly* 6 (1975):133–48.

Gayton, Anna H. "Yokuts and Western Mono Ethnography." *University of California Anthropological Records* 10 (1948):1–302.

Genovese, Eugene. *Roll Jordan Roll: The World the Slaves Made*. New York: Pantheon, 1974.

Gibson, Charles. *The Aztecs under Spanish Rule: A History of the Indians of the Valley of Mexico, 1519–1820*. Stanford: Stanford University Press, 1964.

Goodrich, Chauncy Shafter. "The Legal Status of the California Indian: Introductory." *California Law Review* 14 (1926):81–100.

Griswold del Castillo, Richard. *The Los Angeles Barrio, 1850–1890: A Social History*. Berkeley: University of California Press, 1979.

Groth, A. Nicholas. *Men Who Rape: The Psychology of the Offender*. New York: Plenum, 1979.

Guest, Francis F., O.F.M., "An Examination of the Thesis of S. F. Cook on the Forced Conversion of Indians in the California Missions." *Southern California Quarterly* 61 (1979):1–77.

Gutiérrez, Ramón A. "From Honor to Love: Transformations of the Meaning of Sexuality in Colonial New Mexico." In *Kinship Ideology and Practice in Latin America*. Edited by Raymod T. Smith. Chapel Hill: University of North Carolina Press, 1984.

———. "Honor Ideology, Marriage Negotiation, and Class-Gender Domination in New Mexico, 1690–1846." *Latin American Perspectives* 12 (Winter 1985):81–104.

Gutman, Herbert G. *Work, Culture, and Society in Industrializing America: Essays in American Working-Class and Social History*. New York: Vintage, 1977.

Harlow, Neal. *California Conquered: War and Peace on the Pacific, 1846–1850*. Berkeley: University of California Press, 1982.

Harris, Dennis. "The California Census of 1852: A Note of Caution and Encouragement." *The Pacific Historian* 28 (Summer 1984):59–64.

Hawgood, John A. "John Augustus Sutter: A Reappraisal." *Arizona and the West* 4 (Winter 1962):345–56.

———. "Patterns of Yankee Infiltration in Mexican Alta California." *Pacific Historical Review* 27 (1958):27–38.

Heizer, Robert F. "The California Indians: Archaeology, Varieties of Culture, and Arts of Life." *California Historical Society Quarterly* 41 (1962):1–28.

———. "Walla Walla Indian Expeditions to the Sacramento Valley." *California Historical Society Quarterly* 21 (1942):1–7.

Heizer, Robert F., ed. *Handbook of North American Indians*. Vol. 8, *California*. Washington, D.C.: Smithsonian Institution, 1978.

Heizer, Robert F., and Alan Almquist. *The Other Californians: Prejudice and Discrimination under Spain, Mexico and the United States to 1920*. Berkeley: University of California Press, 1971.

Heizer, Robert F., and Albert B. Elsasser. *The Natural World of California Indians*. Berkeley: University of California Press, 1980.

Hill, Dorothy. *The Indians of Chico Rancheria*. Sacramento, California: State of California, Department of Parks and Recreation, 1978.

Hill, Edward H. *The Office of Indian Affairs, 1824–1880: Historical Sketches*. New York: Clearwater, 1974.

Hill, Joseph J. "Ewing Young in the Fur Trade of the Southwest." *Oregon Historical Society Quarterly* 24 (1923):1–35.

Hine, Robert V. *In the Shadow of Frémont: Edward Kern and the Art of Exploration*. 2d ed. Norman: University of Oklahoma Press, 1982.

Holterman, Jack. "The Revolt of Estanislao." *The Indian Historian* 3 (Winter 1970):43–54.

———. "The Revolt of Yozcolo: Indian Warrior in the Fight for Freedom." *The Indian Historian* 3 (Spring 1970):19–23.

Hoopes, Alban W. *Indian Affairs and Their Administration with Special Reference to the Far West, 1849–1860*. Philadelphia: University of Pennsylvania Press, 1932.

Horsman, Reginald. *Expansion and American Indian Policy, 1783–1812*. East Lansing, Mich.: Michigan State University Press, 1967.

———. *The Frontier in the Formative Years*. New York: Holt, Rinehart, and Winston, 1970.

———. *Race and Manifest Destiny: The Origins of American Racial Anglo-Saxonism*. Cambridge: Harvard University Press, 1981.

———. "Well-Trodden Paths and Fresh Byways: Recent Writing on Native American History." *Reviews in American History* 10 (December 1982):234.

Hoxie, Frederick E. "Positively Paternal." *Reviews in American History* 13 (September 1985):393.

Humphreys, Alfred Glenn. "Thomas L. (Peg-leg) Smith." In *The Mountain Men and the Fur Trade of the Far West*. 10 vols. Edited by LeRoy R. Hafen. Vol. 4:311–30. Glendale, Calif.: Arthur H. Clark, 1966.

Hunt, Rockwell D. *John Bidwell: Prince of California Pioneers*. Caldwell, Idaho,: The Caxton Printers, 1942.

Hurtado, Albert L. "Controlling California's Indian Labor Force: Federal Administration of California Indian Affairs during the Mexican War, 1846–1849." *Southern California Quarterly* 61 (1979):217–38.

———. " 'Hardly a Farm House—A Kitchen without Them': Indian and White Households on the California Borderland Frontier in 1860." *Western Historical Quarterly* 13 (1982):245–70.

———. " 'Saved so Much as Possible for Labour': Indian Population and the New Helvetia Work Force." *American Indian Culture and Research Journal* 6, no. 4 (1982):63–78.

Hussey, John Adam, and George Walcott Ames, Jr. "California Preparations to Meet the Walla Walla Invasion, 1846." *California Historical Society Quarterly* 21 (1942):9–21.

Hutchinson, C. Alan. "The Mexican Government and the Mission Indians of Upper California." *Americas* 21 (1964–65):335–62.

Jacobs, Wilbur R. "Sherburne Friend Cook: Rebel-Revisionist (1896–1974)." *Pacific Historical Review* 54 (1985):191–99.

Jeffrey, Julie Roy. *Frontier Women: The Trans-Mississippi West, 1840–1880*. New York: Hill and Wang, 1979.

Jennings, Francis. *The Invasion of America: Indians, Colonialism, and the Cant of Conquest*. Chapel Hill: University of North Carolina Press, 1975.

Jones, Oakah L. *Los Paisanos: Spanish Settlers on the Northern Frontier of New Spain*. Norman: University of Oklahoma Press, 1979.

Kappler, Charles J., comp. *Indian Affairs: Laws and Treaties*. 5 vols. Washington, D.C.: Government Printing Office, 1904–41.

Kelsey, Harry. "The California Indian Treaty Myth." *Southern California Quarterly* 55 (1973):225–38.

Kennedy, Joseph C. T., comp. *Population of the United States in 1860*. Washington, D.C.: Government Printing Office, 1864.

Kenny, Robert W. *History and Proposed Settlement: Claims of California Indians.* Sacramento: State Printing Office, 1944.

Kroeber, Alfred L. *Handbook of the Indians of California.* 1925. Reprint. Berkeley: California Book Company, 1967.

Kroeber, Theodora. *Ishi in Two Worlds: A Biography of the Last Wild Indian in North America.* Berkeley: University of California Press, 1961.

Kroeber, Theodora, and Robert F. Heizer, comps. *Almost Ancestors: The First Californians.* San Francisco: Sierra Club, 1968.

Kroeber, Theodora, Albert B. Elsasser, and Robert F. Heizer. *Drawn from Life: California Indians in Pen and Brush.* Socorro, N.M.: Ballena Press, 1977.

Kuznesof, Elizabeth, and Robert Oppenheimer. "The Family and Society in Nineteenth-Century Latin America: An Historiographical Introduction." *Journal of Family History* 10 (1985): 215–34.

Lamar, Howard. "From Bondage to Contract: Ethnic Labor in the American West, 1600–1890." In *The Countryside in the Age of Capitalist Transformation: Essays in the Social History of Rural America.* Edited by Steven Hahn and Jonathan Prude. Chapel Hill: University of North Carolina Press, 1985.

Laslett, Barbara. "Household Structure on an American Frontier: Los Angeles, California, in 1850." *American Journal of Sociology* 81 (July 1975):109–28.

Laslett, Peter. "The Comparative History of Household and Family." *Journal of Social History* 4 (Fall 1970):75–87.

Laslett, Peter, ed. *Household and Family in Past Time.* Cambridge, England: Cambridge University Press, 1972.

Lawrence, Elinore. "Horse Thieves on the Spanish Trail." *Touring Topics* 23 (January 1931):22–25, 55.

———. "Mexican Trade between Santa Fe and Los Angeles, 1830–1848." *California Historical Society Quarterly* 10 (1931):27–39.

Layton, Thomas N. "Traders and Raiders: Aspects of the Trans-Basin and California-Plateau Commerce, 1800–1830." *Journal of California and Great Basin Anthropology* 3 (Summer 1981):127–36.

Lecompte, Janet. "The Independent Women of Hispanic New Mexico." *Western Historical Quarterly* 12 (1981):17–36.

Lockhart, James. *Spanish Colonial Peru, 1532–1560: A Colonial Society.* Madison: University of Wisconsin Press, 1968.

Lyman, George D. *John Marsh, Pioneer: The Life Story of a Trail-blazer on Six Frontiers.* New York: Charles Scribner's Sons, 1930.

Meister, Carl W. "Methods for Evaluating the Accuracy of Ethnohistorical Demographic Data on North American Indians: A Brief Assessment." *Ethnohistory* 27 (1980):153–69.

Merk, Frederick. *Manifest Destiny and Mission in American History: A Reinterpretation.* New York: Alfred A. Knopf, 1963.

Merriam, C. Hart "The Indian Population of California." *American Anthropologist,* n.s. 7, no. 4 (1905):594–606.

Miranda, Gloria E. "Gente de Razón Marriage Patterns in Spanish and Mexican

California: A Case Study of Santa Barbara and Los Angeles." *Southern California Quarterly* 63 (1981):1–21.

Miller, Christopher L. *Prophetic Worlds: Indians and Whites on the Columbia Plateau*. New Brunswick, N.J.: Rutgers University Press, 1985.

Mirandé, Alfredo, and Evangelina Enríquez. *La Chicana: The Mexican-American Woman*. Chicago: University of Chicago Press, 1979.

Mitchell, Annie R. "Major James D. Savage and the Tularenos." *California Historical Society Quarterly* 28 (1949):323–41.

Morgan, Dale. *Jedediah Smith and the Opening of the West*. Indianapolis: Bobbs-Merrill, 1953.

Myres, Sandra L. *Westering Women and the Frontier Experience, 1800–1915*. Albuquerque: University of New Mexico Press, 1982.

Norton, Jack. *Genocide in Northwestern California: When Our Worlds Cried*. San Francisco: The Indian Historian Press, 1979.

Nugent, Walter. *Structures of American Social History*. Bloomington: Indiana University Press, 1981.

Nunis, Doyce B. "A Mysterious Chapter in the Life of John A. Sutter." *California Historical Society Quarterly* 38 (1959):321–27.

Palmer, Lyman L. *History of Napa and Lake Counties, California*. San Francisco: Slocum, Bowen, 1881.

Pate, Bernice. Interview with author. July 1, 1976, Auburn, California.

Paul, Rodman W. *California Gold: The Beginning of Mining in the Far West*. Lincoln: University of Nebraska Press, 1947.

Pearce, Roy Harvey. *The Savages of America: A Study of the Indian and the Idea of Civilization*. Baltimore: Johns Hopkins University Press, 1965.

Phillips, George Harwood. *Chiefs and Challengers: Indian Resistance and Cooperation in Southern California*. Berkeley: University of California Press, 1975.

———. "Indians in Los Angeles, 1781–1875: Economic Integration, Social Disintegration." *Pacific Historical Review* 69 (1980):427–51.

———. *The Enduring Struggle: Indians in California History*. San Francisco: Boyd and Fraser, 1981.

Pilling, Arnold. "Yurok." In *California: Handbook of North American Indians*. Edited by Robert F. Heizer. Washington, D.C.: Smithsonian Institution, 1978.

Pitt, Leonard. *Decline of the Californios: A Social History of the Spanish-Speaking Californians, 1846–1890*. Berkeley: University of California Press, 1966.

Pollard, Sidney. *The Genesis of Modern Management: A Study of the Industrial Revolution in Great Britain*. Cambridge, Mass.: Harvard University Press, 1965.

Population of the United States in 1860, Compiled from the Original Returns of the Eighth Census. Washington, D.C.: Government Printing Office, 1864.

Prucha, Francis Paul. *American Indian Policy in the Formative Years: The Indian Trade and Intercourse Acts, 1790–1834*. Lincoln: University of Nebraska Press, 1962.

———. *The Great Father: The United States Government and the American Indians*. 2 vols. Lincoln: University of Nebraska Press, 1984.

Rawls, James. "Gold Diggers: Indian Miners in the California Gold Rush." *California Historical Quarterly* 55 (1976):28–45.

———. *Indians of California: The Changing Image*. Norman: University of Oklahoma Press, 1984.

Riley, Glenda. *Women and the Indians on the Frontier, 1825–1915*. Albuquerque: University of New Mexico Press, 1984.

Rogin, Leo. *The Introduction of Farm Machinery in Relation to the Productivity of Labor in the United States during the Nineteenth Century*. Berkeley: University of California Press, 1931.

Ronda, James P. *Lewis and Clark among the Indians*. Lincoln: University of Nebraska Press, 1984.

Rothman, David J. *The Discovery of the Asylum: Social Order and Disorder in the New Republic*. Boston: Little, Brown, 1971.

Rotter, Andrew J. " 'Matilda for Gods Sake Write': Women and Families on the Argonaut Mind." *California History* 58 (1979):128–41.

Satz, Ronald N. *American Indian Policy in the Jacksonian Era*. Lincoln: University of Nebraska Press, 1975.

Sauer, Carl O. *The Early Spanish Main*. Berkeley: University of California Press, 1966.

Schwendinger, Julia R., and Herman Schwendinger. *Rape and Inequality*. Beverly Hills: Sage Publications, 1983.

Seed, Patricia. "The Church and the Patriarchal Family: Marriage Conflicts in Sixteenth- and Seventeenth-Century New Spain." *Journal of Family History* 10 (1985):284–93.

Servín, Manuel P. "The Secularization of the California Missions: A Reappraisal." *Southern California Quarterly* 47 (1965):133–49.

Sheehan, Bernard W. *Seeds of Extinction: Jeffersonian Philanthropy and the American Indian*. New York: W. W. Norton, 1973.

Sievers, Michael A. "Malfeasance or Indirection? Administration of the California Indian Superintendency's Business Affairs." *Southern California Quarterly* 56 (Fall 1974):273–94.

Simpson, Lesley Byrd. *The Encomienda in New Spain: The Beginnings of Spanish Mexico*. Berkeley: University of California Press, 1950.

Simpson, Richard. *Ooti: A Maidu Legacy*. Millbrae, Calif.: Celestial Arts, 1977.

Slotkin, Richard. *Regeneration through Violence: The Mythology of the American Frontier, 1600–1860*. Middletown, Conn.: Wesleyan University Press, 1973.

———. *The Fatal Environment: The Myth of the Frontier in the Age of Industrialization, 1800–1890*. Middletown, Conn.: Wesleyan University Press, 1985.

Smits, David. "The 'Squaw Drudge': A Prime Index of Savagism." *Ethnohistory* 29 (1982):281–306.

Stavrianos, L. S. *Global Rift*. New York: Morrow, 1981.

Steger, Gertrude. "A Chronology of the Life of Pierson B. Reading." *California Historical Society Quarterly* 22 (1943):365–71.

Swagerty, William R. "Marriage and Settlement Patterns of the Rocky Mountain Trappers and Traders." *Western Historical Quarterly* 11 (1980):159–80.

Takaki, Ronald T. *Iron Cages: Race and Culture in Nineteenth-Century America.* Seattle: University of Washington Press, 1979.

Teitelbaum, Michael S. "Factors Associated with the Sex Ratio in Human Populations." In *The Structure of Human Populations.* Edited by G. A. Harrison and A. J. Boyce. Oxford: Oxford University Press, 1972.

Templeton, Sardis. *The Lame Captain: The Life and Adventures of Pegleg Smith.* Los Angeles: Westernlore Press, 1965.

Thompson, Gerald. *Edward F. Beale and the American West.* Albuquerque: University of New Mexico Press, 1983.

Trennert, Robert A. *Alternative to Extinction: Federal Indian Policy and the Beginnings of the Reservation System, 1846–51.* Philadelphia: Temple University Press, 1975.

Turner, Frederick Jackson. "The Significance of the Frontier in American History." In *The Frontier in American History.* 1920. Reprint. New York: Holt, Rinehart, and Winston, 1962.

Unruh, John D., Jr. *The Plains Across: The Overland Emigrants and the Trans-Mississippi West, 1840–1860.* Urbana: University of Illinois Press, 1979.

Utley, Robert M. *The Indian Frontier of the American West, 1846–1890.* Albuquerque: University of New Mexico Press, 1984.

Van Kirk, Sylvia. *Many Tender Ties: Women in Fur Trade Society, 1670–1870.* Norman: University of Oklahoma Press, 1980.

Walker, Francis A., comp. *A Compendium of the Ninth Census (June 1, 1870).* Washington, D.C.: Government Printing Office, 1872.

Wallerstein, Immanuel. *The Modern World System: Capitalist Agriculture and the Origins of the European World-Economy in the Sixteenth Century.* New York: Academic Press. 1976.

———. "Household Structures and Labor-Force Formation in the Capitalist World-Economy." In *Households and the World-Economy.* Edited by Joan Smith, Immanuel Wallerstein, and Hans-Dieter Evers. Beverly Hills: Sage Publications, 1984.

Weber, David J. "American Westward Expansion and the Breakdown of Relations between Pobladores and 'Indios Barbaros' on Mexico's Far Northern Frontier, 1821–1846." *New Mexico Historical Review* 56 (1981):221–38.

———. *The Mexican Frontier, 1821–1846: The American Southwest under Mexico.* Albuquerque: University of New Mexico Press, 1982.

Weinberg, Albert K. *Manifest Destiny: A Study of Nationalist Expansionism in American History.* Baltimore: Johns Hopkins University Press, 1935.

Welter, B. "Cult of True Womanhood." *Am Qtrly* 18 (1966):151–74.

White, Richard. *The Roots of Dependency: Subsistence, Environment, and Social Change among the Choctaws, Pawnees, and Navajos.* Lincoln: University of Nebraska Press, 1983.

Willoughby, Nona C. "Division of Labor among the Indians of California." In *California Indians.* Vol. 2. Garland American Indian Ethnohistory Series. 6 vols. New York: Garland, 1974.

Wilson, Iris Higbie. "William Wolfskill." In *The Mountain Men and the Fur Trade in the Far West*, edited by LeRoy Hafen, vol. 2. Glendale, California: Arthur H. Clark, 1965.

Winchell, Lilbourne Alsip. *History of Fresno County and the San Joaquin Valley*. Fresno: A. H. Cawston, 1933.

Wishart, David J. *The Fur Trade of the American West, 1807–1840*. Lincoln: University of Nebraska Press, 1979.

Wood, Peter H. *Black Majority: Negroes in Colonial South Carolina from 1670 through the Stono Rebellion*. New York: W. W. Norton, 1975.

Wright, Doris Marion. *A Yankee in Mexican California: Abel Stearns, 1798–1848*. Santa Barbara, Calif.: Wallace Hebberd, 1977.

Zillmann, Dolf. "Excitation Transfer in Communication-Mediated Agressive Behavior." *Journal of Experimental Social Psychology* 7 (1971):419–34.

Zollinger, James Peter. *Sutter: The Man and His Empire*. New York: Oxford University Press, 1939.

Index

Titles of related interest available from Yale University Press

Cheyenne Memories
Second Edition
With a New Preface
John Stands In Timber
    and Margot Liberty

"This is an extraordinarily fascinating book, . . . a book that all Americans, Indians as well as non-Indians, will treasure."   —Alvin M. Josephy, Jr.

The Last Days of the Sioux Nation
Robert M. Utley

"By far the best treatment of the complex and controversial relationship between the Sioux and their conquerors yet presented and should be must reading for serious students of Western Americana." —*St. Louis Post Dispatch*

YALE WESTERN AMERICANA SERIES

Sun Chief
The Autobiography of a Hopi Indian
Edited by Leo W. Simmons
With a New Foreword by Robert V. Hine

"An autobiography which gives us not merely glimpses into Indian life but many opportunities for sustained and detailed observation of what goes on inside an Indian community."
            —*Western American Literature*

YALE WESTERN AMERICANA SERIES

Blacks in Gold Rush California
Rudolph M. Lapp

"Thoroughly researched, intelligently organized, and effectively presented."
            —Kenneth Wiggins Porter,
            American Historical Review

YALE WESTERN AMERICANA SERIES

Gold Seeker
Adventures of a Belgian Argonaut
during the Gold Rush Years
Jean-Nicolas Perlot
Translated by Helen Harding Bretnor
Edited and with an Introduction by
    Howard R. Lamar

"A superb, remarkable narrative [that] contributes an invaluable perspective on the California era between 1850 and 1857."
            —Wayne A. Saroyan, *San Francisco*
                Examiner-Chronicle

YALE WESTERN AMERICANA SERIES

The New Encyclopedia of the
American West
Edited by Howard R. Lamar

With more than 2,400 entries and over 600 illustrations and maps, this authoritative encyclopedia provides a comprehensive and indispensable introduction to the American West.

Religion and Society in
Frontier California
Laurie F. Maffly-Kipp

"A well-crafted, carefully reasoned, and artfully written account of an important aspect of life in gold rush California."
            —Eldon Ernst, *Southern*
                California Quarterly

YALE HISTORICAL PUBLICATIONS

For other books on these subjects, visit our website at http://www.yale.edu/yup/